# Stars and
# Revised & ι

## Roger Aubrey

To John and Pauline:
With love and deep
appreciation of all that
you mean to us.

Roger and Dianne.

**Lulu Publishers**

**ISBN 978-1-291-82595-4**

Also by Roger Aubrey

*The Elijah People*

*The Circle of Life*

*Discovering God*

*Angels*

*The Little Book of Hope*

*About the author*

Roger Aubrey was born and raised in Cardiff, Wales. He lives in the city with his wife Dianne. He has been a Christian since 1966. Roger serves on the leadership team of All Nations Church, with responsibility for teaching and preaching. He enjoys cricket and rugby, and visits Churches and Bible Colleges throughout the world, teaching the Word of God and building up the Body of Christ. Roger has a Master's Degree and a PhD in Christian Theology from Cardiff University. He likes to read biographies of those who shape history.

**Foreword to the revised and updated edition**

The original edition of Stars and Sand contained articles from my blog, dating from November 2004 to June 2008. This revised and updated edition contains over eighty new articles: some that were not included in the first edition, plus a large selection of those composed up to 2013, when Stars and Sand concluded. My new blog, VOICE, was launched in January 2014.

As with the first edition, this new edition comprises observations, meditations and teaching, all based in the Word of God. Even though they were written a while ago, I believe that each one of them is relevant today, and trust that they prove to be an encouragement, challenge and blessing.

Once again, a huge thanks to all those who take the time read my blog: I appreciate it very much. God bless you. Special thanks also to my dear friend David Shutt for designing the front cover.

*Roger Aubrey*
*Spring 2014*

## Foreword to the original edition

In the autumn of 2004 I was staying at the home of my friends Erling and Solveig Thu in Bergen, Norway. Erling had become a passionate devotee of the Internet phenomenon known as blogging. To be honest, I had been rather dismissive of blogging, thinking it was a passing fad that would soon go the way of all latest crazes.

One evening Erling opened his laptop, logged on to his site, and began to type a blog post. It took him about ten minutes to write what he wanted to say: a short, devotional piece on a Bible verse he had been studying that day. Intrigued, I began to quiz him about what he had done. Erling explained how easy it was to blog, and why he blogged. He could communicate with the world immediately, publishing truth from God's Word simply and quickly. He opened his laptop again and showed me the responses his post, written only thirty minutes ago, had created. From several parts of the world, people had already left comments appreciating what Erling had written.

Something began to stir within me. A few months previously, the Holy Spirit had spoken to me that people from many nations were waiting to hear from me, that I had something to say to them, and that I would affect people right across the world. Initially I thought, 'How can I travel to all these nations?' It dawned on me that night in Erling's home that I didn't have to physically go to all these nations: I could visit them through blogging. I decided to give it a go.

I asked Erling to help me get started, which he graciously did. When I returned home a few days later I was excited by the prospect of blogging. But I didn't want it to be a fad, so I promised the Lord that if I started I would take it seriously and stick at it. Seven years later, I am still blogging.

Sure enough, just as the Lord promised, I regularly receive supportive and appreciative responses from across the world. People read the blog in all corners of the globe. What is even more thrilling is to physically meet some of them from time to time when I travel. They are always very kind and encourage me to keep on blogging.

This book is a selection of blog posts from the very first one in November 2004, up to June 2008. Those of you who have been readers know that the blog comprises many things, including video and audio clips, quotes from other writers and links to news stories. I have collected together here posts that I think are still relevant today.

Early on I decided to call the blog 'Stars and Sand.' God promised Abraham that his spiritual descendants would be as numerous as the stars in the sky and the sand on the seashore (Genesis 22:17). Abraham's descendants are all those who have confessed Jesus as their Lord: his church throughout the world. I believe God has a purpose that encompasses the whole world:

> *The earth will be filled with the knowledge of the glory of the LORD as the waters cover the sea. (Habakkuk 2:14)*

It is my hope and prayer that over the years my blog has played some small part in the fulfilment of God's eternal purpose for his world.

## November 25, 2004: Every day is Thanksgiving Day

Today is an important day for our American friends. It is Thanksgiving Day, the annual occasion when they remember the goodness of God to the early settlers who survived that first harsh winter. Earlier today I was in conversation with some Americans who belong to our church; they will be celebrating tonight with a traditional Thanksgiving meal - lots of everything! It is good that they give thanks to God; it should also be a fundamental characteristic of all Christians at all times. 1Thessalonians 5:18 says, 'give thanks in all circumstances, for this is God's will for you.' I used to think that circumstances were the really big things in life: marriage, jobs, or bereavement. But how I respond in those times is largely determined by how I give thanks at other times, especially when things are going well. This verse says that we should give thanks to God in all circumstances.

Recently I have been learning that my life is full of all kinds of circumstances every day. In fact, my first circumstance each day is when I wake up. What is my first response to the new day? I am learning to give thanks to God the moment I wake up - simply for the fact that I am alive, because for many people there was no today.

Then in each circumstance I face during the day I give God thanks for his goodness - for my wife and children; for the water in the shower; for the food on my table; for the money in my pocket. If I can learn to live like this in good circumstances then when bad things happen, I can still give God thanks. However, I don't give God thanks for the bad circumstance; I am not a masochist. Nevertheless, even in the hard times, I still give thanks to God that he is good and is the Source of my life, no matter what happens.

This attitude has transformed my life. I still face difficult situations, but since I have begun to adopt the attitude of gratitude my relationship with Jesus through the

Holy Spirit has been much closer and warmer. He really is a good God.

Think of one thing that has happened to you today: the breakfast you ate; the bus or train was on time; your child's smile; that difficult person who sits opposite you in work; or the doctor's appointment. Try giving thanks to the Lord. See what happens.

### November 28, 2004: Prove it

Have you ever had one of those days when the Holy Spirit tests the reality in your own life of something you have been teaching others to live by? A couple of days ago I wrote about giving thanks in all circumstances. Today, my wife Dianne and I were visiting a church in Taunton, Somerset, which is just over an hour from our home. We had a marvellous time there, sharing on making good confessions and giving thanks to God all the time. On our way home, about thirty minutes from the house, we found the road closed. We were diverted to another road that added another forty-five minutes to our trip. That was not too bad; but when we got off this road on to what we hoped would be the final leg we were diverted again! This added another hour to our trip. Furthermore, we had no food with us, and nothing to drink. What did we do? We decided to keep our attitude good and give thanks to God. We arrived home two hours after we should have, tired, hungry, thirsty, but still in good heart. Giving thanks in all circumstances works!

### December 1, 2004: The magnitude of mercy

*I was shown mercy so that in me, the worst of sinners, Christ Jesus might display his unlimited patience as an example for those who would believe on him and receive eternal life. (1Timothy 1:16)*

The life of Saul of Tarsus, better known to us as the apostle Paul, is a tremendous example of the magnitude of God's mercy. It is a powerful reminder to us never to write people off because of the apparent hopelessness of their present condition. Before Saul met Jesus he was a murderous, religious bigot. He was in some ways just as dangerous as today's Islamic terrorists: he killed in the name of his god. However, the gospel of Jesus Christ is powerful and life transforming. God had chosen Saul before the foundation of the world. That day, on the road to Damascus, Saul encountered the risen and ascended Lord Jesus Christ in person. In that instant he was changed by the mercy of God. He was never the same again.

### December 4, 2004: Back Home

The best thing about coming home is being back in the presence of my family. That word 'presence' is the key; it isn't the house that I look forward to coming back to, although we have a lovely one. It's not the city of Cardiff, although it is a great place to live. It is people – my wife and children – that make the difference. Their presence is what I miss when I am away, because they are the most precious part of my life. Gordon Fee describes the Holy Spirit as 'God's empowering presence'. Fee also says:

> "Nothing can take the place of presence, not gifts, not telephone calls, not pictures, not mementos, nothing. Ask the person who has lost a lifelong mate what they miss the most; the answer is invariably 'presence'".

Whenever Christians come together we should seek the presence of God. So often we settle for the gilt edged - 'the songs were great, lots of people came to the meeting, the preaching was good, the meeting finished early' - instead of the gold, 'The Lord was among us'. Once you have tasted the presence of the Lord anything less leaves an awful smell in your nostrils. You will have been ruined for anything else. You were born for God's presence.

### December 16, 2004: Teach your children

I once read an article in *Time* magazine about how languages die. Experts note three distinct stages in the process:

1. A language is considered *endangered* when children no longer speak it.
2. A language is considered *moribund* (about to die) when only a handful of elderly speakers are left.
3. A language is *extinct* when there are no speakers left.

There are important lessons for us Christians in this concerning the passing on of our 'language' from one generation of faith to another. Our 'language' is our revelation of the plan and purpose of God for his world, that 'the earth will be filled with the knowledge of the glory of the Lord as the waters cover the sea' (Habakkuk 2:14). Psalm 48:12-14 tells us to walk about Zion (the Kingdom people of God, the church), to have a good look at her so that we can tell the next generation what we have seen and are building so they will do the same.

We see in Judges chapter two how this trans-generational impartation of revelation broke down. Verse eight of this chapter records the death of Joshua; verse ten says that 'after that whole generation had died, another generation grew up, who neither knew the Lord *nor what he had done for Israel*...they did evil in the eyes of the Lord'.

Something terrible had happened. The previous generation of God's people failed to impart to the next generation any sense of knowing God or his purpose. Their 'language' moved from being endangered, through the moribund state, to extinction. The result was that by the time the previous generation died, the next generation had no moorings to hold them. They had no root, no foundation.

Who was to blame? Not the younger generation, surely. No, the responsibility lay with the previous generation; they failed to prepare and equip their children for God's eternal purpose. There is a divine responsibility on those of us who have walked in the ways of God and his purpose that our revelation does not die with us. I have a priority to give myself to impart to the younger generation of men and women of God the truth I have walked in and the vision of the restored bride that the Church is becoming. And if I die before Jesus returns, then the next generation will play their part fully in bringing him back. Fathers, let's turn our hearts to our children; we owe them their destiny.

## December 21, 2004: Why the angels sang

I began to think about Christmas last week when my son James and I bought the Christmas tree; it is one of our annual traditions. But the real meaning of what this season is all about usually affects me at our carol service, which we held last Sunday night. There we sang what has to be the best carol in the world: 'Hark, the herald angels sing, Glory to the newborn King.' I have always loved it and always sing it with great gusto, perhaps because the angelic realms have always fascinated me.

Luke chapter two tells us that an angel of the Lord appeared to the shepherds the night Jesus was born. Soon the angel was joined by a great company of the heavenly host, who praised God and shouted and sang, 'Glory to God in the Highest!' These were not just angels; a large number of the heavenly host turned up to celebrate. The heavenly host includes the whole angelic realm: cherubs, seraphs, angels, rulers, thrones, principalities, powers, dominions, and mighty ones. God is often described as the LORD of Hosts in the Old Testament; it is a military image in which God is said to be the Commander of a great army; at all times he has absolute supremacy in the heavenly realms, with all the angelic powers ready and poised to do his command.

The angels had waited a long time for this moment and they were going to let the heavenly realms know that what had happened in Bethlehem had cosmic repercussions. The birth of Jesus was not only wonderful for humanity; it meant so much to the heavenly host too. It is true that Jesus came to die for us humans, but his birth, life, death, resurrection, ascension and the sending of the Holy Spirit reversed the curse that one of their own – Satan – had caused.

We should understand something about Satan: he is not a bad version of God; he is not god at all. In fact, he himself is an angelic being – a cherub. Ezekiel 28:12-17 describes what he was originally like; he was an anointed cherub, 'the model of perfection, full of wisdom and beauty.' But it was not enough for him. Lucifer ('Light-Bearer,' as he was known) became proud and wanted to replace God as the Most High (see Isaiah 14:12). All the angelic beings witnessed Lucifer's rebellion. The angels witnessed the creation of the world (Job 38:6-7). They witnessed the creation of Adam and Eve; they saw the pleasure of God as he brought the pinnacle of his creation into being. Then they witnessed the Fall into sin as they saw one of their archangels, who had led the heavenly host in their worship of God, who was magnificently beautiful, become the ultimate evil and slither like a snake in the Garden of Eden, bringing the cancer of sin, death, decay, sickness, hatred, murder, pride – all that was a stench in the nostrils of God – into God's beautiful creation.

The Heavenly Hosts heard the judgement on Satan as God promised him that the Seed of the woman would be born and would crush his head (Genesis 3:14-15). They had waited a long time for the fulfilment of this promise. And now, in an obscure little town in an outpost of the most powerful empire the world had yet seen, the first cries of a newborn baby sent shudders of fear and doom through all the demonic hosts who had done everything they could to prevent this happening. But here he was: the promised Seed of the woman, who would not only undo all that Lucifer had brought into being but would restore everything that God had planned in the first place: to fill the world with a people in his image. No wonder the angels sang for joy over Bethlehem that night!

### December 22, 2004: Days of Elijah

*Elijah said to the widow of Zarephath, 'The jar of flour will not be used up and the jug of oil will not run dry until the day the LORD gives rain on the land'...there was food every day...for the jar of flour was not used up and the jug of oil did not run dry, in keeping with the word of the LORD spoken by Elijah. (1Kings 17:13-16)*

A young man called Abraham came to our church from India in June 2003, to work as a doctor in our local hospital. When he arrived in the UK he bought a small bottle of shampoo and a small can of shaving foam. Abraham used both shampoo and foam each day. Unusually, they did not run out. During this period, Abraham was unable to obtain the post he wanted, so he had to do other less well-paid jobs, which meant that he had to rely on God for his finances, and for everyday items such as shampoo and shaving foam. As the months went by he was surprised that they had still not run out, when other things had. He began to realise that the Lord was providing for him just he had looked after the widow at Zarephath.

Eventually, in October 2004, Abraham began the job he had come to the UK for. Just three days before he started in his new employment, the shampoo and shaving foam finally ran out.

### December 24, 2004: He came

*The Word became flesh and lived among us. (John 1:14)*

When we strip away all the paraphernalia that surrounds Christmas, this one sentence from the Bible is really what it is all about: God became one of us in the Person of Jesus Christ. He came:

- He came because he was sent by his Father;
- He came because he was the Obedient Son;
- He came because he wanted to;
- He came to save us from an eternal hell;
- He came to destroy the works of the devil;
- He came to crush the serpent's head;
- He came to take away our sins;
- He came to set us free;
- He came to give us hope and a future;
- He came to take away our sicknesses and diseases;
- He came for us all;
- He came because he loves us;
- He came to restore us to the image of God;
- He came to make us children of God;
- He came to make us brand new;
- He came to fulfil the eternal purpose of God;
- He came to fulfil the Word of God;
- He came to be King of his Kingdom;
- He came to be Head of the Body;
- He came knowing the inevitable Cross faced him;
- He came to rise again from the dead;
- He came so that we would be baptised in the Holy Spirit;
- He came to give us life in all its fullness;
- He came to make us one as he is one with the Father and the Spirit;
- He came to go back to his Father as the Lord of All;

- He came so we could see God;
- He came so we can know God as our Father.

And one day he will come again.

## January 4, 2005: No other Foundation

*No-one can lay any foundation other than the one already laid, which is Jesus Christ. (1Corinthians 3:11)*

The recent earthquake in the Indian Ocean, which triggered the destructive tsunami, was so powerful it changed the face of the earth. The island of Sumatra is now one hundred feet (thirty metres) west of where it stood before the earthquake. The very foundations of the earth shook. We know that the plates that are beneath us move, causing constant tremors, but we think that the bedrock on which we build is secure. But it is not. The earth itself is moving beneath us. Even the land we build our homes on is on the move. We cannot place our ultimate security even here where we often feel the safest.

There is only one foundation that is totally secure: Jesus Christ. The Bible speaks about *the* foundation, which is Christ; not belief about him nor teaching based on him, but actually him. Christianity is not a set of beliefs or doctrines; it is not a code of behaviour or morals. It includes those things, but they are not the essence of what Christianity is.

The essence is Jesus. He is a real person, alive today, who sits in heaven as Lord of all and who lives in his people, the Church, by the person of the Holy Spirit. So often we substitute the real foundation for the furnishings; but that is a disaster waiting to happen. If anything takes the place of the foundation in my life, I am in real trouble. I cannot build my life on anybody else than the person of Jesus. If I skimp on just part of the foundation then when the storms of life come I cannot stand.

That is what Jesus meant when he told the story of the two men who built their houses on rock and sand respectively (Matthew 7:24-28). The foundation that the wise man built on was *'hearing my words and putting them into practice.'* He was not merely following a teaching but taking into his life the words of Jesus. In doing so he took the person of Jesus into his life. Then he actually did the words of Jesus; he put them into practice.

The foundation of Jesus has to be laid in every believer; that is what the opening verses of Hebrews chapter six are all about. These 'elementary teachings' (literally 'first principles') about Christ are necessary for all of us: repentance, faith in God, baptism in water, baptism in the Holy Spirit, laying on of hands, resurrection of the dead, and eternal judgement. These are all to do with the proper formation of Christ in me; they are not only for teaching 'foundation classes' for those who wish to join our churches. Therefore, I must ensure that each one of these elements of the One Foundation that they comprise is properly laid in me.

### January 6, 2005: Suddenly but not surprising

*Suddenly a sound came from heaven and filled the whole house where they were sitting. (Acts 2:2)*

Around nine o'clock in the morning on Pentecost day something happened in Jerusalem - suddenly. It wasn't gradual and there was no prior warning; it happened suddenly. One moment: nothing. The next: all heaven broke loose among one hundred and twenty men and women. Suddenly. It was the arrival of the Holy Spirit; and when he came suddenly in that moment he came like the blowing of a violent wind and fire that came on all of them. Suddenly. They were all filled. Suddenly. They all spoke in tongues. Suddenly. They were all empowered. Suddenly. They were all changed. Suddenly. The world was not the same. Suddenly.

But they were ready; the suddenly did not take them by surprise. Why? They had been expecting it and were waiting for it. Jesus had told them that 'in just a few days' they were going to be baptised in the Holy Spirit (Acts 1:5). He had told them clearly and they were ready.

Recent events, such as the tsunami in Asia, have shown us how important it is to have early warning systems, for things happen suddenly and we have to be ready. Did you know that the Holy Spirit is about to do something in this world the like of which we have never seen before? These are the greater days that Jesus promised in John 14:12. There have been some amazing moves of the Holy Spirit in recent times, but there is another on the way. The warning signs are there. Will you be ready?

## January 11, 2005: No new questions

Every day on the BBC Radio 4 news programme *Today* someone gives a 'Thought for the Day.' The contributor usually comments on current the issues from a wide range of religious and moral viewpoints.

I was impressed by the contribution of Clifford Longley on yesterday's programme; Longley is a commentator on religious issues and he raised the issue of belief in God being questioned and shaken at this time. Longley made the excellent point that the media and those in Christian ministry come from two opposing poles. Those in the media are too interested in the sound bite and the immediacy of things. So, when a tsunami strikes and kills vast numbers of people, the media will immediately ask Christian leaders, 'Doesn't this shake your faith in God?'

Christians meet this question all the time. However, one is not very long in ministry before one has to come to terms with it. I have had to bury a child that lived just twenty minutes; I conducted the funeral of a Christian friend aged twenty-five who died from a fit; I have lost friends to cancer who were very young; I have had to help parents whose son committed suicide. In my own family we have had to deal with life threatening illnesses where the doctors talked about the possibility of a child not surviving. The question of faith in God during times of suffering is not new for us. The media are too quick to ask such questions as if nobody has thought of them before. Anybody engaged in knowing God and serving him will have already faced this a thousand times, often at the sharp end of things when we are the ones who comfort those who mourn.

What is the answer? Simply that God is a good God, no matter what happens. That is not a trite truism that easily falls of the tongue; it is an essential moral quality of our Creator. This must be so, for if God is not good then nothing makes sense. And if nothing makes sense, then life is meaningless.

### January 14, 2005: Royal responsibility

Last weekend, Prince Harry (third in line to the British throne), was photographed at a fancy dress party wearing the uniform of the Second World War German Army Afrika Korps, complete with a Nazi swastika armband. The incident has created uproar in the UK press, and has spread to the worldwide media too. What has upset so many people is the fact that since Prince Harry is a prominent member of the royal family he has been incredibly irresponsible. His timing was also bad; in a few weeks, events will be held at Auschwitz to commemorate the sixtieth anniversary of the death camp's liberation. Harry should have known better and acted more responsibly. He has issued a statement of apology.

Christians have a royal responsibility. The Bible says that *'we are a chosen people, a royal priesthood, a holy nation, a people belonging to God, that we might declare the praises of him who called us out of darkness into his wonderful light'* (1Peter 2:9). We have incredible privileges as children of God: forgiveness of all our sins; joy; hope; peace; prosperity; health; purpose; a sense of belonging; eternal security; living with God as our Father, with Jesus as our Lord, and the Holy Spirit as our empower.

Along with that comes responsibility; we have to *live a life worthy of the calling we have received'* (Ephesians 4:1). Christians are called to live a life that truly represents God. Whenever people come into contact with us, they are actually meeting the living God in us. That means we have to learn how to live in God's royal family:

- We conduct ourselves with the bearing and dignity of children of the King;
- We realise that people formulate their opinion of what Christianity is all about by watching us;
- We are aware that people often gain their understanding of what God is like by their interaction with us;
- We are proud to be part of the family with our heads held high;
- We walk humbly with our Father and with people;
- We are approachable and normal;
- We always remember that the 'royal robes' we wear are by the grace of God;
- We never switch off being who we are;
- We live every moment to serve our Majesty.

We now live in a world of digital cameras and camera phones, which means that off guard moments like Prince Harry experienced are soon flashed around the world and make the headlines. Imagine how wonderful it will be when the world realises that it is inhabited by billions of princes and princesses who live to demonstrate their royalty by living to please the honour of the One on the throne.

**January 26, 2005: The surpassing value of knowing Jesus**

> *I consider everything a loss compared to the surpassing value of knowing Christ Jesus my Lord, for whose sake I have lost all things. I consider them human excrement, that I may gain Christ. (Philippians 3:8)*

Imagine for a moment that your house caught fire. What would you try and rescue? The cat? The children? Jewellery? Family photos? It is likely that you would go for what you value the most; the rest you could live without. That is what Paul is talking about in this passage of Scripture.

Paul used to think that he had everything going for him, but he came to see that what he thought was to his profit was actually to his loss, all because of one thing - he had met Jesus Christ. After that, nothing could compare with the surpassing value of knowing Jesus. This word 'surpassing' is a very powerful one in the New Testament; it means 'to hold above, be superior, rise above'. Paul used this term to describe what Jesus now meant to him: everything. For Paul, compared to knowing Jesus everything else was dung, excrement. Many of the English versions sanitise this verse for the sensibilities of their readers; they do us wrong. Everything is rotten manure compared to knowing Jesus.

**January 27, 2005: Return to Auschwitz**

Today is the sixtieth anniversary of the liberation of Auschwitz. World leaders are gathering in Cracow, Poland, to commemorate the day when the Russian Army freed the survivors of the Nazi death camp. I had the opportunity of visiting Auschwitz a few years ago, when I was speaking at a conference in Cracow. It is an appalling place. What shocked me was how 'civilised' it was; I was expecting a haphazard, hastily built prison camp. What I found was a carefully thought out, designed, functioning killing city. As I walked around the gas chambers and ovens, I realised that this was a more 'sophisticated' version of the first murder when Cain killed Abel. Mankind had come up with an even more perverse way of doing what sinful men have always done. That is what made it so horrific.

I was moved by this morning's news to see one particular little old lady's return to the camp. She was only ten when she was liberated and had been imprisoned there with her twin sister, who also survived. In fact these two sisters feature in a famous film clip of a line of twins being escorted out of the camp by nurses on the day of liberation. Dr Josef Mengele used twins for his evil experiments on humans, including this woman and her sister.

This little old lady was remarkable. As she shuffled through the snow-covered camp she was interviewed by a reporter. She held no bitterness or hatred towards those who committed these atrocities, even Mengele, but walked in dignity and peace. When asked how she could behave in such a way after all that had been done to her, she spoke about forgiveness: that there was no point in hating those who abused and mistreated her all those years ago. If she had not forgiven them then her life would have been wasted, eaten away by her bitterness and refusal to forgive. She had chosen to live free. In a powerful statement she said, 'Forgiveness is self-healing; it is a gift you make to yourself.'

### February 3, 2005: The slave apostle
*Paul, a slave of Jesus Christ, called to be an apostle and set apart for the gospel of God. (Romans 1:1)*

In his opening sentence to the believers in Rome, Paul tells his readers much about himself. The order in which he introduces himself is very important. First, Paul describes himself as a slave of Jesus Christ. He did not address the church waving his ministry badge - 'I am Apostle Paul'. Writing to the Romans, where status and title meant everything, he made it very clear that any calling he had from God was invested by the ascended Lord Jesus Christ in a slave. Elsewhere in the New Testament, Paul often called himself a servant. He knew his place and his function.

We are first and foremost slaves and servants of Jesus Christ. Without recognising our identity in this way we get lopsided. Calling without servant-hood leads to pride and an abuse of the call. We serve the Christ who called us, not the calling itself.

The incarnation brought about a paradigm shift in all structures of leadership that represent God. Jesus completely destroyed the lust for power and authority that epitomised Lucifer in Isaiah 14:13-14. Philippians 2:5-8 tells us how he did it. He refused to grasp for position; he made himself nothing (literally 'insignificant'); he took the nature of a servant and humbled himself. Jesus was obedient, even to death. These are very powerful statements about how Jesus lived as a man on earth. He knew he had a calling and he knew he was Lord of all; but he carried his calling with the attitude and bearing of a servant. Jesus nailed all ungodly lust for power:

*'You know that the rulers of the Gentiles lord it over them, and their high officials exercise authority over them. Not so with you. Instead, whoever wants to be great among you must be your servant, and whoever wants to be first among you must be your slave - just as the Son of Man did not come to be served, but to serve and to give his life a ransom for many.' (Matthew 20:25-28)*

Jesus did not deride his disciples for wanting to be great. Neither should we discourage our people from their sense of destiny and calling in God. But Jesus defined true greatness: being a servant.

### February 7, 2005: Jesus and the Word

Today I was teaching at our Bible School. We were studying the authority of the Word of God and especially

Jesus' relationship with the Old Testament. Two things in particular stood out to me about how Jesus treated the Old Testament.

Firstly, Jesus never imposed his authority as God over the Old Testament; in fact he deferred to it in his Messianic ministry. Zechariah 9:9 says that the coming Messiah would enter Zion riding on a foal of a donkey. This prophetic scripture, written some five hundred years before Jesus was born, was binding; 'it is written'. Therefore, when Jesus, the Messiah, duly arrived, he could not and would alter it in any way. Jesus could not say, 'I am the Messiah, I am God's Son, I am the One who wrote it, so I can change it if I want to.' No, the Word of God has a real authority given it by God and even he is bound by it. That demonstrates how powerful the Word of God is: God never overrides it.

Secondly, the Old Testament had a self-fulfilling authority over Jesus. Read John 19:23-24; 31-36, and you will see what I mean. In these passages Jesus was hanging on the Cross, in agony, suffering for the sins of the world, and naturally speaking out of control of the situation. At his feet were godless Roman soldiers doing what they did every day; dividing up the goods of those they were crucifying. They had no idea of what was unfolding before them. Suddenly one of the soldiers had a bright idea: they should not tear the clothes of this particular man, but gamble for them. So they did. Even here, in this moment, these ungodly soldiers were fulfilling the Word of God: '*They divided my garments among them and cast lots for my clothing*' (Psalm 22:18, written by David under the inspiration of the Holy Spirit one thousand years before).

Even after Jesus died, the Word of God was still working to fulfil itself. The soldier sent to break the legs of those crucified walked up to the first thief and smashed his legs (this was done to hasten death by suffocation - the victim could no longer stand to breathe). He walked past Jesus (who we know was in the middle) and went to the other thief, and broke his legs. Then he started towards Jesus; on seeing that Jesus was dead he decided not to break his legs. So he took out a spear and thrust it into his side. In that moment this Roman soldier, who had no comprehension of the significance of what he was doing, fulfilled not one but two Old Testament prophecies (Psalm 34:20 and Zechariah 12:10).

When I taught this today it reminded me again of just how wonderful the Word of God is; its authority over my life must be as complete as it was in Jesus and even in its fulfilment of itself through men who had no idea of it. If we who claim to be people of the Word really submit to it in everything then we can release its power in an incredible dimension.

### February 9, 2005: Following means leaving

> The LORD said to Abram, 'Leave your country, your people, and your father's household and go to the land I will show you'. (Genesis 12:1)

Whenever God asks us to follow him, inevitably we have to leave something. Following always demands leaving. Abraham embarked on a nomadic journey; it is true he did not know where he was going, but he knew whom he was following and what he was looking for (Hebrews 11:8-10). He had seen something: the God of glory and the city that God was building; and he was prepared to leave all that he had in order to pursue it.

Jesus said the same thing to his disciples: he said to them, 'Follow me.' They had to leave their boats and nets, their tax-collecting booths, their livelihood. Can you imagine Peter dragging a big fishing net around with him while trying to follow Jesus up the Mount of Transfiguration? Where he was going he would not need it anymore.

When God says, 'Follow me,' he never leads us into an aimless existence. He calls us for purpose. When Abram left

Ur it was because God told him to 'go the land I will show you.' Jesus said his disciples would fish for the souls of men and women, and they would be his witnesses throughout the world. Whenever God calls us to follow him and leave, it is always for something greater than what we were in before he called us. Abram, the 'exalted father', became Abraham, 'the father of many nations.' The disciples became the vehicle for the Holy Spirit to break into the world at Pentecost and were the means of the Gospel going into all nations. If we were to ask any of these men at the end of their lives if they would like to go back to what they were and what they had before God called them to follow him and leave everything, I doubt if any one of them would wish to go back, even though they all had the opportunity to do so. God always leads us out of the mundane and into the extraordinary.

### February 11, 2005: Room for more?

*They all ate and were satisfied, and the disciples picked up twelve basketfuls of broken pieces of bread and fish. (Mark 6:42-43)*

I love the story of when Jesus fed the five thousand. In fact there could have been ten thousand or more, because the gospels tell us that there were five thousand men besides the women and children. The numbers, however, made no difference to Jesus: one hundred or one million, he continued creating the bread and fish. That is what Jesus does; he is the Creator of heaven and earth, so this was no big deal for him.

This incident does not only fill me with faith for the miraculous; it also tells me something about the generosity and overflowing nature of Jesus and the sheer enjoyment he derived from performing these incredible signs. The miracle stopped only when all of the people had enough to eat; but there was far more food for them. Jesus fed them as long as they were hungry and he wanted them to be really full. So he did not just give them a little scrap of bread and fish each; they had such a meal that they were full to bursting. And it was free! Even if they did not like fish they loved this meal.

Their stomachs groaned; they had to loosen their belts and lie down for a minute to sleep it off. Jesus gave them such a feast that he even had leftovers. The disciples needed twelve doggy bags to contain what the crowd had left behind. I always imagine Jesus doing this miracle with a big smile on his face and a twinkle in his eye, saying to the people, 'Sure you can't manage another piece?' Jesus is not stingy or mean spirited. We serve a 'how much more' God! No matter what amount of blessing you need he has more than enough and he never turns off the tap.

### February 16, 2005: God IS into numbers

The other day I received a newsletter from a Christian organisation. The writer was reporting on a man who is working with the Aborigines in Australia. God is blessing this work; the reporter said that the church this man is working in has grown from twenty to six hundred. Then he made the statement that I have heard so often from Christians and makes me cross every time: 'Not that God is into numbers.'

May I make a heartfelt appeal to Christians not to come up with this statement of false humility anymore? It is simply not true. God *is* into numbers: vast numbers; huge numbers; enormous numbers; countless numbers! How do I know? Because God says so in his Word:

*I will make your offspring like the dust of the earth, so that if anyone could count the dust, then your offspring could be counted (Genesis 13:16)*

*Look up at the heavens and count the stars - if indeed you can count them...so shall your offspring be. (Genesis 15:5)*

*I will surely bless you and make your descendants as numerous as the stars in the sky and as the sand on the seashore. (Genesis 22:17)*

*I looked and there before me was a great multitude that no one could count, from every tribe, every nation, every people and every language, standing before the throne and in front of the Lamb. (Revelation 7:9)*

God is into numbers because each number is a person, uniquely made by their Creator. Each one is important to God. Each one has a destiny within God's eternal purpose. Each one counts. Galatians 3:29 tells us that we are the offspring that God is speaking about in Genesis, because Jesus is the Seed who would bring many offspring to God (Isaiah 53:10). God has a big family. So, please: no more of this small thinking. I am proud to be part of a massive number of people - millions and millions of us - who are filling the earth with the glory of God. We are as countless as the sand on the seashore. That is a huge number.

### February 22, 2005: Whose life is it anyway?

A few days ago the writer Hunter S Thompson committed suicide. He was the creator of 'gonzo' journalism and best known for his book 'Fear and Loathing in Las Vegas.' Thompson was an interesting character; no doubt about that. Even if you have never heard of him his writing style has become a well-known feature of modern journalism. What caught my attention this morning was what one commentator on the radio said about him. Thompson is reported to have said that the possibility of committing suicide gave him the ultimate control over his life - he was the ultimate master of his own destiny.

But whose life is it? As a Christian I cannot agree with Thompson, that my life belongs to me. God created me for his sake. I do not have the right to live my life independently of

God, or of his people. God gave me life in the first place and every breath I breathe is only by his grace and mercy. My life is not my own; it is not mine to determine what I will do with it; how I will live it; or when I will end it. In receiving Jesus Christ as Lord I acknowledged that he is the Owner, Master and Lord not of just my moments, possessions, ambitions and desires: he is the Owner, Master and Lord of life itself. If we settle that fundamental truth once and for all then life becomes truly meaningful, because it has meaning only within the desire of the One who created it in the first place. Sadly, this is something that Hunter S Thompson is just discovering.

### February 23, 2005: You're not going out dressed like that

*Clothe yourselves with the Lord Jesus Christ. (Romans 13:14)*

*Stay in the city until you have been clothed with power from on high. (Luke 24:49)*

*Clothe yourselves with compassion, kindness, humility, gentleness and patience. (Colossians 3:12)*

'You're not going out dressed like that!' How many times have we as parents said that to our children? (I vividly remember my parents saying it to me). It is currently the middle of winter, pouring with rain, bitterly cold yet I see loads of youngsters outside; all they have on is a pair of jeans, a T-shirt and a lightweight top that would not protect against the slightest puff of wind. My mother's words ring in my ears: 'You'll catch your death of cold.'

Imagine going to a wedding in your scruffiest, dirtiest clothes - the ones you wear to paint the house, to do the gardening, or clear the garage in. There is no way we would do that; and if we did we certainly not be allowed in! We have to wear the right clothes for the right occasions.

I was intrigued by the verse in Romans 13:14 - *clothe yourselves with the Lord Jesus Christ*. Paul does not often put these three titles/names of Jesus together in one phrase; so when he does it is very important that I take note of it. When I clothe myself the material I actually use is visible to all; people might even admire or pass comment on it - 'nice jacket'; 'great sweater'; 'like the shirt.' They actually can see something on me. That is what Paul says here: the invisible Lord Jesus Christ becomes visible through me. How does that happen? Through the indwelling Holy Spirit who 'clothes' me with him by taking up residence within me. These three words: Lord - Jesus - Christ - all have their own 'material' that must be visible in and on me:

## 1. Lord

The Greek word is *kurios* – 'lord or master.' In New Testament times your lord had the power of life and death over you, without question. For Romans, and indeed for all citizens of the empire, depending on who the emperor was, Caesar was lord. But Romans 10:9 says I have to confess Jesus as Lord. I cannot become a Christian unless and until I do so. That is not just a formula; I believe, I have faith in my heart that Jesus died and rose again from the dead - for me - and then I confess, I speak the word of agreement with God the Father, that Jesus is my absolute ruler and master. I surrender my life to him. I don't *make* Jesus my Lord: he *is* my Lord - Lord of everything - and I submit to his already existing Lordship.

However, there is more to *kurios* than just Lord. In the Septuagint, the Greek translation of the Old Testament, *kurios* is used over six thousand times to translate *Yahweh*, the name of God. So, for the early Church, to say 'Jesus is Lord' was to say 'Jesus is God.' Therefore, in the right sense, and I choose my words carefully here - when I am clothed with 'the Lord' (God), people who look at me look at God. Now don't panic: I am not God; I am not divine; I am not Jesus. I know we hold this treasure in earthly vessels, but the treasure is real and he is really in me. Therefore he must be visible in and on me.

## 2. Jesus

*Jesus* means 'Saviour', or 'the Lord saves.' That is his name - he is Jesus, the Saviour. He saves us from our sins; he takes them all away through his blood shed on the Cross. He removes them completely so that we are no longer sinners but saints. You do not have to be dead or a special Christian to be a saint; when Paul writes to the Philippians he calls them saints - holy ones (Philippians 1:1). That is what we are: as Christians we are no longer sinners. Our nature has changed; we are now born again of the Holy Spirit of God and the Saviour of the World now lives in us. The old has gone, and the new has come. If we are in Christ we are new creations (2Corinthians 5:17); we have never lived before. We are brand new people. From now on we sin only when we choose to do so. We lived saved; put that jacket on.

## 3. Christ

*Christ* means 'Anointed One.' It is the Greek form of *Messiah*. Jesus is the Messiah, the Anointed King (that is what the term came to mean in its strongest form in the Old Testament). Acts 10:38 says that God the Father anointed Jesus with the Holy Spirit and power, and he went around doing good and healing all who were under the power of the devil. At this very moment Jesus is ruling and reigning over the whole universe as the Anointed One, the Messianic King, as the Christ. He is the King of the kingdom of God. Christians are those filled with the Spirit of the Messiah: we too are 'anointed ones.' Again, we are not Christ, we are humans, but we are seated with him in the heavenly realms (Ephesians 1:3; 2:6) and the same Spirit that anointed him is now clothing us (Luke 24:49; Acts 1:8).

Therefore the visible anointing of the invisible Messiah will be seen in and on us. That is what happened at Pentecost: when Peter wanted to prove to his hearers that Jesus is the Messiah who is now exalted to the highest heavens as Lord of all, he pointed to one hundred and twenty people 'drunk' with the Holy Spirit as his only proof. See for yourself; that is what Acts 2:33 says – 'you can see and hear the proof.'

One final thought on all this. Note that Paul says in Romans chapter thirteen that we must clothe *ourselves*. It is in the plural, the clothing is corporate. Jesus is really only fully manifested through his Body, not his toenail, not his left eyebrow. The church is the Body of Christ (1Corinthians 12:12-28; Ephesians 1:22-23; Colossians 1:18). Peter did not point to one person at Pentecost, he pointed to the church, empowered by the Holy Spirit. That should tell us something about the nature of our salvation and the church, and deal a deathblow to the independent, individualistic, 'me and Jesus' mentality and subsequent way of life that pervades and cripples western Christianity. I long for the day when the world looks at the church and says, 'We like your dress sense; you look just like the Lord Jesus Christ.'

## March 18, 2005: Lack of faith displeases Jesus

*Jesus appeared to the Eleven as they were eating; he rebuked them for their lack of faith and their stubborn refusal to believe those who had seen him after he had risen. (Mark 16:14)*

Previously, whenever I read this passage, I was taken aback by Jesus' attitude to the disciples. Now I realise why he had to speak to them like this. Mark 16:10 says that they were hidden away, mourning and weeping not only over Jesus, but over their own situation. Yet he had constantly told them that three days after he died he would rise again and that they would see him again (see Mark 10:33-34). Jesus spoke plainly about it. If they had believed him then they would not have been in this state. They would have been filled with anticipation and excitement, because this was the third day.

Even when Mary Magdalene came running from the tomb to tell them that Jesus was alive, that she had seen him and spoken to him, they did not believe her. In fact Luke 24:11 says they thought she was speaking complete nonsense. Their unbelief was not even challenged by the two disciples who had been with Jesus at Emmaus; they didn't believe them either (Mark 16:13). All this despite the fact that Jesus had spelled out for them clearly, simply and emphatically: 'Three days after they kill me I will rise again from the dead.'

If you do not have faith in the resurrected Jesus, you too will be always mourning and weeping. You have nothing to live for. That night the resurrected Jesus, the one they did not believe was alive, walked through the wall and appeared before them - alive! The one they did not believe in turned up in the room. And he was not happy with them. Jesus did not sit down with his friends as if nothing had happened; immediately he challenged them. In fact he rebuked them. That word is a very strong Greek word; it is used in the New Testament elsewhere:

- In Matthew 27:44 where the thieves who died with Jesus *insulted* him;
- In Matthew 11:20 when Jesus himself *denounced* those cities that did not believe in him;
- In James 1:5, which talks about *finding fault*.

Jesus spoke to his disciples in the strongest terms about their lack of faith in him. Faith was so important for these men that he could not let them off the hook. He did not care for their sensitivities or dignity; he stood on their toes - and it hurt.

Why did Jesus speak like this to the disciples? Because where they were headed in life every one of them would have to be a man of faith. They would be men who would do the works of Jesus and also do the greater works (John 14:12); they had to become men of faith. So do we. Hebrews 11:6 says without faith it is *impossible* to please God. Romans 1:17 stresses that the righteous *live* by faith. Faith pleases God; only faith gets the job done. Therefore, if only because it pleases God, I will be a man of faith.

In order to fulfil their commission, these disciples needed faith. The gospel they would take into the world would be one of faith: they would call people into a relationship with the unseen Jesus, whom they would know by faith. Notice in the following verses how important faith is (*believe* is the same word as *faith* in the New Testament):

*Whoever believes and is baptised will be saved, but whoever does not believe will be condemned. And these signs will accompany those who believe... (Mark 16:16-18)*

Now the great thing about God is that he knows we need faith - so he gives it to us:

- *Ephesians 2:8* - he gives us faith to be saved and to live as Christians;
- *Galatians 5:22* - faith is part of the fruit of the Holy Spirit. Faithfulness is being full of faith, resulting in being trustworthy, persevering;
- *1Corinthians 12:9* - faith is a gift of the Holy Spirit to be exercised just like we exercise the other gifts.

God gives you faith, and he expects you to use it. You are responsible for your faith. When God speaks to you he expects you to believe him and to act on what he says. That is why Jesus was not pleased with the disciples that night - they were no use to him in that state. He had told them he would die and rise again; they should have been waiting for him with faith and anticipation. Instead, they were depressed, sad, and without any motivation. Understand this fundamental truth: when God speaks to you, you either move forward in faith or backwards in unbelief. You never stand still. Where you and I are headed in life we will need faith.

### March 22, 2005: Jesus unwrapped

*This will be a sign to you: You will find a baby wrapped in cloths and lying in a feeding trough. (Luke 2:12)*

*Joseph of Arimathea went to Pilate and asked for Jesus' body. He took it down from the cross, wrapped it in linen cloth and placed it in a tomb. (Luke 23:52-53)*

There are two occasions in the New Testament when Jesus was wrapped in cloths. The first was in those moments just after he had been born into this world as the God-Man. The second was in the hours immediately following his death thirty-three years later. In both instances Jesus was wrapped up by those who loved and cared for him; they wanted him to be safe. At his birth his mother did not want him to be cold; in his death Joseph wanted him to be buried properly and with dignity. Both had sincere motives; they cared. I am sure that Jesus appreciated it.

And yet, even at these times of apparent 'limitation' the cloths wrapped around him did not hinder Jesus. As he lay in the feeding trough in Bethlehem he was still the Eternal Son of God, still *'upholding all things by his powerful word'* (Hebrews 1:3). Even though the Creator had become one of us in the Person of the Son, this divine Person - this baby - was actively at work in his limitless eternity sustaining the very fabric of the universe. Some people think that when Jesus came he left behind in heaven some of his divine attributes; they claim that is what Philippians 2:7 means - 'he emptied himself'. Nothing could be further from the truth. That scripture literally means, 'he became insignificant.' The glory of God was fully and completely present in a baby.

Then, all those years later, as his body lay wrapped in those burial clothes, Jesus was still at work. He had taken the thief who died with him to Paradise. Peter tells us that at this time also Jesus went and preached to the spirits in prison

(1Peter 3:19). Much debate surrounds the meaning of that verse, but all agree that Jesus was active during the period between his death and resurrection. No grave clothes would hinder him.

This set me thinking. What 'cloths' do we attempt to wrap Jesus in to make him ineffective? Here are a few that can stop me enjoying and moving in his unconfined freedom:

- Empty religious tradition;
- Fear;
- Ignorance;
- Unbelief;
- Apathy;
- Cynicism;
- Resistance to change;
- Compromising our convictions;
- Sin;
- Focussing on what Jesus did in the past rather than on what he is doing now.

The antidote for these is to allow the Spirit who raised Jesus from the dead and who now lives in us (Romans 8:11) to release the full power of the Eternal Son in us. That is resurrection life!

Oh, and one last thought for all teenagers. John 20:6-7 tells us that when Jesus rose from the dead he left the grave clothes tidy. He did not just walk out of them and leave them in a heap on the floor. Put your dirty clothes in the laundry basket.

## March 25, 2005: It is finished

*They crucified him. (Mark 15:24)*

This stark, simple statement affects me every time I read it. After a night of torture in which he was beaten up by soldiers, had a crown of sharp thorns thrust deep into his head, was whipped with a Roman scourge, had been sleep-deprived, and dragged through the streets: now came the ultimate degradation. This man who had done no wrong was stripped and nailed to a cross. They crucified him. The Bible makes no attempt at sensationalism; it just states the fact. Jesus, by now barely recognisable, was slowly killed in the most brutal, agonising way.

And he planned it all, along with his Father and the Holy Spirit. That is what it took to remove once for all the sins of the world; to crush the head of Satan; to inaugurate the Kingdom; to release the Spirit at Pentecost; to make disciples of all nations; to reconcile mankind to God; to bring healing; to defeat each and every enemy - including death.

What appeared to the natural eye to be an abject, humiliating, ignominious end of a man's life was in fact the victory of victories and a glorious, overwhelming triumph. That is why with his last breath, Jesus did not cry out, 'I am finished'; he declared to all the creation: 'IT IS FINISHED!'

### March 27, 2005: Get a life

*Why do you look for the living among the dead? He is not here; he has risen! (Luke 24:5-6)*

It is Easter Sunday, just after five o'clock in the afternoon and still light. The clocks went forward last night, which means longer daylight. Warm summer evenings are just around the corner. I love Easter Sunday; it was the day I got saved back in 1966. The past thirty-nine years have been interesting to say the least; but by and large it has been a walk in and into the light. I determined long ago that I would never devote my life to something dead: Jesus was dead for only three days and I was not going to spend my life in the cemetery of dead religion. For me the resurrection is not only an event, it is actually living in a resurrection relationship with Jesus, who is very much alive. And the miracle is that I can get a life - his life! Happy Easter.

## March 29, 2005: Authority must be accountable

I am presently reading Robert Service's outstanding biography of Joseph Stalin. It is a fascinating and horrifying story of how Stalin manipulated, cajoled, abused, terrorised and killed his way to become the most powerful man in the USSR. He was prepared to betray his friends and colleagues, condemning them to the Gulag or the grave. Stalin literally held the power of life and death over the people.

This morning I was listening to the news about this week's forthcoming election in Zimbabwe, which the totally corrupt regime of Robert Mugabe is expected to win by deceit, corruption and violence. This evil man is prepared to see his nation starve to death so he can cling to the trappings of power. All opposition is systematically crushed, but it keeps coming back to challenge him.

I am reminded that all authority structures must also have commensurate accountability structures to ensure that authority does not become autocracy, despotism, or mob rule. Neither can true authority be exercised through mere democratic means; for democracy, while being extremely valuable is still a human invention. This principle must also be present in the church, which represents the nature of God in a unique manner. I believe that leaders such as apostles and elders have real authority. I do not believe the Bible teaches that the church is a democracy; it is a theocracy. Our leaders have an authority from God to do what they have been called to do; they cannot be subject to the whims and political controls of church boards or the fickle and unpredictable voting patterns of church meetings.

At the same time leaders also have to be accountable, because only the one under authority has authority. Totalitarian regimes like Zimbabwe and the former USSR do away with all forms of proper accountability. Church leaders must ensure that whoever has the authority to lead God's people must also be subject to accountability. That is why I am glad to be joined to the men I work with throughout the world. What keeps us safe is that no man is above accountability - even and especially the apostles. While they have real authority and are first among the gifts of Christ to his church, they are not above the rest of us. They understand that their authority can only be exercised by mutual submission to one another, to the church itself, and to those other gifts of Christ to whom God has joined them. This gives them the freedom to exercise a real authority, one that builds up the Body of Christ with free people who are slaves of Christ.

### April 8, 2005: Familiarity breeds intimacy

I am sure you have heard the saying: 'familiarity breeds contempt.' You see someone or something so often you take them or it for granted and no longer value them. I suppose it is true; but in other ways familiarity breeds more appreciation. Familiarity can breed faith. This came home to me today when I was listening to a piece of music.

It was the opening bars of 'Layla' that did it to me. For those of you who don't know the song it is one of the great timeless rock classics: Eric Clapton in his Derek and the Dominoes era. As I heard those notes I immediately knew what the song was and where it was going. I also knew how I would feel, what emotions would be stirred in me. It is music for driving with one arm on the wheel and one hanging over the window. As I listened, a familiar song became even more appreciated. Clapton's guitar soared as he croaked 'Layla, you got me on my knees...' Then it switched into that long piano section that goes on and on, always leading on to the climax of the song. I have heard 'Layla' hundreds of times; but each time as the familiar notes go through my head I find new things to appreciate in the song. Just hearing those opening bars sets me off.

It is the same with God. Every time I open the Bible I have that same anticipation; I know what is coming. Then I begin to read: *How great is the love the Father has lavished on us that we should be called the children of God. And that is what we are!... If the Spirit of him who raised Jesus from the dead is living in you...Anyone who believes in me will do what I have been doing...and even greater things than these...You will receive power when the Holy Spirit comes on you...There is no condemnation to those who are in Christ Jesus...The earth will be filled with the knowledge of the glory of the LORD as the waters cover the sea...In the beginning was the Word...there they crucified him...Through you all nations will be blessed...he healed them all...for God so loved the world...the old has gone; the new has come!...you will lay hands on sick people and they will recover...you will speak in new tongues...they were all filled with the Holy Spirit...the blood of Jesus...*

Familiar words, yes; but breeding contempt? Never. As I cast my eye over these words or they come back to my mind and I speak them out they become even more precious and powerful. The Holy Spirit stirs me and excites me through them; he gives me increasing revelation and wonderment about the power of the Word of God and how it is to be worked out in me. Just as 'Layla' gets into me so does the Word, only in a vastly different dimension and manifestation. I not only remember the words of the Bible; the Holy Spirit takes hold of me and I see the Word fulfilled in me. It becomes such a part of me that it is 'playing' in me all the time, producing the life of God.

Of course, if I never heard 'Layla' it could not affect me. If I do not open my Bible the Word cannot 'sing' to me. And just hearing 'Layla' once was not enough; it took several listenings to know the song. Now each time I hear it I not only know it I know what it will do to me. It is the same with the Word. An occasional 'listening' will never get it into me and change me. Don't be contemptuous: get familiar. That familiarity will breed intimacy.

### April 11, 2005: Santo Subito - Immediate sainthood

*To all in Rome who are loved by God and called to be saints. (Romans 1:7)*

*To the church of God in Corinth, together with all the saints throughout Achaia. (2Corinthians 1:1)*

*To the saints in Ephesus, the faithful in Christ Jesus. (Ephesians 1:1)*

I am a saint. And I am still alive. Amidst the emotion and grief at last week's funeral of pope John Paul II, a cry went up from a section of the crowd, along with raised banners, calling for the dead pope to be recognised as a saint immediately. Roman Catholics believe that a saint first of all has to be dead. Then among other things, a prayer offered to that person results in at least two proven miracles done by them; or they will have done these miracles in their lifetime. After a time of testing and checking they are eventually elevated to sainthood. The only problem with this is that it is totally at odds with what the Word of God says. (I am not attacking Catholics; many Protestants also have views that are against the Word: for example, those who believe in infant baptism or deny the baptism in the Holy Spirit).

The verses above show that Paul was writing to people who were very much alive; and he called them all saints. That is what they were. They were not a special class of Christian: they were what every Christian is - a saint. That word 'saint' literally means 'holy one' and it describes exactly what we are as Christians. The moment we repent of our sins and receive Jesus Christ as Lord our old sinful nature dies - it has gone completely (see Colossians 2:11-15). We become brand new creations (2Corinthians 5:17), and become partakers in the divine nature (2Peter 1:3-4).

We become saints immediately when we receive Jesus as Lord. We are as holy and righteous in that moment of new birth as we will ever be – it is our new nature. Now it is true that we then grow and mature, but only as what we already are - holy and righteous sons of God. We are no longer sinners but saints. I am so glad God does not have a special class of a few holy people, while the rest of the Church is supposed to struggle on in sin, hoping one day to make it to a stained glass window long after we are dead. I received my sainthood thirty-nine years ago yesterday: on 10 April 1966 God declared me holy when I put my faith in Jesus Christ and declared him to be my Lord. And now I am really alive.

### April 13, 2005: The legacy of faith

*...who through faith conquered kingdoms, administered justice, and gained what was promised; who shut the mouths of lions, quenched the fury of the flames, and escaped the edge of the sword; whose weakness was turned to strength; and who became powerful in battle and routed foreign armies. Women received back their dead, raised to life again. (Hebrews 11:33-35)*

A vibrant, living faith in God enables us to do the most amazing exploits. It empowers us to gloriously overcome every obstacle and enemy of our faith. There is nothing that faith cannot achieve; it is the controlling force of so much. Faith even has the power to create. Yet, paradoxically, we have to be honest and say that faith in God also brings difficulties, sometimes severe ones:

*Others were tortured and refused to be released, so that they might gain a better resurrection. Some faced jeers and flogging, while still others were chained and put in prison. They were stoned; they were sawn in two; they were put to death by the sword...They were all commended for their faith, yet none of them received what was promised. God had planned something better for us so that only together with us would they be made perfect. (Hebrews 11:35-40)*

Many of our forefathers in the faith suffered terribly because of their faith in God. They even died for it; yet the Bible says they were all still living by active, vibrant faith when they died. They did not stop having faith in God just because they were going to die. What they believed God for was alive to them; it already existed even though they never saw it with their natural eyes. Even though they themselves would die and not see it in physical reality, it was still real to them; so real that they were happy to die in faith. Faith changes a person completely; a coward becomes a hero.

That is where we come in. This legacy of faith now lies with us, those on whom *the fulfilment of the ages has now come* (1Corinthians 10:11). We New Covenant believers have a responsibility not only to God, but also to all our forefathers of faith. We are the inheritors and the means by which they are made perfect (Hebrews 11:40). That is nothing to do with salvation; the word 'perfect' means 'complete', 'to reach a goal', 'to finish.' It is to do with the fact that we have the privilege of working with them now to complete and finish what they saw and began and died for. We are bringing into physical reality the very same things that they saw by faith. These things were just as real to them as they must be for us, so we can bring these things into a physical, tangible manifestation.

That is why we must have a sense of the presence, by the help of the Holy Spirit, of the great cloud of witnesses of Hebrews chapter twelve who surround us. We must have an understanding of the combined, cumulative faith of all those who have gone before us. Biblical faith is not merely my own personal, individual walk, even though I must have my own faith. Faith is also a walk of the people of God that has been gathering in force and pace since the first person exercised it.

We are walking not only in our faith but also in theirs; we join our faith to that of Abraham, Moses, David, Esther, and Rahab. It is a multiplied, present, now faith. Abraham's faith is still being exercised today through us.

It is vital that we grasp this dimension of faith; I join my faith to those who have gone before as well as those living with me now. The cloud of witnesses are not just a group of watchers or bystanders; they are our encouragers who have left a deposit of faith for us to agree with and walk in and bring to completion what they started. All these people were living by faith when they died. Even though they are now physically dead they still speak, and they speak faith.

Therefore, we take up what they saw and spoke of in faith and we bring it into this physical reality. That is why to agree with Abraham's faith I have to see exactly what he saw. Jesus said that Abraham saw 'my day' (John 8:56); he saw it and was glad. Abraham did not just see Jesus walking around on the earth; he saw much more. This is the day of Jesus - the day we live in now. Abraham saw the church, the Bride, the Body of Christ, mature, beautiful, complete and finished. Hebrews 11:10 tells us he saw the city of God - the same thing. No wonder he died in faith - he had seen it and it was real to him, even though it would be thousands of years before it would come into physical reality.

Faith is too important merely to be focussed only on my personal needs or my blessing. We have to understand that God is looking for a people of the faith of Abraham so they can agree with Abraham in faith that what Abraham saw will come to pass.

## April 19, 2005: Avoiding nostalgia down memory lane

*I was so much older then, I'm younger than that now. (Bob Dylan: My Back Pages)*

I had two strange encounters with my past yesterday. My daughter, Naomi, is training to be a teacher and is on placement in the same school that I attended from age five to eleven. The school was an old building even when I was there; next year it celebrates its centenary. A couple of weeks ago Naomi was telling me about her tutor at the school and mentioned his name. I said that I used to be in high school with someone of that name and asked her to describe him. As she did I felt sure that it was the same man; so I asked to her to enquire if that was so. Naomi did. She said to him that he might know her dad; when she mentioned my name he said, 'Know him? We were really close friends!' He asked Naomi to contact me and ask me to pop in and say hello when I collected her.

So yesterday afternoon I entered the school I last walked into over forty years ago with my daughter in tow, to meet a friend I had not seen for many years. We met in a classroom I had last been in as an eleven year old. Many memories came flooding back; the room even smelled the same. Inevitably we talked about the past and the intervening years - marriages, school friends and characters, families; the years rolled back and we laughed about many of the things we got up to. We were both really good at sports - about the same level at cricket; I was better than him at rugby; he was an absolutely brilliant footballer. We played side by side for over ten years; we even joined the same football team after school. Then life separated us.

All the time as we spoke I was trying to hold two sets of memories and associations together - standing again in my childhood school and being with a man with whom I shared my adolescent years in high school. As we talked we were sixteen again and facing our futures. He is now a grandfather; my own daughter walks the corridors where I once trod with awe so long ago. Then he gave me a tour of the school, asking me to recall memories of those rooms: Miss Esscott, who taught us to write using pens dipped in inkwells...Mr Hughes, the funniest teacher I ever had...the sleep room where we had to go after lunch to sit and put our heads down for fifteen minutes...the playground where we played British Bulldogs...the old wartime air raid shelter whose wall was one of our football goals.

Memory began to be haunted by nostalgia and I suddenly had to catch myself. Those were good days - great days; but not the best days. I honestly have to say that my life is better now than then, even with all the things that have come my way over the years. God has been good to me. I remember standing on the Great Wall of China a few years ago and thinking, 'How did a little Welsh boy from Cardiff get here?' I could easily have allowed myself to become nostalgic and become trapped in a moment of time. But I have learned that nostalgia is a liar; it does not interpret the truth of the past as it really happened.

While I was really thrilled to see my old friend again - and will try and keep in touch with him - I cannot live in my past. I'm younger than that now.

### April 20, 2005: Principles are not negotiable

Cardinal Joseph Ratzinger is now pope Benedict XVI. His election has satisfied the conservatives and saddened the liberals within Roman Catholicism. Mind you, these are relative terms when you talk about Rome; they prefer to use the term orthodox to describe the new pope. That is probably a better term.

The pope's critics within the Church claim that he, like his predecessor, is too dogmatic in sticking to the traditional teachings of the Church concerning issues such as the ordination of women, homosexuality and birth control methods. They hoped that somehow the new pope would be someone who would move with the times and make accommodations for these issues. But they forget that the pope will remain true to what he sees as the fundamentals of Roman Catholicism. While I may not agree very much with Roman Catholic theology, doctrine and practice, I do admire the fact that they stick to what they believe. 'If you want to be a Roman Catholic', they say, 'this is what you must believe and practise.' If you do not want to believe and do these things, then do not call yourself a Roman Catholic. The same principle holds true in the golf club: 'this is a golf club and we play golf; and we play according to the rules of the Royal & Ancient. If you want to play golf, you play this way.'

The pope will hold to his principles; and these principles are not negotiable. I admire him for that, even if I do not agree that his theology is correct (although I agree concerning the ordination of women and homosexuality). Too many church leaders are led along by the spirit of the age, accommodating their beliefs and theologies to the shifting sands of popular culture and opinion. Christianity cannot do that: it offers a culture contrary to the world. It is prepared to offer salvation to the lost, but on God's terms.

Ratzinger was right when he said, 'We are moving towards a dictatorship of relativism that has as its highest goal one's own ego and one's own desires.' The gospel we offer to the world is not one that accommodates itself to the prevailing views of the day; it is one that cuts right across every worldly philosophy with the radical and eternal message that God loves this world, but he will only accept us on his terms. He is not only a God of love; he is a God of light.

Dean Inge said, 'The church that is married to the spirit of this age will be a widow in the next.' We must stand for objective truth no matter what the pressure is to conform, compromise or yield. That is not being bloody minded; it is simply being true, and remaining faithful to eternal truth.

## April 21, 2005: The hand of God
*His hands formed the dry land. (Psalm 95:5)*

*Filled with compassion, Jesus reached out his hand and touched the leper. 'Be clean', he said. (Mark 1:41)*

*'These signs will accompany those who believe: In my name...they will place their hands on sick people and they will get well.' (Mark 16:16,18)*

God does not have literal, real hands; but as I read these words I was reminded and stirred again that because he lives in us through the wonderful Person of the Holy Spirit, whenever we lay our hands on people to bless them or heal them, then our hands are actually at that moment the very hands of God. They have the same creative power in them that formed the universe in the first place. If we can grasp this incredible fact then we will not spend so much time trying to convince God to bless and heal; we will just put his hands on those to whom he guides us.

## April 27, 2005: The test of praise
*Don't praise yourself; let others do it! (Proverbs 27:2)*

*A person is tested by being praised. (Proverbs 27:21)*

It is obvious that we must never praise ourselves; but neither do we seem to want to accept praise from others – which, according to the verse first above, seems to be wrong. It says *let* others praise you. When others want to praise you, let them (if their motive is right). It is fitting to give honour and esteem to those who are worthy of it. So if I refuse to allow people to praise me for something worthy I have done, or to show me appropriate honour, then I rob them of any praise or honour that will subsequently come their way. They have sown honour and praise and cannot reap it if they are refused the opportunity to do so in the first place. For me to refuse praise from others robs them and is in fact false humility on my part, which is inverted pride.

Furthermore, God uses the praise we receive to test our hearts to see if we are really humble. First, we have to be big enough to accept the praise of our friends: 'Thanks for being such an encouragement;' 'That was a tremendous prophecy;' 'You really are a credit to this church;' 'I want to thank you for the way you served last night.' If our hearts are humble we can receive such praise. And if nobody ever praises us, it makes no difference to us. It really does not matter to us, because we know that it is only by the grace of God that we are what we are. If we constantly crave the attention and praise of our friends there is something amiss; but if we can handle it when it comes, knowing it is real appreciation of us and therefore of the Christ within us, then we pass the test of praise.

### May 1, 2005: God's honest truth

*In my holiness I cannot lie. (Psalm 89:35 NLT)*

It is impossible for God to lie, because it is impossible for him to be or do anything contrary to his nature. God does not even consider lying and then chooses not to; it is actually impossible for any option like that to enter his thought process. He is morally incapable of sin. He is holy - absolutely morally and ethically perfect. To be holy God does not have to meet any standard - he *is* the standard. Therefore, for God to lie would deny his very nature as holy. What would happen if he did lie? Nothing would exist anymore, including God himself; everything would go back into nothingness, because the existence of everything depends on the unchanging nature of God and his unchanging word. The fact that the sun came up this morning demonstrates again that God never changes. And it will come up tomorrow. And the next day. And the day after that.

## May 4, 2005: Bread on the table

*In the days when the judges ruled in Israel, a man from Bethlehem in Judah left the country because of a severe famine. (Ruth 1:1)*

The story of Ruth is an excellent example of the sovereign purpose of God in history: how he took a foreign widow, who, to all intents and purposes had no future, and destined her to be an ancestor of the Saviour of the world.

Elimelech, was forced to leave his country because there was a famine. He came from Bethlehem, which means House of Bread; but he had to go away from there because there was no bread in Bethlehem. The result: he died in a foreign land; his wife Naomi (meaning 'pleasant') became Mara ('bitter'). His sons lost a father; then they died and their wives became widows. Elimelech and his sons became food for the worms in a foreign land. All because there was no bread in the house of bread.

It is the responsibility of leaders to feed God's people with the Bread of Life; we must never send them away hungry, starving or feed them scraps. We must feed them so they can live. If our people do not receive bread from us they will starve and become desolate. Or they will wander off and feed on whatever they can get their hands on; they will devour food they are not designed to eat. Jesus wants his sheep well fed (John 20:15-17); not so they can lie around with full and fat bellies, but that they may fulfil the wonderful, unique purpose God has for each one of them.

Being a leader means that we are not at liberty to feed God's people with our own fanciful ideas or latest fads. Neither are we here to extend our own reputations; we are dealing with the lives of real people. Our responsibility is to prepare God's people for eternity and for their heavenly reward. It is an awesome privilege. Let us make sure that there is always fresh bread from God on our tables.

### May 18, 2005: The rich widow

I am always inspired by the story in Mark 12:41-44 about the widow who came to the Temple to give her offering to God. She put in all she had to live on, two *lepta*. Two *lepta* made a *kodrantes*, a Roman copper coin worth about one sixty-fourth of a *denarius*, which was a day's wage for a labourer.

This woman was dirt poor; however, she made a great impression on Jesus as she gave her offering. People far richer than she threw in larger amounts, but none gave as much as she did. Why? Because the *measure* of her giving was much greater than anybody else's. I know millionaires who put £500 in an offering; they give out of their wealth. I know widows who give £5; but the measure of their giving is greater than the millionaires'. To be at the same measure the millionaire would have to give hundreds of thousands of pounds. God is not only concerned with the amount we give; he is concerned about our measure of faith and the measure of generosity we use in our giving.

What happened to this lady? I cannot prove it from the Word, because she is never mentioned again. But I just have a sneaking feeling that she did not remain poor. Why do I say that? Well, Jesus told us:

> *'Give and it will be given to you. A good measure, pressed down, shaken together and running over, will be poured into your lap. For with the measure you use, it will be measured to you.' (Luke 6:38)*

This law of sowing and reaping must have worked for her; she certainly used a good measure - for her it was really large. Therefore, she must have reaped a pressed down, shaken together and running over blessing, don't you think? In fact, she should be called the rich widow.

## June 6, 2005: The world at the end of my street

The street I grew up in had a park at the end of it – about twenty yards (sixty metres) from my house. Maitland Park was my world; I spent most of my waking, non-school, daylight hours there from my earliest memories until we moved when I was eleven. That park was my life.

It was divided in two: a vast grass arena where we played cricket test matches, FA cup finals, Grand Slam rugby (Wales always beat England). It was a battleground where we played 'best faller' (the one who could die the best was the winner). In one day I could score the winning goal, the winning try, take the final wicket and die a hero.

The other section of the park was a massive paved area with a huge slide, monkey bars, a roundabout that we spun as fast as we could then jump off, and swings that could take you twenty feet into the air. It was on those swings that one day I started itching; when I told my mum she got out the calamine lotion (it was pink and dried to a crust on me), poured it all over my body and told me I had chicken pox. I didn't see my beloved world for two weeks.

Maitland Park was a vast world to me; it seemed to stretch out into the far distance, an endless horizon. But of course, it didn't. I just saw it and lived in it through the eyes of a small boy.

Occasionally I have to walk through the park. Every time I realise how small it really is, even though it is still the same size as it always was. The difference is in me: I have grown. I am bigger. I am now a man. The park is too small to contain me now; my world is now much larger. I cannot be confined by that little world that once excited me and filled my life. Leaving the park was painful when I was eleven. Within a short time I found a bigger one. Not long after I left park life behind altogether. I was a teenager. Knew it all. Or so I thought. I became a teenage omniscient and lost the wonder of discovery and imagination. Then I met Jesus. He became my world, and I have not been able to outgrow him. I never will.

### June 8, 2005: Abraham the worshipper

*Abraham looked up and there in the thicket he saw a ram caught by its horns. He went over and sacrificed it as a burnt offering instead of his son. (Genesis 22:13)*

The story of Abraham's obedient and willing sacrifice of Isaac is one of worship. When the angel of the LORD called to Abraham not to kill Isaac, Abraham looked up and saw a trapped ram. He was not looking around beforehand, hoping for an alternative or a get out; he was totally focussed on obeying the Lord in sacrificing Isaac. Only then did he look up.

Now, as far as I can see, the Lord never asked Abraham to sacrifice the ram (I know there is typology at work here - the Lord providing the sacrificial ram prefiguring the Lamb of God). But for Abraham, the purpose of his being on that mountain was not yet complete. Back in Genesis 22:5 he had told his servants that he and Isaac were going to worship God and that both would return (that is real faith). Abraham had worshipped; now the Lord had put a ram in his sight. Abraham could have taken it home with him - it was the blessing of God. But he did not do that: he was such a worshipper, his heart was so overflowing in love and praise to God that he did what came naturally - he sacrificed the ram to the Lord. God had asked for a burnt offering (Genesis 22:2); he received one. Abraham worshipped the Lord with anything he could: son, ram, whatever. He could not return to his servants until he had worshipped. True worshippers are extravagantly generous people; they do not even hold on to life.

## June 9, 2005: Put your money where your mouth is

*Abraham left everything he owned to his son Isaac. (Genesis 25:5)*

Abraham was one hundred and thirty seven when his wife Sarah died. God continued to bless Abraham the rest of his life: he married again and his new wife Keturah bore him six children. He died full of faith at the age of one hundred and seventy five. Abraham gave gifts to all his sons before he died; but he left everything he owned to Isaac. Why did he do that?

He did it because he wanted to sow his wealth into the purpose of God, into his own future. In Genesis chapter fourteen Abraham told the king of Sodom that it was the Lord who had made Abraham wealthy; he understood who his source was. Now, as he prepared to die, he knew that he must sow that wealth into the one who would carry on the purpose of God – Isaac. Isaac's descendants would one day produce the Seed of Abraham - Jesus Christ, who would himself produce many seeds/offspring - the church (see Isaiah 53:10 and Galatians 3). Abraham knew that even though he was about to die, his vision would continue. He had seen the city of God, the day of Jesus, the whole earth filled with his seed - millions and millions of people from every tribe, tongue and nation. Abraham saw us. So he made provision; the purpose would continue through Isaac - his only son as far as that purpose was concerned; he sowed again to the God of the Seed of Abraham. Abraham's wealth represented his life, his time, and his energy. He was not going to leave it to godless

Ishmael or to his other children. He left it to the son of the promise.

I know a godly man whose adult children are totally godless. He is getting very old now. He has told his godless children that they will not receive the major part of his estate. He will bless them as the scripture says he should, but he will not leave them everything. He is sowing it into the purpose of God, into his own future. I know another Christian man, none of whose grown up children walk with God. He plans to leave his vast wealth to them. His choice of course; but why invest 'purpose money' into the godless?

Of course, it is not just to do with money. My whole life must be sown into the purpose of God. I must therefore focus all on that purpose - absolutely everything. That will determine who I see is able to carry on that purpose into the next generation, or until Jesus comes. Then I have to invest all I can into them. This may cause me to appear to be narrow: I prefer to say I am focussed. I will put my money and my life where my faith is - in the God of Abraham.

### June 17, 2005: What a difference a day made
*Rebekah said, 'Yes, I will go'. (Genesis 24:57)*

I love that classic Dinah Washington song, 'What a difference a day made.' For Rebekah, it was certainly true. There she was one afternoon, fetching water from the local well, just like she did every other day, when she came across a man sent from God - Abraham's servant. He had been sent by Abraham to find a wife for Isaac. This man had been asking God for a sign to show him the one destined to play a vital role in the promise made to Abraham concerning his offspring.

It became clear to him very quickly that Rebekah was the one (you can read the whole story in Genesis 24). As the servant later recounted his story to Rebekah's brother Laban and her father Bethuel, they all agreed that she would be the wife for Isaac. Rebekah agreed too (she was not a piece of property to buy and sell; she was a valued and precious woman, loved by her family). The timing was the only problem. Early the next morning Abraham's servant was eager to be on his way with Rebekah. But her brother and mother tried to play the emotional card: *'But we want Rebekah to stay another ten days. Then she can go'* (verse 55). The servant would have none of it: he was on a mission and had to complete it. Sitting around for another ten days, twiddling his thumbs, would be pointless.

They agreed to ask Rebekah. 'Are you willing to go with this man?' they asked her. She replied, 'Yes, I will go.' What was the point of her staying even another moment when her future was waiting for her elsewhere? Just as Abraham had left everything many years before, so now his future daughter-in-law had the same spirit. To stay another day would be a waste. Rebekah's destiny lay in another place with another people. She had counted the cost; she had heard the word of God for her life. It was time to go. In the space of less than twenty-four hours this young lady was on her way to fulfil the purpose of God for her life. She left her family, her place of security, to pursue God. Once you know it is time to go, then go. Your future is waiting.

## June 24, 2005: The doctor will see you now

*Healthy people don't need a doctor - sick people do. I have come to call sinners, not those who think they are already good enough. (Jesus, in Mark 2:17)*

Jesus can help us only when we finally arrive at the point of recognising that we are sinners. Until then his power to save us cannot be properly released. The person who thinks he is already good enough has no awareness of his awful predicament in the sight of a just and holy God; and he cannot acknowledge his need to be saved from that fate which awaits him - eternal punishment. One of the best pieces of news we can receive is that we are sinners.

Once a person knows he is a sinner then there is hope for him; it is good news to realise that you are in trouble with God. That is the beginning of your coming to Christ. Any Gospel preaching or presentation that takes little or no account of the sinfulness of mankind and his need to repent is really no gospel at all. It is not good news to keep from somebody that without Christ he is doomed. The preaching of repentance from sin must be a major aspect of our gospel. Merely encouraging people to decide for Christ or praying a little prayer of invitation to Jesus will not do the job. We have to understand that God is a God of hate as well as a God of love: *you love what is right and hate what is wrong* (Hebrews 1:9). The old adage, *God loves sinners but hates sin* is so true. God is not a benign grandfather, sitting in a rocking chair, blissfully unaware, approving of anything. He is the righteous God who is passionate about sin - he hates it. He is righteous and he sits on a throne that is established on righteousness.

Some might say to me, 'Roger, the world has moved on; we see things differently now. You have to be more tolerant; it is just the way people are.' Well, the world may have moved, but it has not moved on. The issues of sinfulness remain what they always have been. We only delude ourselves that we are more sophisticated than the ancients, which is an act of supreme arrogance on our part. Just knowing more does not change your nature; you can be the most educated sinner - but you are still a sinner.

Once we come into Doctor Jesus' surgery and hear him give us the diagnosis - 'You are sick in sin'- we had better listen to him. For it is only when we acknowledge the expertise and skill of this Doctor and his assessment of our condition, that we are ready to hear his remedy and take his prescription: *'Repent of your sin, put your faith in me, be baptised in water, and receive the gift of the Holy Spirit.'* In that moment of our response, when we take that medicine, the repentant sinner becomes the righteous saint.

## August 5, 2005: Faith and Citizenship

During recent weeks Islam has come under intense scrutiny here in the UK. The sheer horror of the 7 July suicide bomb attacks in London was compounded in the days that followed by the news that these Islamic terrorists were not men who slipped into the country from another nation; they were British Muslims, born and raised here. How could they do such a thing to their fellow citizens? Just two weeks later four more Muslims, this time either born here or brought here as children and raised in our country, attempted the same thing. Thankfully they failed and are now in custody.

The media has been full of articles and reports on Islam and its place in British society. How British do Muslims feel? A survey asked Muslims whether they saw themselves as Muslims first or British first. The percentage who saw themselves as Muslims first was around forty-nine percent. I wondered what the response would be from Christians who were asked the same question. I imagine the percentage would be much higher. I am first and foremost a Christian, a subject and a citizen of the Kingdom of God. Before anything else, that is what I am; it touches my very identity.

However, I am a Christian who is also a British subject. My Christianity will determine how I live and act in British society. I like being British; I love being Welsh. This is where I was born and raised; it is where I live. For Christians our relationship with society is one of separation and involvement. We are separate because we belong to God: we are holy unto him. We are meant to expose the sinfulness of a society without God by being the light of the world. The church is meant to stand apart from the world as the representation and manifestation of a holy, just and gracious God. We are not of this world.

Yet we love the world because God loves it (John 3:16). The word for 'world' in this verse is 'people,' not the spirit of the age. Therefore we involve with it; we go into it with the Good News of Jesus for sinners who can become saints. We do not abandon the world; we certainly do not terrorise it; we do not bomb it; we do not let it go to hell. We are the salt of the earth; we live in it as Jesus lived in it.

Being a good citizen is very important for Christians. The Word of God constantly reminds us to live as such. Jesus told us to pay our taxes; we are told to pray for those in government and in places of authority; we interact with our neighbours; we do good to all people. We work hard at our jobs. We are active members of our communities, reaching out with the life of Jesus across all strata of society. We do not live in Christian ghettos; the Church is not an escape from the world, it is the Body of Christ in it.

In fact, during the persecutions that the early church endured from the Roman Empire, their constant appeal to their persecutors was that they were the best citizens of the empire. Even though their allegiance was to another Lord besides Caesar - Jesus - this allegiance meant that they were the most honest, law-abiding, faithful, hardworking upholders of the empire. When they were persecuted for their faith, they never tried to overthrow the Emperor. They were not terrorists; they were motivated solely by the love of God for his fallen world.

Being a good citizen does not mean we agree with or accept just anything and everything about our society. There is much in British society that is ungodly and wrong: our abortion laws; the way that marriage is no longer honoured; the acceptance of homosexuality; spin politics; the cult of celebrity. As Christians who are British our response is not to destroy our society through violence and hatred (and all violence against any and all religious groups must be condemned. A brick through a Mosque window; the desecration of a Jewish cemetery; the physical or verbal abuse of a woman because she wears a hijab - all are utterly vile and must be condemned). We do not attack homosexuals or blow up the places in which they gather. We do not murder doctors who perform abortions. We do not assassinate our political leaders who pass laws contrary to God's Word. We change society through the very real power of the Gospel of Jesus. As an individual is transformed by the risen Jesus living in him through the Person of the Holy Spirit, so his values, morals, ethics and desires change. Society is people; change people and you change society.

I think of the church that I belong to here in Cardiff. We have hundreds of people from all sorts of backgrounds, cultures and nations. I know people here from African nations whose tribes have massacred each other. To see two men from these tribes breaking bread together as brothers in Christ is powerful. To see another man whose nation has been invaded and occupied by the nation of the brother sitting next to him in peace is absolutely amazing. To talk with a man who prays for a nation while he carries shrapnel in his body from a weapon that nation fired at him – that is awesome. The love of God is more powerful than hate.

## August 10, 2005: Life in the slow lane
*What is this life if, full of care, we have no time to stand and stare? (WH Davies)*

Our twenty-first century western lifestyle leaves little time for reflection, meditation, observing the world around us, or taking stock. I heard this morning that the word 'multi-task' is now in the latest edition of the Oxford English Dictionary, which is published today.

Yesterday I did something that I have not done for a while. I was out for a morning walk when I saw a rose bush and stopped to smell a rose. It was exquisite. Now don't worry: I have not gone ephemeral or effete; it was just that I am beginning to realise again the wonderful creation that is all around us. So often we rush through the days/weeks/months/years without taking the time just to appreciate the stuff of life.

I know life is busy: we have deadlines, responsibilities, meetings to attend, home groups to get to, kids to raise, places to be, money to earn, jobs to do, phones to answer, emails to write, food to buy. But sometimes we are in danger of missing the enjoyment and appreciation of the journey. Maybe we need to slow down sometimes. I am not advocating that we become sluggards or sloths; or that we abdicate our genuine responsibilities. Nevertheless, I do believe there is value in reflection, thought, meditation and rest. While there is no redemptive value or meaning in the Sabbath day (Christ is the fulfilment and I now live the Sabbath rest in him, free from the 'work' of sin), the principle of rest still holds. We are designed by God to rest as well as work. I have a call from God that determines my life, and I enjoy it. Part of that life is learning how to appreciate everything about life. Being someone who stops to smell the roses is important. Here are some things you might consider trying:

- Sit in the garden, close your eyes, and listen to birdsong.
- Turn off your mobile phone for twenty-four hours.
- Go for a walk and count how many butterflies you see.
- Smell a rose!
- Go outside, sit in a chair, and gaze at the moon and stars on a clear night.
- Go for another walk and notice something you missed the last time.
- Just sit and think.

- Read Isaiah 40 out loud, but really slowly.
- Listen to a piece of music that makes you emotional.
- If you have kids, watch them playing.
- Have a meal with your wife/husband at the table, and don't talk about church or jobs.
- Read a joke book.
- Tell God why you love him.
- Count your blessings.
- Hug someone.
- Do a jigsaw puzzle.
- Laugh (just look in the mirror).
- Put your feet up for thirty minutes - don't move.
- Take up a hobby.
- Get an answer machine.
- Read a long classic novel.
- Listen to God without saying anything in return.

## August 11, 2005: Grace, mercy and peace

*Paul...to Timothy...Grace, mercy and peace to you from God our Father and the Lord Jesus Christ. (2Timothy 1:1-2)*

Second Timothy was Paul's last New Testament letter before he was executed. Written from a Roman prison cell under sentence of death, Paul took a final opportunity to encourage and exhort his son in the faith. Paul's natural circumstances were dismal in the extreme; he knew he was not coming out alive. There would be no deliverance. Yet he faced death with faith, in peace, knowing he had run his race and was ready to receive his reward (4:7-8). He was about to see his Lord.

Knowing all this was going to happen to him did not throw Paul into turmoil. His opening words to Timothy were not a tirade of self-pity, frustration, anger or injustice. Rather, they resounded with power. Even though he was in such dire straits, he was still able to minister to this young man the grace, mercy and peace of God. How could he do that? Because he himself was living in that grace, mercy and peace. Our circumstances and situations should not determine what goes on inside us. We should be controlled by the Spirit of grace, mercy and peace - the same Spirit who was at work in Jesus. This same Jesus was the one who could say just hours before his crucifixion, 'Peace I leave with you; my peace I give to you' (John 14:27).

Elsewhere, earlier in his life, Paul said that he had learned the secret of being content in any and every situation (Philippians 4:12); and that is the key. If we as the people of God lock into this secret then no matter what our circumstances we will always be spreading the grace, mercy and peace of God - which is the very life of God himself.

### August 17, 2005: You've changed

*'Where did he get all his wisdom and the power to perform such miracles? He's just the carpenter.' (Mark 6:2-3)*

I'm sure we have all met people we haven't seen for some time: old work colleagues, fellow students, or family members. Sometimes people say to me at those times, 'Oh, you haven't changed a bit!' But in all honesty I know there are just a few signs of the years about me. Last Christmas, while out buying the tree, I bumped into a man I had not seen since high school. The only thing that was the same about him was his voice; otherwise I would never have recognised him.

When Jesus went back to his home at Nazareth after a short time away, his neighbours and friends noticed something different about him. They had known him all his life: watched him grow from a baby to a thirty year old man. They knew Jesus. Some of them had played with him, sat next to him in school, eaten with him, or bought from him. He had always been one of them and yet different. But in their eyes he had changed; there was a discernible difference about him.

This began to intrigue me because Jesus was always perfect, he never sinned, always obeyed his parents, always told the truth, always was honest, never got depressed, and never lost his temper. There was nothing to change; Jesus was perfection in flesh.

Nevertheless when he stood up in the synagogue that Sabbath they noticed something: he had a new wisdom and the power to perform miracles. This man was different. Yet Jesus was always God in the flesh; he did not become God. He already was in fullness what he had been since his birth: the whole miracle of the Incarnation is fully God becoming fully man. He was always perfect God and perfect sinless man, full of wisdom. He was by nature the miracle working God who was upholding the whole universe by his powerful word as he crafted in the carpenter's shop. But something had changed - they were right.

What had happened to Jesus in that time away from Nazareth? Very simple: he had been filled with the Holy Spirit. The tangible difference was the personal presence of the third Person of the Trinity, who had torn heaven open and descended on him in anointing power at his baptism. Even though Jesus was God he was showing us what a man filled with the Spirit could be like. This same Spirit would come from heaven in a windstorm and burning fire just a few years later upon one hundred and twenty people who changed the world. They were never the same again. He is the same Holy Spirit who birthed you into the Kingdom and baptised you in power.

When the Holy Spirit fills us there has to be a tangible, manifest difference in us. And it is a difference that others must notice. The New Testament constantly distinguishes between those who have the Spirit and those who do not:

- Holy Spirit filled people manifest the fruit of the Holy Spirit (Galatians 5:22-23);

- They live in righteousness, peace and joy (Romans 14:17);
- They use all the gifts of the Holy Spirit (1Corinthians 12 and Romans 12);
- They love to worship Jesus (John 4:23-24);
- They do the works of Jesus (John 14:12);
- They are active members of the Body of Christ (1Corinthians 12:13).

I find it very difficult when I meet someone who claims to be filled with the Holy Spirit, but who is short-tempered, cynical, sarcastic, rude, mean, miserable, unkind, lacking in compassion, independent, selfishly ambitious and yo-yoing all the time (up and down, in and out). That is not meant to be critical, but if the Holy Spirit made a difference in Jesus' perfect life, don't you think it reasonable to expect that the difference in us should be even more stark?

### August 18, 2005: Remember the ravens

*The LORD said to Elijah...'Eat what the ravens bring you, for I have commanded them to bring you food'...The ravens brought him bread and meat each morning and evening. (1Kings 17:4-5)*

I wonder what Elijah's reaction was when God spoke these words to him. Elijah had just prophesied to Israel that there would be no rain until he said so. That meant no harvest, no food. God said to him, 'don't you worry; I will look after you in all this. I will feed you. And this is how: I will send ravens twice a day with breakfast and dinner. They will bring you bread and meat.'

Anybody who knows anything about ravens knows one thing: they love meat. What an apparently crazy thing for God to do: to provide meat for his servant via a bird that loves carrion, that eats anything. It would carry the food in its beak; who knows where that beak had been! And what if the raven helped itself to the meal on the way and left Elijah only the scraps? And what exactly would it bring to eat? A vole? A rat? A sparrow? To the natural mind, this sounds like one of God's less clever ideas. But guess what happened? The ravens came, just like God said they would, and fed Elijah with fresh meat. A prophet was well fed by a creature that by nature would not do this.

We must never limit God and the ways he works. We can rest assured that he will always act according to his nature; being omnipotent does not mean he can do just anything. God cannot lie, sin, deny himself or act against who he is. It is impossible for him to do so. He does not even think about the possibility of doing wrong; he is good and everything he does is good. If we settle that truth then we can expect him to work in the most incredible, unimaginable ways that will sometimes blow our minds and upset our neat theologies, but which will always increase our faith and love for him.

Do not tell God what he can and cannot do - he might just want to meet your need through a 'raven', in a way that you never thought he could. Once we learn that he is the source of everything then we are ready to accept that he will meet our need from any resource he chooses. Do not let the resource become the source (the ravens only fed Elijah for a while); and do not refuse a God-sent resource. Remember the ravens!

### August 25, 2005: Through new eyes

*We have stopped evaluating others by what the world thinks about them. Once I mistakenly thought of Christ that way, as though he were merely a human being. How differently I think about him now! (2Corinthians 5:16)*

It is only when we see Jesus Christ as he really is that we are in a position to evaluate anything or anyone else. That is because we are not making our own natural evaluations, since we are no longer natural, we are spiritual. Therefore we must have a *revelation* of Christ. That is a word we use a lot as Christians, and it is right to do so because it is a biblical word. *Revelation* literally means 'the unveiling of something hidden so it can be seen and known for what it really is.' So when God reveals himself we know him for who he really is. He does not say to us, 'Here I am, this is me;' but we are still left wondering, 'What was that?'

Sometimes we say to each other, 'You must get revelation on that,' but that is not what revelation is all about. It is not the same as human investigation, or seeking after God, which is also vitally important and something the Bible says we have to do (Isaiah 55:6). We can only seek God because he has revealed himself to be sought and found. Revelation is not us finding God, but God revealing himself to us so we can know him for who he is. Since Jesus is the final, ultimate revelation of God, we have to know Jesus as he really is. Only then do we know God as he really is. That is what Jesus meant in John 14:9 when he said, '*Anyone who has seen me has seen the Father.*' How do we know or see Jesus? That is where the Holy Spirit comes in. Ephesians 1:17 calls the Holy Spirit '*the Spirit of wisdom and revelation.*' The Holy Spirit is the difference between the natural and the spiritual. When he makes us new creations in Christ, everything changes, everything is new (2Corinthians 5:17). We are totally new people who have never lived before.

Having this new nature by the Spirit includes the fact that we see everything differently from the way the old 'us' did. We no longer make any evaluation of anything or anybody by natural means. Our value systems have changed completely; our views of everything are diametrically opposed to what they were. I thought initially it is like putting on a new pair of spectacles. But then I thought no, it is actually having totally new eyes - the eyes of Jesus Christ himself.

## August 26, 2005: Bring a Bottle

*Enter his gates with thanksgiving; go into his courts with praise. (Psalm 100:4)*

Have you ever hosted a party where everyone is supposed to bring something, only for one of your guests to arrive empty handed, with no present, no food or nothing to drink?

The Bible tells us we should never come into God's presence like that. We are always meant to come with something. In fact, in the Old Testament you were not allowed to come before God empty handed (Exodus 23:15; Deuteronomy 16:16). It was not permissible; if you had nothing in your hand you did not make it into his presence. Bringing something 'to the party' of God was not an attempt to buy his favour; it was an act of gratitude, of worship, acknowledging that everything you were and had was simply because of God. You were not coming to abuse the host, but to give of yourself.

For us as New Covenant believers, the principle still holds. Just think of next Sunday when you join with all the saints at the party (it should be full of life shouldn't it? Who wants to attend a funeral every seven days?). Here are some of the things you can bring to the party this Sunday:

- Come: accept the Lord's invitation. Don't stay away.
- Be on time. Don't come late to this party - the Host is waiting for you.
- Come with thanksgiving and praise: before you get there be ready to praise the Lord. The leader of worship is not there to convince you it is a good thing to worship God. Sing to the Lord in the shower; speak in tongues, read the Bible. Sharpen yourself spiritually

before you arrive, so you come with thanksgiving and praise flowing out from you as you arrive.

- Come to contribute something: what are you going to give to this meeting? Prayer, testimony, stewarding, playing in the musicians, working with the kids?
- Come with the gifts of the Spirit. Same old people prophesying each week? Same few pray-ers? Shake it up.
- Come with your tithe and offering. Bring your tithe to the Lord and give him a generous offering. Ask if you can take up the offering; instead of just passing the basket around have the people come and give it to the Lord. Make sure those who receive it are smiling!
- Come to hear and obey the word. Give agreement to the word; speak your amen.
- Come with friendship. Greet your fellow saints; don't just sit in the same old seat in the same old place. Sit somewhere else. Speak to somebody new.
- Come with the attitude of a servant. Maybe there are tasks and jobs to be done that the faithful few perform each week. I appreciate it when the guests at a party help clear up.
- Come to meet the needs of others: a word of kindness, a practical gift, or an invitation to lunch.
- Come with an expectation of divine visitation. God is in the House!!

### August 30, 2005: RFA
*Be prepared in season and out of season. (2Timothy 4:2)*

*Always be prepared to give an answer to everyone who asks you to give the reason for the hope that you have. (1Peter 3:15*

When I was around eighteen I was part of a group of young people who were being discipled by an evangelist called Mervyn Morgan. He would take us on crusades up and down the country, into schools, colleges, Christian coffee bars, summer camps, anywhere to share the gospel. It was great experience and I will always be grateful to Mervyn for those years.

There was one golden rule when travelling with Mervyn: as soon as we set out he would say, 'OK everyone, are you RFA?' And we would reply 'RFA, Merv'. RFA was our code: *Ready For Anything.* Part of the deal of travelling with Mervyn was that we had to be ready for anything - preach, give a testimony, sing, take an offering, lead someone to Christ - anything. He believed that we should be ready to face anything that came our way. He taught us that we had all the resources in Christ to do what was necessary. It was nerve-wracking, we often made huge mistakes, but it was great fun and an incredible time of learning. This came home to me again the other day.

Dianne and I were walking around Roath Park Lake, one of the best places in Cardiff to stroll. It is about a mile all the way around, and if you are a people watcher, it is the ideal place. The lake is also home to swans, geese, ducks and other wildfowl. Part of living in Cardiff for many residents is feeding the birds at the lake. It is something of a rite of passage. My parents took me when I was a child; I have taken my own. Any walk around the lake also involves negotiating a path through the hordes of birds, waddling up to you looking for a feed, as they did to Dianne and me. And that is when the Holy Spirit spoke to me.

The problem for the birds was that I had no bread with which to feed them. As the swans, ducks and geese gathered round me I said to them, 'Sorry guys, I have nothing for you.' Suddenly these birds were people (not literally of course): needy people, sick people, hungry people, hurting people, lost people, all looking to me for 'bread.' One of those Holy Spirit reminder moments was on me. I always have to be RFA, even 'out of season' as Paul put it to Timothy. Jesus was never caught off guard, unprepared or even under prepared. He always had all the resources within him to meet and deal with every situation. I have the same resource within me; the anointing is a Person, the Holy Spirit. I do not have to say to anybody who genuinely comes to me looking for Jesus, 'Sorry, I have nothing for you.' The Bread of Life is in all of us who are filled with his Spirit; and his power and ability to heal, save, restore hope and meet all needs has not diminished one jot since he walked among us. In fact, it is now magnified and extended because of the Spirit of God who is at large in all the earth. And next time I go to the lake, I will take some bread to feed the birds.

### September 9, 2005: The joy of being you

*You love what is right and hate what is wrong. Therefore God, your God, has anointed you, pouring out the oil of joy on you more than anyone else. (Hebrews 1:9)*

God really enjoys being God. He loves being who he is; he enjoys doing everything he does. God has a great life; it is never a drudge, a drag or a drain. God never wishes he were someone else or somewhere else. He does not have good days or bad days. He never looks longingly at someone else's life and wishes he were like them. He never feels inadequate or lonely. He does not sit in heaven all alone drinking his cocoa waiting for the phone to ring while everyone else is out having the time of their life. God is not a 'Billy no-mates.'

God gets on with himself really well. He has no self-loathing; he does not come under pressure to be a better God, to work harder and meet unreachable targets. If God slept, he would sleep peacefully, with no tranquilisers to calm his shattered nerves. God has no peer pressure; he is totally secure. God believes in himself. He believes what he says about himself. God has a wonderful life, life in all its fullness - and he has given that life to you.

## September 15, 2005: Let's talk

*The LORD...delights in the prayers of the upright. (Proverbs 15:8)*

God loves to hear my voice. Whenever he hears me clear my throat and say, 'Father...' it causes him pleasure. He does not put his hands over his ears; he does not turn up the volume on his iPod or ask the angels to sing louder to drown me out. He is attentive to every word I speak to him; and he enjoys hearing me to talk to him. I never bore him with my prayers; it is never a tedious affair for him to listen to me. He delights in listening and answering.

And I delight in hearing his voice. To think that the Creator of the universe speaks to me! Prayer is not just me talking to my Father; it is also him talking to me. In fact, the longer I have known God the more I just want to listen to him speaking to me. There are times when the words just pour out of me, praising him and loving him, speaking in tongues and in English, and asking him to do things - to bless my family, to heal somebody, to save the lost, to send revival. But there are also those precious times when I just sit in his presence, listening to his magnificent voice, being still and knowing he is God.

Do you think that you have no one to talk to? Think again; then just open your mouth and speak to the One who has all the time in the world to listen.

## September 16, 2005: You met WHO?

I was getting ready for bed last night when my daughter Naomi arrived home. She had been in town for a friend's birthday. Suddenly I heard a shriek and the usual commotion when my two kids get together - next thing she and her brother James were running up the stairs. James was almost apoplectic. The cause of the hoo-ha? Naomi had casually said to James, 'I met that cricketer Shane Wall tonight. He was in the restaurant and one of the girls asked him if he'd have his photo taken with us.' When James got off the floor he said, 'Do you mean Shane Warne?' Naomi replied, 'Oh yes, that's him.' As you can tell, Naomi is not a great cricket follower; unwittingly she had just met the greatest bowler in the history of cricket! Apparently he was really nice and had his photo taken. He is in town playing for his county, but she did not appreciate the moment as much as James and I would have done. The significance of it all had passed her by.

Needless to say, this got me thinking. This coming Sunday, we have the opportunity of a lifetime to meet the greatest, most significant, incredibly talented, beautiful, awesome and outstanding Person of all time - Jesus Christ. He is not a past figure from a book or the latest celebrity; he is alive and well and still making public appearances. He is still the main attraction.

I wonder if we really appreciate and know who exactly Jesus is. And does it truly fill us with excitement and anticipation to think that we will be in the presence of such a Person? Or will it be another same old, same old, just going through the motions? 'Oh, it's only Jesus.' Will we grasp with both hands the opportunity of meeting Jesus Christ or will it pass us by because we couldn't be bothered, we came late, or he doesn't really mean that much to us?

### September 22, 2005: The Paraclete

*I will ask the Father and he will give you another Counsellor to be with you forever - the Spirit of truth. (John 14:16-17)*

*We have an Advocate with the Father: Jesus Christ the righteous. (1 John 2:1)*

These verses explain what we mean when we sometimes say 'Jesus lives in me.' How can this be, since Jesus is actually in heaven, sitting at the right hand of God the Father, ruling and reigning over all things as the ascended King of Kings and Lord of Lords? Yet we are correct in affirming that he does live in us.

Jesus promised that the Father would send us another Counsellor. This word means 'another of the same kind' - another as the same kind as Jesus. The same kind of what? The same kind of Counsellor. That word is *parakletos* (literally 'one who is called alongside to help'). The English name is the Paraclete. Jesus himself is called the Paraclete in 1John 2:1; so in receiving the Holy Spirit we are receiving someone just like Jesus. Having the Holy Spirit is just like having Jesus.

In Jesus' time a teacher's disciples were called his children; and when he died they thought themselves to be orphans (an orphan in those times was someone without a father). However, Jesus promised his disciples they would not be left as orphans (John 14:18); he said he would come to them. He did so in the Person of the Holy Spirit.

Therefore, we have two Paracletes: one in heaven - Jesus; one on the earth - the Holy Spirit. Everything that Jesus is doing in heaven, the Holy Spirit is also doing on earth. The ascended Paraclete - Jesus - lives in us through the Person of the other Paraclete - the Holy Spirit.

## September 28, 2005: Don't fence me in

I have been watching Martin Scorsese's excellent film of Bob Dylan - *No Direction Home*. It follows Dylan from his early life, through his breakthrough to fame via the folk/protest singer movement, to the time in the mid sixties when he created a furore by going electric. 'Folkies' turned on him, even calling him 'Judas' at the famous concert in the UK.

Dylan has always resisted confinement. He was once called the spokesman of his generation - he denied it. He refused to be labelled as the voice of the anti-war movement. He infuriated people; yet he still fascinated and attracted them through his obstinate unwillingness to be pigeon-holed, stereotyped, controlled or owned by any movement or philosophy. He is still like that today.

Jesus sometimes drove people crazy too. He would not fit into their pre-conceived ideas of what the Messiah should be. They wanted him to be a political or military figure - he refused. They tried to make him king - he refused. They tried to localise him - he kept moving on. His hearers and observers constantly attempted to label him, trying to bring him to their level so they could control him, work him out, and make him safe. He never played their game. He said and did controversial things, sometimes just to deliberately provoke and elicit reactions from religious people. He was not vague or obtuse, like Dylan was and is; he would reveal his true self to those who really wanted to know him. But he would not play the religious and political game to win acceptance and understanding with the establishment.

This characteristic should be an aspect of our identity and behaviour as Christians. It is true we have a mission to explain and make things clear to the world; but I hate any label or epithet besides *Christian*. I like it when people ask me what kind of Christian I am; I answer I am a Christian. I can see the cogs in their brains trying to categorise me, and I refuse to be put into any of their accepted criteria. It is a great source of open conversation. As they ask me question after question it enables me to draw them in and to tear down their deeply held conclusions on what Christianity is, what the church is, who Jesus really is. For example, I will often say, 'I'm a Christian, but I have never gone to church in my life.' It gives me opportunity to explain that church is not something to which we go, church is who we are. A friend of mine often greets people by saying, 'It's a great privilege for you to meet me.' You should see their faces!

We are in a time when we have to shatter the world's view - often reinforced by the media - that we are a bunch of insipid, mindless, irrelevant doormats who wouldn't say boo to a goose. No. We are Christians.

## October 3, 2005: The truth will set you free

*'You will know the truth and the truth will set you free.' (Jesus, in John 8:32)*

*'I am the Way, and the Truth and the Life. No one comes to the Father except through me.' (Jesus, in John 14:6)*

I was in the kitchen last night when I heard the sound of a TV commercial coming from the living room. I think it was advertising something like women's hair and beauty products and the voiceover said confidently in trying to convince all the ladies to buy this essential product: 'Twelve thousand people can't be wrong.'

I immediately thought, 'Oh yes they can.' The more I pondered it the more ludicrous that claim became. Just because twelve thousand people all believe something does not make it true. In fact, one million or even three billion people can believe the same thing and they can all be wrong. Most people used to believe that the world was flat or the sun went round the earth. They were wrong.

The truth of something does not depend on how many people believe it. Neither does it depend on the kind of people who believe it. Truth is nothing to do with that. Something is true because it is true, not whether we accept it as true. In these days when relativism attempts to erode the place of objective truth because the truth might offend someone or cut across their religion, their ethics, their morality or their philosophy, there is an increasing cry in the hearts of ordinary men and women for truth. This is not surprising, since the truth is really *the* Truth - the Person of Jesus Christ. He is the objective truth of the objective, eternal True God who never changes.

### October 21, 2005: The measure of mercy
*God...is rich in mercy. (Ephesians 2:4)*

I was blessed in reading again the story of the Good Samaritan in Luke 10:25-37. He was not merely kind to the Jewish man, who was his natural enemy. He did not only perform the bare minimum act of kindness. He expressed measures of mercy and grace that not only saw the other man tended and cared for; he ensured that he was brought to a complete restoration of life and health.

God is like that; he is rich in mercy and grace. In his mercy he does not give us what we deserve: death and separation from him in hell. But he does not leave it there; he expresses his grace to us. In his grace he gives us what we do not deserve: complete forgiveness, a new nature, sonship, hope and a future. When God restores us to himself in Christ he does not only cancel our sin; he gives us a brand new nature. We get much, much more. Amazing grace indeed!

### October 28, 2005: Joyful generosity
*We want you to know about the grace that God has given the Macedonian churches. Out of the most severe trial, their overflowing joy and their extreme poverty welled up in rich generosity...They gave as much as they were able, and even beyond their ability...They pleaded with us for the privilege of sharing in this service to the saints. (2Corinthians 8:1-4)*

I like the way Paul commended the believers in Macedonia. They were a true example of abundant life, even though at this particular time they were experiencing extreme financial poverty. Their joy in the Holy Spirit ruled over their poverty; their lack of material wealth did not control their joy. They were not poor Christians; they were rich in grace, rich in faith, and rich in joy. They just didn't have much money. These believers were so full of the life of the Spirit that they could not help but be rich in generosity to their fellow brothers and sisters who were in need. They didn't adopt a poverty mentality that only receives but never gives. They were not more concerned about their own lack than the needs of others. They pleaded with the apostle that he would give them the privilege and joy of blessing their fellow saints.

Out of their extreme poverty they sowed generously to the Lord. They gave out of a large measure (Luke 6:38), even though the actual amount might have been small in comparison with other churches (it is not the amount we give, it is the measure of our wealth that we give which measures our generosity). And because we always reap what we sow (Galatians 6:7), the Macedonian believers would have reaped back from the Lord much more than they sowed. These were the richest of believers.

### November 11, 2005: Remember me

> *This is my body, which is for you; do this in remembrance of me...whenever you drink this cup, do it in remembrance of me. (1Corinthians 11:24-25)*

Today is Armistice Day. At the eleventh hour of the eleventh day of the eleventh month, we remember and pay tribute to those British servicemen and women who fell in two world wars, as well as those who have died in more recent conflicts. Like many millions of people in this country today, I wore my poppy with pride; and I stopped work at eleven o'clock to stand in silence and pay my respects. We do it to remember. For many the moments are spent remembering friends and comrades, fathers and mothers, brothers and sisters, sons and daughters, who are gone forever and will never return. They are poignant moments, ones we should respect.

Each time Christians break bread together we also remember somebody. But this remembrance is different. The person we remember is not dead; he is not even absent. Therefore we don't eat and drink with sadness or nostalgia; we don't reminisce about former times, recalling the good old days. We don't raise a glass to an absent friend. Our remembering is actually done in fellowship with the One we have come together to celebrate. Our eating and drinking together in the Lord's Supper is a celebration. Jesus is alive!

### November 15, 2005: All Change

I have the most comfortable pair of deck shoes that I love to wear around the house. I've had them quite a while; they just slip on and are so soft and easy on the feet. I'm wearing them now. True, they're a little past their best; but they're just so comfy.

But I'm worried. Dianne, my dear wife, has begun to make comments about them. After twenty-six years of marriage I can read the signs and interpret the signals: my shoes and I will soon be parted. She'll insist that I actually have to throw them away and get another pair. But the new pair won't be as easy to slip on; they'll pinch a bit. It will take time to make them just how I like them. And then she'll do it again. Change, change, change.

It's often said that constant change is here to stay. Like it or not, change is a necessary part of life. Ann Lindbergh said, 'in nature, there is no greater sin than the sin of resistance to change.' As I write these words it's a winter's afternoon; the season long ago changed from autumn and summer is a distant memory – the seasons must come and go. My geraniums, fiery red in the heat of summer, are now fading fast. The frost will soon kill them. As much as they resist, they will die.

Change is sometimes painful and risky, but it's necessary. The purpose of change for us as Christians is that we grow up and become mature. We cannot remain babies all our lives. In 1Samuel 2:19 we read about Hannah, who each year would bring her son Samuel new clothes when she visited him. Why? Simply because he was growing up. He would have looked ridiculous in the clothes of a three year old when he was sixteen. So it is with the Christian: the attitudes of a babe in Christ are not befitting a man of God. The continued immaturity of a disciple of Jesus is unacceptable to God.

That's why the kingdom of God is all about change, maturity and increase. When we are born again by the Holy Spirit and Jesus becomes our Lord we enter into his kingdom (John 3:3). Everything changes: where we were once sinners we now become the very righteousness of God in Christ (2Corinthians 5:21). This kingdom is in the Holy Spirit (Romans 14:17); we truly are as righteous in that moment of new birth as we're ever going to be. We're really in the kingdom.

However, that is not the end, only the beginning. The prophet Isaiah says that the kingdom of God – he called it God's government and peace - will never stop increasing (Isaiah 9:7). Hebrews 12:28 says that 'we are receiving a kingdom that cannot be shaken'; God is actually proactive in shaking things so that only his kingdom remains. Therefore, if we are going to reach our full potential as children of God, the process of change towards maturity is a constant one that accompanies our walk with God at every stage of life. We never stop changing, growing all the time in our likeness to Jesus 'from one degree of glory to another' or with 'ever increasing glory' (2Corinthians 3:18). Living in this ever-increasing kingdom inevitably means constant change, because change is necessary to bring the kingdom of God to maturity and fullness. The process of maturing demands change when and where necessary.

It's vital, therefore, that we recognise a refusal to change does not guarantee that what we care about remains the same, it doesn't. In fact, it gets worse. If we don't change for the better then we don't stay the same, we actually go backwards. The kingdom advances; if we don't let its characteristics mature us we end up fighting its progress. We never stand still. A refusal to change only assures us that what we once cared about has been deprived of what it needs to survive and grow. If we actually took time to think about it, things we sometimes hold on to and refuse to change were themselves originally produced by change.

We must always remember that the changes God brings are always according to his kingdom purpose. God keeps shaking things to ensure that his kingdom comes in all its fullness. He is not just following the latest trends or fads; he does not make changes for change's sake; he is not playing games with us. Just like Samuel's natural body, the Body of Christ is growing. It's perfectly natural for the church to do so. Here some of the things the Holy Spirit challenges me to do so that I can change:

1. Focus my faith – Abraham looked for the city (Hebrews 11:9-10).
2. Let the past be the past – forget the former things (Isaiah 43:18).
3. Don't control the uncontrollable (John 3:8). The nature of the kingdom of God is that it's in the Holy Spirit. He must control it.
4. Don't be self-centred – it's not about me and my agendas, plans and personal self-fulfilment.
5. Be a steward not an owner. Hold everything lightly. Even though he was God, Jesus never grasped at

anything (Philippians 2:6). He died with his hands open.

6. See change as an opportunity to grow.
7. Be prepared to change again.

Now, if I can just distract Dianne's gaze away from my beautiful shoes...

## November 28, 2005: King of kings

*'You are a King, then!' said Pilate. Jesus answered, 'You are right in saying that I am a King'. (John 18:37)*

When we are born again by the Holy Spirit we are born into the Kingdom of God. This kingdom has a King – the Lord Jesus; he is the very real King of this very real kingdom. King Jesus is full of love, mercy, grace and compassion; but as the King of the kingdom he also makes incredible demands on the subjects of his kingdom.

When we enter the kingdom, the kingdom enters us. A real life King takes up residence in us to establish his kingdom. When King Jesus comes into my life it becomes his life. He does not enter as a constitutional monarch, like the one we have in the United Kingdom. Our present monarch, Queen Elizabeth II, has all the trappings of royalty, majesty and power; but she is devoid of any ultimate authority. The authority that was vested in her ancestors now lies with our Parliament; it decides the laws of the United Kingdom and the way the nation will function. The monarch has to sign into law what Parliament decides. Each year the monarch comes to Parliament to read out what her government will carry out in the next year. Yet she has no real authority to change, veto, or even decide anything her government will do. She cannot even say whether she agrees with it or not.

King Jesus is no such monarch. He is no democrat. When he comes, he comes as an absolute ruler. He is King over kings and Lord over lords. He comes as a benevolent dictator; he rules as a kindly and loving despot. When he came into my life it ceased to be my life. He came to demolish my kingdom; he dethroned me and made my heart his throne. He entered my life to dominate and control my every thought, every action, every word, every motive, every moment. That is what it means for the Christian to declare, 'Jesus is Lord.' The season of Advent reminds us that Christmas is about the birth of a King; and that this King now reigns over the whole universe, including you.

### December 7, 2005: I am a Christian

*The disciples were first called Christians at Antioch. (Acts 11:25)*

I am puzzled why Christians so often describe themselves with additional adjectives - Evangelical, Spirit-filled, Charismatic, Bible-believing, born again. I understand that they are trying to explain a theological position or doctrinal belief; but such language often confuses people and does not help the cause. Often when I am sharing my faith with unbelievers they say they are at a loss to understand these labels we put on ourselves.

The New Testament knows nothing of such labels. The early believers in Jesus were called just that - believers. They were also known as brothers and followers of the Way; but they never demarcated themselves beyond that. The scriptures know nothing about any kind of Christian but a Christian. Some might think I am being unrealistic or idealistic; but some time ago I decided not to use any description of myself besides Christian. It gives me so many opportunities to explain to people what a Christian is that a lot of foggy perceptions are blown away for them. Try it for a while and see what happens.

## December 14, 2005: Speaking in tongues

*Anyone who speaks in a tongue...speaks to God. (1Corinthians 14:2)*

Recently I have become more appreciative of speaking in tongues. Those of you who know me will agree that it has been a very important part of my life ever since I was baptised in the Holy Spirit twenty-five years ago. But its vitality and power came home to me afresh in the summer.

One day I was sitting in my chair and began to speak in tongues. Suddenly the Holy Spirit spoke to me and said, 'What are you doing?' A little nonplussed, I replied, 'I am speaking in tongues.' He said, 'No you are not; you are just babbling.' I realised that the Spirit was right: I was not concentrating on what I was doing or to whom I was speaking. Speaking in tongues had become a habit; I was merely going through the motions. Then I thought about how I speak to Dianne; I don't start off in a torrent of words aimed into the air while thinking about something else entirely. I speak to her. In fact, every conversation I have with somebody means proper communication: I am speaking to another person. That made me grasp again what I am doing when I speak in tongues: I am speaking in another language to a Person - to God. I am having spiritual conversations with my Father. Tongues became alive to me again.

I have shared this insight in different conferences and churches in recent months and have lost count of the numbers who have testified that they have also rediscovered what I have: the power that the Holy Spirit has given us in this ability to converse with our heavenly Father in other languages.

### December 20, 2005: The fool

*Altogether, Adam lived 930 years, and then he died. (Genesis 5:5)*

This morning was my last engagement before Christmas; it was something I was never designed to do. I conducted a funeral. Praise God it was a lovely Christian lady, the mother of close friends. It is incredibly powerful to read Jesus' declaration of himself at these events: *'I am the Resurrection and the Life. He who believes in me will live, even though he dies'* (John 11:25). Even so, every time I stand in front of the coffin or say the words of the committal, I think, 'God never intended this; we were not born to die'. It is unnatural.

Even though Adam lived such a long time he was meant to live forever. If he had never sinned he would have lived on and on, fulfilling the purpose for which he had been made. But he was a fool, choosing instead to live outside of obedient fellowship with his Creator. He paid the ultimate price for his folly: he died spiritually in the moment he sinned and then years later he died physically. Death got him. That body, wonderfully created by God and breathed into by the creative Spirit, intended to fill the earth with the glory of God, ended up a rotting corpse, as worm food. What a fool. Praise God for the Obedient Son who set us free from the law of sin and death!

### December 23, 2005: One of us

*What if God was one of us / Just a slob like one of us / just a stranger on the bus trying to make his way home? (Joan Osborne: One of Us)*

*The Word became flesh and lived among us. (John 1:14)*

'If God had a name what would it be and would you call it to his face if you were faced with him in all his glory? If

God had a face what would it look like?' I really like that song by Joan Osborne, it has some perceptive lines in it, like these for example. I know some Christians do not like it; and I know God is not a slob. But the song asks some very good questions, coming from a non-Christian, especially that chorus - what if God was one of us?

The wonderful answer to that question is that God *has* become one of us. The miracle of the Incarnation is that fully God became fully man in the Person Jesus of Nazareth, God the Son. Jesus was a flesh and blood, genuine man. He lived a full human life, doing all the things other humans do. He even cleaned his teeth and went to the toilet. Jesus was not some ethereal, otherworldly figure who floated through life six inches off the ground. He lived in a real world as a real man. He laughed, cried, ate, slept, learnt how to walk and talk, he spilt his food. He was ordinary, just like us.

Except in one regard. He never sinned. Never. He was tempted just like the rest of us, but uniquely he never succumbed. Not once. Those temptations were real; don't let anyone ever kid you otherwise. If they weren't then he is less than us and does not understand what it means to be human. But he lived as a man in total obedience to God, thus qualifying to be the sinless Saviour of the world.

Jesus put a face on God. Jesus said that if we saw him then we had seen God. It was no coincidence that he was born in humble circumstances, lived in a large family (he was the eldest of at least seven children), worked hard for a living, was misunderstood and labelled a bastard, a troublemaker, a religious fanatic, and a demoniac. He brought God down to us, showed him to us in all his glory, and opened the way for us to know him. And now, as the great Bible teacher Ern Baxter said, 'One of us is on the throne!' That is why I love Christmas.

### January 3, 2006: Living in the 'now is'
*A time is coming and now is. (John 4:23)*

Sometimes I have been guilty of delaying to the future what God wants to do in the present. Over the years I have received several specific prophetic words from proven servants of God about what God wanted to do in me and through me. Many of them spoke about 'you will be;' 'you will do;' 'you will go.' Some were fulfilled while others remain waiting to be enacted. I know that there are seasons of fulfilment and of waiting and the timings of God in our lives; but I began to realise that some things had not been fulfilled simply because I had not acted on them in the here and now.

I found the same tendency with things in the church: people say 'this year will be,' 'I'm going to do so and so.' We tend to project into the future what God wants to do now. We can so easily live too much in the 'time is coming' dimension of faith. Recently I was reading this scripture again and the Holy Spirit distinctly spoke to me. He said, 'Stop living in the *time is coming* and start living in the *now is.*' That shook me to the core. I believe I am a man of faith and expect God to do things on a daily basis. But I was slipping into the habit of projecting into the future, even if only by weeks, what God wanted to do in the here and now - this very minute. This has caused a new sense of immediacy to rise in my spirit, and brought a new release of increased faith. Even though Jesus lived with an eternal, long-term perspective he also lived and acted in the here and now. That is how I am going to live. No: that is how I am living today.

### January 9, 2006: The danger of superstition
Sometimes I come across an item in the paper that angers and perplexes me. Saturday's *Times* was one of those occasions. It contained the story of nineteen-year-old Christos Meletis from central Greece, who tragically died of drowning

last week. Very sad, but in itself not that different a news story to make an impact. It was the circumstances of Mr. Meletis' drowning that affected me. He died while trying to retrieve a cross from a frozen lake. Apparently, each year as part of the Epiphany ceremony, the local Greek Orthodox priest throws the cross out over the lake. The person who retrieves the cross is believed to be assured of a year's good luck.

What kind of man of God would make his people do such an insane, stupid thing? A young man has lost his life because a priest gave approval to an unfounded, superstitious act of folly. A year's luck for catching a cross? On a frozen lake? How can these people claim to be the representation of the living God? No wonder the world is turned off by religion; it has more sense.

## January 19, 2006: In his presence

*Eli...was lying down in his own place. Samuel was lying in the temple of the LORD, where the ark of God was. (1Samuel 3:2-3)*

The stark contrast between the old man Eli and the young boy Samuel is vividly portrayed in this incident: the night that God called Samuel by name. Eli was the priest of God; he was a man who should have been at home in the presence of the Lord. Instead he was content to lie down and sleep 'in his own place.' Perhaps he had never been a man who was hungry for God's presence; maybe he just went through the routines of priesthood because that is what Levites did. Or perhaps he had once lived every moment just to be in the presence of the Lord; now he had lost his fervour, his passion, his longing to dwell and soak in the presence of God; to fellowship with his Creator; to hear his voice. It meant little to him anymore. Now it was only a habit, a ritual. Even when the young lad came running in to his room, convinced that Eli had spoken to him, Eli could no longer discern that it was God who had called the boy by name. God did not ignite Eli anymore; it took three visits from Samuel before Eli realised what was going on.

Samuel, however, was different. He did not yet know the LORD, but he was positioned to meet him, even at night when he was in bed. He laid down where the Ark of the Covenant was, the place where God met with his people in glory; the place of his presence. And even though he did not know whose voice it was when God spoke, he heard the voice and responded immediately. Samuel's destiny was to be a judge and prophet, one of the greatest in the Word of God. He would grow to be a man who loved and lived in the presence of God, hearing the voice of his Lord and speaking that word of God to his generation. And this night, once he knew it was God speaking to him he said, 'Speak, Lord, your servant hears.' He began the best way: let God do the talking; let God be God.

That is the great need of our time: for God's people to be concerned with his presence. It is not about meetings or services; not campaigns and faddish initiatives. True: we must present our gospel in contemporary ways for modern people to understand. But the presence of God cannot be advertised or presented in a slick multimedia presentation. It comes from a humble people wanting nothing less than for God to be God. For the presence of God is not detached from God; it is God himself in manifestation in our midst. And those times are not for us to bombard him with inane and petty little things; it is time to say, 'Speak, Lord, your servant hears.' The presence of God is the distinguishing mark of his people. It is what sets us apart from any other people. Sometimes people ask me: 'How will we know when we are in the presence of God?' I reply: 'Oh, you will know.'

## January 23, 2006: What about the animals?

I am slightly wary about today's subject: it concerns animals. Let me make it very clear that I like animals, not in that Disney-esque, schmaltzy sentimental way. But they're part of God's creation that he made for himself (only he could create a giraffe). So I like them. I believe that Christianity must have an ecology in its theology. However, when animals make headline news ahead of the issues of the hour I have to wonder if we're going too far.

Last weekend a northern bottled-nosed whale appeared in the river Thames, hundreds of miles from its normal habitat. For the next 24 hours all the news channels here ran it as their lead story, especially when the whale died while being transported back to sea. Over £50,000 was spent in the attempted rescue operation. Now this is why I am wary, because of the reaction my next statement might cause: I think the whole thing was way over the top. Sure, a whale died. Thousands of sea creatures die every day. Throughout the world people also die in tragic circumstances every day, with no news reporting at all. A shark kills a man in Australia: it features about ten items down on the running order, if at all. But the moment a story like this breaks, the media go crazy, showing every moment of the drama.

In the great scheme of world news a whale swimming down the Thames and dying is not that big a story. What if it had happened on 7 July 2005, or on 11 September 2001? Was it just a slow news day, or do we really need the breaking news that the poor creature died spread constantly across our television screens? What about the thousands of children who died of AIDS related diseases in Africa on the same day and every other day come to that? We ought to get things into perspective.

## January 24, 2006: The right perspective

*God raised us up with Christ and seated us with him in the heavenly realms in Christ Jesus. (Ephesians 2:6)*

Theologians sometimes talk about theology from below and theology from above. Roughly put, the former starts with our subjective experiences and works everything from there. The latter starts with the objective truth of God and works out everything from there. For example: my life experience might lead me to conclude that God is not really that good, because of something that happened to me. Therefore I end up living with a concept of God that is my own making, because of my experience. But if I start with the objective truth of God - that he is good - then I interpret and understand my experience in the light of that truth. My circumstances have no bearing on the goodness of God. It is all a matter of perspective.

For me it is vital to always do my theology from above; to start with the nature of God and work out doctrine from there. Every doctrine and every practice tells us something of the nature of God: baptism, marriage, head-covering, breaking of bread, disciplining children, eldership, you name it. These are not meaningless practices of an empty tradition. If we understand what they represent of the Godhead then we are able to practise them meaningfully. That is why it is important, for example, when we read a letter like Ephesians, not to dive in at chapter four or five. Start at the beginning, where Paul paints that wonderful picture of the purpose of God in Christ. Only when he has explained that purpose does he move on to describe the place of the church, marriage, family and employment within that purpose. Having a heavenly perspective makes living on earth much more meaningful.

## January 26, 2006: Who do you think you are?

*Those who believe are children of Abraham. (Galatians 3:7)*

*If you belong to Christ then you are Abraham's seed, and heirs according to the promise. (Galatians 3:29)*

Over the past few weeks there has been an interesting series on the BBC. It is called *Who do you think you are?* and it features well known British personalities. Each week one of these people traces their family line, often making some fascinating discoveries along the way. Last night's programme was about the broadcaster Stephen Fry; it was especially interesting and poignant. Fry's mother's family originally came from Slovakia; her father had come to the UK in the 1930s to work. The rest of the family stayed in Slovakia. Nobody knew what became of them, but they suspected that the Nazis had killed them (they were Jewish). Sure enough, that is what happened. It was very moving to see Fry in Slovakia tracing his family line and breaking down when he discovered their names, where they lived, and that most of them had perished in the hell of Auschwitz.

Programmes like this always interest me because I cannot trace my family line back very far. My father was illegitimate. I didn't discover this until after both he and my mother had died. I never had a chance to ask him, and after he and mum had gone it was too late. So, on his side of the family, that is where our known genealogy stops.

However, I can trace my genealogy back to 2,000 BC, to another father: Abraham. The Bible tells me that because I am a Christian, I am part of a massive family with millions and millions of brothers and sisters from every tribe and nation. And we have a common father, the father of all the faithful: Abraham. I am a direct descendant of Abraham; I am not Jewish by birth, but I am a true Jew, one inwardly (Romans 9:6-9), because the true children of Abraham are those who believe. Therefore, the children of Abraham comprise all who have faith in Jesus Christ, who is the Seed of the woman (Genesis 3:15) and the Seed of Abraham (Galatians 3:16). The promise of God to bless the nations given in Genesis 12 was never meant to be the natural, physical offspring/seed of Abraham. They are spiritual children, from every people group, who are the sons of God through faith in Jesus Christ. More than that: I also have a heavenly Father and an elder Brother (Hebrews 2:11-12), a Father who chose me to be his adopted son before the foundation of the world (Ephesians 1:4-5). And it is all so the Father can have sons like his Only Son.

It would be nice to know who my blood grandfather was; but I don't feel inadequate or incomplete in any way. My genealogy is easy to find: I just have to open the Word of God and there it is.

### January 31, 2006: Audible obedience
*Samuel said, 'What, then is this bleating of sheep in my ears?' (1Samuel 15:14)*

Sometimes you don't need words of knowledge or the discernment of spirits to know that somebody is living in disobedience to Jesus as Lord. You just need ears and eyes. Their behaviour is like that flock of sheep that Saul failed to kill. God had told Saul to destroy everything to do with the Amalekites, including those sheep. So, when Samuel turned up to check on the progress of obedience it was abundantly clear to him, long before he arrived at the scene, that Saul had disobeyed. Those bleating sheep exposed Saul. They might have been hidden behind a barn, or a hedge; but that bleating gave them and Saul away. There was no hiding place for his disobedience.

It is amazing how stupid we can be on occasions; pretending that all is well while we are faking it in sin. We think that our religious habits will mask the sound; or our self-justification for that tiny amendment to the clear commanded will of God. 'God knows my heart,' we cry. Yet all the time we pose and posture, there is a flock of sheep right behind us giving us away. And they will keep on bleating until they are slaughtered through our repentance and God's gracious forgiveness.

## February 1, 2006: Consanguineous

Here is a fabulous word for all you Scrabble fans. The word is consanguineous: it means to be of the same blood, to have the same parents or ancestors. All of us who are Christians are consanguineous. The same blood has redeemed us all; we all have the same Father; we all have the same royal blood flowing through us. That must be worth a triple-word score.

## February 2, 2006: On your bike

*The LORD said to Samuel, 'How long will you mourn for Saul, since I have rejected him as king over Israel? Fill your horn with oil and be on your way.' (1Samuel 16:1)*

God does not mess about. As we say in this country, he calls a spade a spade. Even though he is eternal and not driven by time, he is on a Divine mission. Since we are involved in that mission, he wants us as focussed as he is on that plan and to keep on track with it. That is why God had no time for Samuel to be sitting around mourning for Saul. God finished with Saul the moment that Saul had wilfully disobeyed him. It was time to move on and Samuel had work to do: the work of God. There was a king to anoint and a kingdom to establish; this was serious work. And God could not afford to have his prophet moping around, filling his head with all sorts of nostalgia, and wasting God's time. I know

God is patient with us; he is faithful, forgiving and longsuffering. But I am talking about something else here.

As God's servants we cannot be sitting around when God is up and doing. Neither can we stay involved in that which God has moved on from. I used to try and convince God that I could change the denomination I was in: 'just give me one more year, Lord. I know that if we get one of the deacons saved the pastor will get on board with the move of the Spirit.' One more year: that is three hundred and sixty five days; twelve months; fifty-two weeks. God told me. 'Be on your way.' I am glad I obeyed; and that principle has stayed with me all these years. The pioneer is a person who has seen the future and lives in it now; we are always 'being on our way.'

### February 3, 2006: Cartoon time

It has been another week full of headlines about religion. A few days ago the UK government's plans to introduce new religious hatred laws were rejected in the House of Commons. The proposals were opposed by all sorts of people: comedians, writers and people of all religious persuasions and none, claiming that these laws would mean that to say anything negative about a religion could lead to prosecution.

Then some European papers published cartoons of Mohammed, lampooning him and Islam. (The cartoons first appeared in a Danish newspaper last autumn, without the current violent reaction). Now the backlash has begun: Islamic communities are burning flags, occupying EU offices, destroying Danish goods in their shops, calling for the death of all those journalists, writers and publishers who have insulted Mohammed.

I thought about putting those cartoons on my web site for all to see. They are easily obtainable on the Internet; I have had a look at them. Satire is part and parcel of our press;

whether that is a good thing or not depends on the target and purpose of it. Some of the anti-Nazi cartoons in the World War II were brilliant. But I decided not to publish the Mohammed cartoons. I am not afraid of Islamic violence against me; but as a Christian I know what it is like to have the object of your worship and adoration ridiculed. Jesus has been the target of some scurrilous and obscene stuff over the years; the recent Jerry Springer musical is quite tame compared with some of the really bad material that has been put out (some of it is too disgusting even to mention).

Does such material offend me? Of course it does. Does it anger and upset me? Yes. Do I complain about it? Indeed I do. I am grateful when other people who are not Christians step in and say that they will not show such terrible things. I was blessed over Christmas by an article by Julie Burchill in the *Times*. Burchill, who is usually no friend of Christianity, wrote a brilliant piece on the state-sponsored persecution of Christians in Pakistan. So, simply because as a Christian I have been the target of this kind of satire I will not show these cartoons here.

Nevertheless, at the same time I totally condemn the hateful response of some Muslims. Their violent outbursts and death threats are vile. Watching the hatred pour out of the mobs is no advert for their religion. I agree that they have the right to stand up and condemn the insults. But to behave in this shameful manner demonstrates only too powerfully the chasm that divides Christians and Muslims. When the world came to perform the most obscene act against our faith, the Saviour of the world allowed himself to be spat on, beaten and nailed to a cross. He defeated his foes by loving them and forgiving them, because he came to save them. Then he rose from the dead to secure their salvation.

### February 10, 2006: It's alive!
*All scripture is God-breathed. (2Timothy 3:16)*

The Bible **is** God-breathed, not **was** God-breathed. I know that the canon of scripture is complete; no more Bible is to be written. And I know that the actual breathing out process of God covered about one thousand five hundred years from Moses to John. In that sense God has breathed out the Bible once and for all.

Nevertheless, every time I read it I discover anew that it is still alive and breathing, just as fresh as when God first breathed it out and communicated it to us via the inspired writers. It has a life of its own. Therefore, every time I open it I can expect God to breathe through it again. The Holy Spirit, the breath of God, will speak to me with the very voice of God.

### February 15, 2006: Fresh blood
*[Jesus] entered the Most Holy Place once for all by his own blood, having obtained eternal redemption. (Hebrews 9:12)*

Last Sunday at All Nations Church, Bob John, one of our members, gave an outstanding testimony. Bob is a dear friend of mine and prays for me several times a day. In recent years he has not been well; and some time ago he had to have his lower left leg amputated. He also suffers from cancer and diabetes; but you will never hear him say anything but constant words of faith and praise in God. Last week Bob was at the hospital having a blood test and was chatting away to the phlebotomist who made a comment about blood: that once it is exposed to air it becomes easily contaminated and only fresh blood is any good for testing. The Lord spoke to Bob and said, 'My blood is always fresh.'

I thought that was amazing. Even though the physical blood of Jesus was shed from a physical body two thousand years ago, it is still as fresh as ever. That is because it is actually eternal blood; Jesus was the holy Lamb slain before the creation of the world. His blood is always fresh because it is not affected by time, but works into time. Jesus' death justified all those who lived by faith before the incarnation and cross. The power of his death works backwards for them and forwards for us.

The practical thing about all this is that the power of Jesus' blood is still as powerful today to do all that it ever did. Later in the meeting last Sunday I had the opportunity to pray for Bob; I claimed the power of that fresh blood of Jesus to work in my brother in Christ. On Monday he went to the doctor for tests on his cancer; they told him it is now in remission. Praise the Lord! His blood is always fresh.

## February 16, 2006: covenant friends

*Jonathan became one in spirit with David, and he loved him as himself...And Jonathan made a covenant with David because he loved him as himself. (1 Samuel 18:1,3)*

The relationship between David and Jonathan is a powerful example to us of the kind of friends that covenant people are. These men became one in spirit; it literally means 'their hearts were tied together.' Covenant is not some kind of legalistic externalism; it is the very life of God himself who exists as a covenant. God makes covenants because he is a covenant. Covenant is the work of the Holy Spirit in joining people together. As far as we know this was the first time David and Jonathan had met or spoken; immediately God did something between them. Only the Holy Spirit could do that. They didn't sit down and have a 'covenant summit' in which they negotiated the terms of their friendship; they became friends because the Holy Spirit attracted them to each other.

What was the key? The Bible says that Jonathan loved David as he loved himself. In doing so he fulfilled the greatest commandment and the Royal Law: he loved God with all his heart, soul and mind: and he loved his neighbour as he loved himself (Mark 12:28-33; James 2:8). Jonathan fulfilled prophetically what each one of us is designed to do in the New Covenant. We love God; we love ourselves; and we love our neighbour in the same way we love God and ourselves. Too many Christians get the order wrong; they try to love God, they cannot or refuse to accept themselves and therefore cannot build successful relationships. You have to get the order correct. When Jonathan looked at David he saw himself; he saw a man who was just like him. It was like looking in a mirror. Therefore he could entrust himself to someone who was like himself - a man of covenant.

### February 20, 2006: Read all about it

*Those eighteen who died when the tower in Siloam fell on them...(Luke 13:4)*

I have read this verse many times and considered carefully what Jesus had to say about repentance and grades of sin. But something new struck me the last time I came across it: Jesus was switched on to what was happening in his world. The incident he referred to is unknown by us; but obviously it was a major talking point with his hearers. Jesus knew what was going on in the world around him; he did not live in 'Jesus-land,' blissfully unaware of the happenings of his day while he lived his isolated, religious life.

Too many Christians have little or no interest in what is happening in the world on a daily basis. They rarely watch the news or read a paper; some seem interested only in listening to Christian radio, watching Christian TV and reading Christian books. We will never reach the world that way. Right now, probably more than ever, we Christians need to have an acute awareness of what is taking place in our world and why. Even in the last two weeks, with the furore over the cartoons of Mohammed, things have moved on again. Soon the world will come knocking at our door and ask if we have anything to say. We have to know what is happening in God's world so we can be God's remedy for it.

## February 21, 2006: Covenant friends: Loyalty
*Jonathan spoke well of David to Saul...(1Samuel 19:4)*

King Saul, to put it mildly, did not like David. Initially he tried to control him; then he became jealous because David was having success. Finally that jealousy festered into hatred and attempted murder. David had to flee for his life. Jonathan, his covenant friend, remained loyal to him, even putting this friendship ahead of the blood relationship with his own natural father. This covenant friendship was marked by practical, tangible loyalty.

It was tested when Saul wanted Jonathan to betray David to him: Jonathan refused to do so; in fact he consistently spoke up for David. Saul spoke badly about David and blamed him for all sorts of nonsense; but Jonathan stood firm for his friend. What is really interesting here is that Jonathan spoke well of David when David wasn't even present. That's one of the proofs of friendship. I don't want a friend who says one thing to my face but when I'm absent says something quite the opposite about me to others. Sometimes I meet my friends and they say, 'We were just talking about you.' I don't have to say, 'Something good, I hope.' I know that these are covenant friends and speak about me in my absence in the same way that they speak to me to my face.

Loyalty can be brought right down to this practical level: it's how I speak about my friend when he cannot hear what I am saying about him. My words will never betray my friend.

### February 22, 2006: Don't own sickness

This morning's news contained a piece about the two and half million people in this country who suffer from asthma. A young lady was being interviewed about her condition; she has been suffering for many years. She purposely spoke about 'my asthma;' she said that she talked like that because it was part of her, something that was so real she could not imagine life without it, even though she hated it and fought against it. She concluded by saying, 'It's like my asthma has a personality.'

I felt compassion for this lady. It is so easy with long-term sickness to speak of it as though one owns it: 'my diabetes, my cancer, my arthritis, my migraines.' People who suffer such long-term illnesses don't need any condemnation. I faced the same situation when I had a heart attack. I determined at the time not to speak of it in terms as if it were mine. It really happened to me, but I never asked for it nor wanted it. It did not belong to me; it was just something that happened to me. I don't deny it happened; the Bible says that Abraham was realistic enough to face the fact that his body was as good as dead. But I refused to own that heart attack; I would not let it become part of my life, or to dominate my life. The abundance of my life is not in sickness, it is in Jesus Christ. I live my life by faith in the Lord Jesus and his power to heal all sicknesses and diseases. I live and speak as a man who is full of health. I cannot live any other way.

### February 28, 2006: Covenant friends: Trust
*David hid in the field. (1 Samuel 20:24)*

Trust is present in varying degrees in any relationship. This is certainly the case in marriage; Dianne and I have had to help several couples over the years where that trust has been betrayed. All too often, when adultery has been involved, the injured wife has said, 'I still love my husband, but I don't trust him anymore.'

Covenant friends are trustworthy: they can always be trusted. David and Jonathan knew this trust in one another in their relationship. To get the full story you'll have to read 1Samuel 20; David was on the run from Saul again and Jonathan was going to Saul to see just how much danger David was in. He told David to go and hide behind a rock in a field while he went to Saul. Thus David found himself all alone in an isolated and extremely dangerous position. He was behind that rock for two whole days while his covenant friend was in the presence of his enemy. During that time there was no communication between them at all.

Do you think David had a little panic or sleepless nights? Do you reckon that his stomach churned with worry in case Jonathan gave him away to Saul? Do you think David felt like a sitting duck? No he did not. He remained calm the entire two days. Why? Because David trusted Jonathan with his life. Absence from one another made no difference to their covenant friendship. David slept like a baby and remained in perfect peace the entire time because he knew that his friend would never betray him. He trusted him. Compare that to Jesus, who was betrayed by his friend Judas in the field of Gethsemane, when Jesus was in his own moment of isolation and danger. The greatest irony is that Judas betrayed Jesus with a kiss - an act of covenant love.

### March 6, 2006: Covenant friends: Vulnerability

*Jonathan took off the robe he was wearing and gave it to David, along with his tunic, and even his sword, his bow and his belt. (1Samuel 18:4)*

Imagine the scene when David and Jonathan first met: David was walking from the battlefield with the head of Goliath in one hand and Goliath's sword in the other. It was not a pretty sight. Despite this, Jonathan did something that appears strange: he gave David his weapons: and his armour, he gave this man the very things that made him feel safe and secure. He realised that he was safe with David and did not need to protect himself; he could let down his guard and be completely vulnerable with his covenant friend.

Vulnerability is a powerful element in covenant friendship. To open ourselves up to others means we run the risk of being abused, rejected or betrayed. But a covenant friend will never abuse you, never reject you, never betray you. We can be utterly open, real and honest with such friends. They know all about us, and still love us! Covenant friends want the best for us and never betray confidences. When I express vulnerability I am putting myself in the hands of others; I can't do that with everybody, but I can do it with some. To be able to be vulnerable is to feel safe.

### March 23, 2006: What time is it?
*Suddenly, a sound like a violent wind came from Heaven. (Acts 2:2)*

Jet lag is weird. Yesterday I arrived home after a trip to the USA. Earlier today my body was operating at 5.00 a.m. while my watch said 10.00 a.m. Experts say the important thing is to adapt to the time zone you are in as quickly as possible.

Even though my body is still operating on a different time zone, I can't live in that time zone; otherwise I would always be five hours behind. I have to embrace the time zone I am in. The adjustment must be made as quickly as possible, otherwise I will always be out of step: asleep when I should be awake; hungry when I should be full; tired when I should be alert.

Pentecost moved the one hundred and twenty believers from one 'time zone' into another; the Holy Spirit came suddenly and jet propelled them into a brand new way of life. In the space of a few moments they entered the age of the Spirit, and all their thoughts, values and understandings had to embrace this new age. Nobody could live at 8:59 anymore; it was now 9.00 o'clock and spiritual jet lag would have left them behind. Well, it's now 8.25 pm on the watch; time for my early afternoon cup of tea.

## March 27, 2006: Principles and methods

There is an old adage: *methods are many, principles are few. Methods often change, principles never do.* This came to mind as I read about the rescue of Norman Kember, the British peace activist. Kember had been held hostage for one hundred and nineteen days in Baghdad after being kidnapped along with three colleagues.

While the media has, on the whole, been positive towards Kember, there has been some considerable criticism of his failure to thank his rescuers. General Sir Mike Jackson, chief of the general staff, suggested that Kember signally failed to express any gratitude to the SAS and other troops who risked their lives to save him. In response, Kember put out the following statement: 'I do not believe a lasting peace is achieved by armed force, but I pay tribute to their courage and thank those who played a part in my rescue.' Kember is a pacifist and a member of the Christian Peacemakers Teams; that is why he was in Baghdad. He had been in the city only three days when he was kidnapped. While we have to respect his principles, the story does raise a few points.

First, should our principles prevent us from being magnanimous? Kember's argument is with the decision makers and those in the corridors of power, not the ordinary soldiers who have to follow the orders required of them. Would it not have helped the cause of peace to say a warm thank you to men who have saved your life, even if you don't agree with their being in the country in the first place? These men are sons, fathers and brothers. They have families; yet they put their own lives in danger to rescue him, a stranger.

To be generous to such men would have made his cause even more honourable, rather than making him appear odd or out of touch. We must hold on to our principles at all costs, if they are worthy ones. Then we have to learn how to apply those principles; we are all things to all men, as Paul said. There is a difference between compromising on principles, which we can never do, and making concessions. For Kember to express thanks, in my view, would not have compromised a principle.

Second: should Kember have been in Baghdad in the first place? Was he foolish or naive? (He used the same term in his statement). He and his colleagues ignored all the accepted forms of protection; it was inevitable that they would be targets. Between ten and forty people are kidnapped in Baghdad every day, and held to ransoms of between £3,000 and £30,000. Four white westerners was too big a prize to resist. Their actions made a rescue by troops unavoidable, even though the four men said that they did not wish to be rescued if they were kidnapped. That was just not going to happen. I don't doubt Kember's bravery; but why act like that in such a volatile situation? David fled from Saul's court when Saul threw a spear at him. Jesus studiously avoided Jerusalem until the appointed time; Paul left Damascus when his life was endangered. It seems to me that to put the lives of others at risk because of one's own actions demonstrates a certain degree of irresponsibility. The whole operation pulled security forces away from other vital duties; costs ran into hundreds of thousands of pounds.

I wish Norman Kember well. I am not a pacifist; and do not believe the Bible teaches it. But it does teach that the sons of God are peacemakers. At least he stood up for what he believed and was willing to lay his own life open for that belief. For that I respect him. Perhaps he could have aided his cause by thinking more of the consequence of his actions on others. I am sure that the death of a soldier in his rescue would have devastated him; I should like to think so.

## March 29, 2006: Death has no dominion

*We know that since Christ was raised from the dead, he cannot die again; death no longer has dominion over him. The death he died, he died to sin once for all; but the life he lives, he lives to God. (Romans 6:9-10)*

Just as death no longer has dominion over Christ - for three days it did its best to hold him in its snares in the tomb - so it does not have dominion over us who are in Christ. Even though we will all die physically until Jesus comes again at the Final Judgement, the power of death is gone from us; it has already lost its sting. We have already begun resurrection life now; the life we live by the power of the Holy Spirit is the resurrection life of Jesus. The resurrection is not merely a wonderful doctrine: it is a life force - the very life of the One who was raised by the Spirit and the Father.

Therefore sin, death and corruption do not dominate us. The physical temple that is our body might be perishing but the imperishable resurrection life of Christ that he lives in us through the Spirit ensures our resurrection in the age to come.

### March 30, 2006: Powerless power

*You will receive power when the Holy Spirit comes upon you. (Acts 1:8)*

*The Kingdom of God is not a matter of talk, but of power. (1Corinthians 4:20)*

An impotent church in no way represents an omnipotent God. The story is told of an old saint being shown around a grandiose, lavishly furnished and expensively finished church building. The guide said to him as he waxed eloquent about the grandeur around them: 'Well, the Church can no longer say, "Silver and gold have I none."' 'True,' replied the saint, 'neither can it say, "In the Name of Jesus Christ of Nazareth - walk."'

### April 3, 2006: Finish the race

*I have finished the race; I have kept the faith. (2Timothy 4:7)*

Late in the evening of October 20, 1968, during the summer Olympics of that year, a few spectators remained in the Mexico City Olympic Stadium. It was cool and dark. The last of the marathon runners, each exhausted, were being carried off to first-aid stations. More than an hour earlier, an Ethiopian, Mamo Wolde, had crossed the finishing line, to win the gold medal. As the remaining spectators prepared to leave, those sitting near the marathon gates suddenly heard the sound of sirens and police whistles. All eyes turned to the gate. Out of the darkness a lone figure wearing the colours of Tanzania slowly entered the stadium. His name was John Stephen Akhwari. He was the last of the seventy-four competitors to finish the marathon. His right leg was bloodied and bandaged, having been severely injured in a fall during the race. His knee had been dislocated. Grimacing with each step, Akhwari hobbled around the 400-metre track.

Realising what was happening in front of them, the spectators rose to their feet and applauded him all the way around the track as if he were the winner. After crossing the finishing line, Akhwari slowly limped away. In view of his injury and having had no chance of winning, a reporter asked him why he had not quit. He replied, "My country did not send me seven thousand miles to start the race. They sent me seven thousand miles to finish it."

### April 5, 2006: Covenant friends: Honesty

*David said to Jonathan, 'What have I done? What is my crime? How have I wronged your father, that he is trying to take my life?' 'Never!' Jonathan replied. 'You are not going to die! Look, my father doesn't do anything, great or small, without confiding in me. Why should he hide this from me? It's not so!' But David said, 'Your father knows very well that I have found favour in your eyes, and he has said to himself, "Jonathan must not know this or he will be grieved." There is only a step between me and death.' (1 Samuel 20:1-3)*

The covenant friendship between David and Jonathan could withstand severe disagreement. They both saw a particular issue from completely different viewpoints and were able to talk about it in complete honesty and reality. Theirs was not a relationship in which they just sat around spouting out nice platitudes of appreciation to each other. Their friendship was forged in the crucible of adversity; and they had to be able to be honest and real with each other. They had to be able to tell each other how they felt, with no holds barred.

On this occasion, both believed the other to be wrong; but neither tried to browbeat the other into submission. Neither threatened the other with the loss of their friendship. They talked it through and resolved the problem (Jonathan was the one in this case who was wrong). There was a line these men could never cross: violating their covenant. Therefore, within those bounds they knew that no matter what came up between them, it would always be resolved. That sense of covenant brings immense security to a relationship.

### April 6, 2006: The Potter's hands

*Who are you, O man, to answer back to God? Has the potter no right over the clay? (Romans 9:20-21)*

There is a missing dimension in our understanding of God today. The sense of his awesome, divine majesty and sovereign power has been replaced in our theology by a God who continually has to justify himself to us, who has to provide an easy life for us, meeting all our needs like a subservient housemaid. God is dumbed down; he is even patronisingly called 'the big man.' Worship and adoration of the One who sits on the throne of heaven has been sidelined for songs about how warm and fuzzy he makes us feel. I have had conversations with Christians who have the audacity to boast that they are not talking to God, as if he were a buddy they fell out with in the schoolyard. God has become a service industry, providing customer satisfaction to the church. And he has some fickle clients.

It is true that the hands of the Potter are a Father's hands (Isaiah 64:8). But he is no indulgent daddy who dotes on his little ones, satisfying their every selfish whim. He is the God who exists for himself, who desires us to be and destined us to become a family of mature sons like his Only Son. He is the God who makes ultimate demands on his people for his own ends. He is interested in us and loves us; but that love is designed to make us like him, not him like us. We have traded the God in whose image we are made for one we have made in our own image. The sooner the church begins to submit to the self-serving hands of the Potter, the sooner we will be formed into the vessel he wants.

## April 14, 2006: It is finished
*They crucified him. (John 19:18)*

None of the Gospel writers dwells on the appalling physical sufferings of Jesus. Their immediate readers would have been familiar with what happened to a crucified man; they saw it all too often. It was the style of execution reserved solely for the lowest of the low, for the commonest criminals. After they had died their bodies were normally thrown in pits or unmarked graves. Jesus was born in obscurity and died in ignominy. And yet this moment was one of absolute triumph; even though to the natural eye it was an abject defeat, the end of the dream.

The Seed of the woman and the Seed of Abraham was being sown into death and the grave so that the Father might reap a family of redeemed sons like his Only Begotten Son. As Jesus gave up his spirit, totally in control of his destiny and the purpose of the Father, he cried out, 'It is finished!' The harvest of a redeemed family was assured, because three days later sin, death and the grave were defeated, totally unable to hold this Occupant. As he burst forth from the dead as the firstfruits of the resurrection of all who would believe in him, Jesus strode out as our Lord and elder brother. And all heaven rejoiced!

## April 20, 2006: The resurrection is not the end
Easter is now over; Jesus has died and risen again. But the resurrection was not the end of the story: something else had to occur to make the resurrection more effective. Forty days after rising victoriously from the dead, Jesus was about to embark on the final stage of what is often called the Christ Event (his virgin birth; sinless life; sacrificial death; burial;

resurrection; and ascension). He would leave this earth to return whence he came – the glory of Heaven. Thirty-three years earlier he had left heaven as God the Son, the second Person of the Trinity, to come to this earth that he had made; to be God incarnate, born of the Virgin Mary as one of us: a real man. He was born in obscurity but now he was leaving in a blaze of glory.

Jesus was no dead hero, about to be carried away on his shield of valour like a slain gladiator. He was no Viking warrior, being transported to Valhalla in a burning ship. He was very much alive and had a mission still to complete. Thus he ascended from the earth into heaven as the all-conquering Saviour of the World and Lord of all. And as he ascended, the cloud of the glory of God received and enveloped him. He sped through the heavens, leading all his defeated captives behind him, gloriously demonstrating his power and authority over them.

As Jesus approached heaven the gates swung wide open for the King of Glory to return home. He swept through those gates in victorious procession. His Father who had sent him welcomed him home; and then that same Father invited him to take his rightful place, to sit on the throne of ultimate honour at the Father's right hand. Thus the Lord Jesus Christ sat down on his kingly throne as King of Kings and Lord of Lords, with the praises of all the heavenly host ringing throughout the universe, with the name above all names, at which every knee will bow and every tongue will confess that he is Lord! Ten days later, this glorified Son and the Father, turned to the Spirit of God and said to him, 'Go!' The result: Pentecost.

### April 25, 2006: Bitterness produces barrenness

*When Michal saw King David leaping and dancing before the LORD, she despised him in her heart...and Michal daughter of Saul had no children to the day she died. (1Samuel 6:16,23)*

Michal is one of those tragic characters in the Bible who, in spite of all the God-given opportunities that came her way, had a wasted life. She married the man she loved, was in a privileged position as the queen of a beloved and popular king, and was a witness to one of the greatest celebrations that Israel had seen for a long time. It meant nothing to her.

Michal had a heart problem: when she saw David dancing in abandonment before the Ark of the Covenant as it was restored to the centre of Israel's worship and life, she despised her husband. But her problem was not with David; it was within herself and her relationship with God. This really was a day to celebrate. It was a day to rejoice in the goodness of God, to praise him for his covenant love and faithfulness. The ark - the symbol of the very presence of God - was coming home. Michal saw nothing of that; all she saw was her husband degrading himself and embarrassing her. (He was not being indecent; that was a false accusation she brought against him). As that bitterness and resentment festered and grew inside her, something died within her spirit. David's worship exposed Michal's heart. And that resulted in her barrenness.

Let me make it clear: I am not saying that every lady who cannot have children suffers from the same attitude as Michal. However, the Bible does show us something here about our attitudes and how they make our lives fruitful or barren. This lady should have involved herself in the celebrations; instead she watched the proceedings from a window. She was an observer, not a participant. She was a critic, a scoffer. She was a watcher from the sidelines, totally unaware of the spiritual significance of what was taking place in front of her. And all the time the One who sees all was observing her heart.

In these days I fear most of all for the cynic, the self-appointed critic, the self-anointed scoffer. I fear for the person, the Christian, who sees the wonders that God is doing and belittles them; who arrogantly denies that it is God at work; who libels and slanders the servants of God; who fills the internet and magazines with withering and inaccurate stories.

We certainly must not just swallow everything just because a well-known Christian says it. Neither must we dismiss everything that does not fit neatly within our theological systems. We have to be like the noble Bereans who 'received the message with great eagerness and examined the Scriptures every day to see if what Paul said was true' (Acts 17:11). That kind of attitude keeps a heart soft and fertile.

### May 3, 2006: Hands off

> *Uzzah reached out and took hold of the ark of God, because the oxen stumbled. The LORD's anger burned against Uzzah because of his irreverent act; therefore God struck him down and he died there beside the ark of God. (2Samuel 6:6-7)*

Some Christians have a problem with this passage of Scripture. They think that God lashed out against a man just because he tried to stop the ark of God falling on the ground. If we read the story from the human viewpoint, then we could quite possibly conclude the same thing. But we must not do that.

The ark was the embodiment of the presence of God; it was where God met with his people; it symbolised his holy and awesome presence. Sinful man was not allowed to approach it; only the Levites could carry it and had to do so on their shoulders. When it was stationed in the Most Holy

Place of the Tabernacle only the High Priest could approach it; and that on just one occasion a year, the Day of Atonement. Even then he had to enter with shed blood and incense. The ark should never have even been on a cart; that is how the Philistines had sent it back after they had captured it. When it was being transported it should have been covered; the eye of sinful man should not have been cast on it. So, when Uzzah touched it he was acting irreverently; a sinful man was 'touching' a holy God.

Uzzah had become over familiar with the holy things of God. The ark had been in his father's house for a long time. He acknowledged that it was holy and important, but he had lived in such close proximity to it that it had lost its meaning to him. I am sure his intention was good, but he had become flippant with the holiness of God. He was involved in the work of God that day, but he had no idea what he was dealing with. There was no sense of divine awe in this man.

This is a salutary lesson for us. While we rejoice in the fact that there is no longer any barrier between God and us because the blood of Jesus has been shed, we must never become flippant and unappreciative concerning who and what we are dealing with. We no longer live in cringing terror of God; neither do we become so familiar with God that he becomes little more than a benign Santa Claus to us. A proper fear of the Lord will keep us in intimacy with him and in awe of him.

### May 16, 2006: Mind blowing

*But you, Bethlehem Ephratha, though you are small among the clans of Judah, out of you will come for me one who will rule over Israel, whose origins are from of old, from ancient times. (Micah 5:2)*

This morning I was with the students of our Bible School, teaching on Christology: the Person of Jesus Christ. It was a great time as we began to unpack the wonderful truth about the God-Man, Jesus Christ. It was a demanding time as we explored the scriptures and discussed the human nature of Jesus. Then we began to study the fact that he is also the long awaited and predicted Saviour/Shepherd King of the Old Testament: the Messiah. Whenever I teach this subject there is one particular verse that always sends shivers up my spine. It is this one from Micah, prophesying in the eighth century BC, about the ruler from Bethlehem. I adore the way that the Word is so specific; that the Messiah would not only come from Judah, but that he would be born in a specific place.

What really gets to me is the phrase about his origins: 'they are from old, from ancient times.' A child will be born in Bethlehem whose existence will not begin at Bethlehem; how can that be? Because the one to be born has no beginning and no end; he is the eternal uncreated Son of God, the One who exists outside of all times and before all times; the Creator of the universe who will uphold all things by his powerful word (Hebrews 1:3), even while in the womb of Mary. Yahweh, the I AM, will become one of us.

### May 17, 2006: Take a deep breath
*All Scripture is God breathed...(2Timothy 3:16)*

The Da Vinci Code bandwagon is gathering pace; along with it is increasing opposition from Churches, religious organisations and pressure groups across the world. It just goes to show that Jesus is still news - he always will be.

To me what the whole thing has done is expose the biblical illiteracy and gullibility of people, including those Christians who say their faith has been shaken by the movie. Such 'faith' needs to be shaken, for it is no faith at all. It has no basis in the Word of God. It only highlights the need for Christians to be People of the Book and to recapture what the Bible really is - the authority of God expressed, the spoken

114

word of God written down. The word 'inspired' in this passage is *theopneustos*, which means 'breathed out by God.' The Bible came from within the 'lungs of God,' from within his very being. God reveals himself to us through speaking, and his ultimate communication is his Word - the Scriptures and even more so, Jesus Christ - the Word of God. God did not find a human book that already had been written and then breathed through it to give it a divine imprint; the Bible originated and came from within the being of God, and was communicated through human authors under the superintendence of the Holy Spirit.

There is no other Jesus but the one revealed in the Word of God. There is no other Scripture besides the Word of God that reveals him. Furthermore, the Scriptures can only be properly understood out of a living relationship with the Living Word through the Holy Spirit. So the Jesus of the Da Vinci Code does not exist, end of story. And the Jesus of the Koran and the Book of Mormon does not exist either.

I am afraid that we are reaping the harvest of years of ignoring and belittling doctrine and theology and replacing them with consumer led drivel. The People of God deserve better; they are fed up with homilies and slickness and Christian marketing techniques. They want to grow to maturity; that will be done only through getting to grips with the Word of God.

### May 19, 2006: Make a profit
*All Scripture is breathed out by God and profitable...*
*(2Timothy 3:16, ESV)*

I like the way the ESV, KJV and NASB translate the word *ophelimos* as 'profitable'. The NIV has 'useful', which does not really draw out the strength of the word. *Ophelimos* means 'advantageous', and comes from a word meaning 'to heap up or accumulate gain.'

The Word of God is breathed out by God so we can gain an advantage, that through receiving it, living by it and putting it into action we accumulate gain in all areas of life. It is much more than useful. It also means that the Word of God will work for us or against us. If we live according to it we will benefit greatly; but if we disobey it or ignore it then we suffer loss. Instead of accumulating profit we suffer spiritual bankruptcy. The Word of God is not neutral, it is living and active and it divides (Hebrews 4:12). It is the very breath of God formed into words. God never speaks neutrally. It will either work for you or against you. You make the choice.

## May 22, 2006: Take your medicine

*All scripture is breathed out by God and profitable for teaching...(2Timothy 3:16)*

So far in this mini series of studies on 2Timothy chapter 3 we've discovered that the Bible is breathed out from within God's very being: that it's his divine breath written down. We've also discovered that it's profitable: we accumulate or heap up again by accepting it as the Word of God and living it out in faith.

Now we must find out what it's profitable for; Paul gives us several different things. First he says that it's profitable for teaching; the Greek word means an instructor, teacher, doctor, master. The Bible is not a book of suggestions or a self-improvement manual. It's not an individualist's charter; it expects to be obeyed without question because it tells us the truth about everything. When we go to school our teachers instruct us that 1+1=2; that is a true fact and if we don't obey that truth we'll get into all sorts of trouble in life. Your bank manager and the taxman will let you know! The Bible does the same; it tells us the '1+1s' about God, ourselves, the world, Jesus, the kingdom, for example. If we believe what it teaches us and put that truth into practice then we accumulate the gain it intends for us.

This word also means 'a doctor'. Imagine you're sick and you go to see your local doctor. He examines you and says, 'You have appendicitis. You need an operation and you'll be fine.' You'd take his diagnosis and welcome his prognosis wouldn't you? I think a person who received such news from a doctor and then ignored it would be an utter fool. But that's what James 1:22-24 is all about! If I don't believe and act on God's Divine Word I am a complete idiot.

I have to adopt an attitude to the Word of God which acknowledges that it knows more than me; that it has to master me, instruct me, teach me, diagnose and heal me. If I adopt such an attitude of faith acceptance and consequent action I'm well on the way.

## May 23, 2006: Gotcha
*All Scripture...is profitable for...rebuking. (2Timothy 3:16)*

Do you enjoy being corrected? How do you feel about being proved wrong? Do you like being shown the error of your ways? Well, that's the next way in which the Bible is profitable for you. The only time this word rebuking (*elegmos*) occurs in the New Testament is in this verse. It literally means 'the conviction of a sinner', 'punishment', 'the refuting of error', 'rebuke'. That doesn't mean we use the Bible to whack each other over the head or to prove a self-righteous point against somebody. It means that whenever we come to the Word it holds our lives, values, sense of right and wrong, opinions, lifestyles, and morals up against the searing light of the truth of God.

The Bible sorts us out; it shows us the errors of our ways outside of Christ and tells us how to change. It exposes our sinfulness as lost sinners then affirms us as saints when we come to Christ. Through the Word of God we discover how right God is and how wrong we are without him - and how right we are within him!

The Bible tells us when and how to do right and avoid wrong. It rebukes us strongly when we think and act contrary to our new nature in Christ. It deals ruthlessly with bad attitudes and sin; it confirms and encourages us when we live and walk in the truth. It's a violent book!

### May 24, 2006: Stand up straight

*All scripture is...profitable...for correcting. (2Timothy 3:16)*

When I was growing up my dad constantly told me not to stoop or slouch but to stand up straight with my shoulders back and head up. It worked and gave me good posture.

The Bible stops us slouching and stooping; the word *epanorthosis* (correcting) literally means to straighten up what is twisted, to rectify, to reform. When the Word of God gets hold of us it's like a spiritual chiropractor or osteopath that gets to work on the twisted joints and limbs of our lives and straightens them out so we can live in wholeness and health. Sometimes the bones crack and the muscles stretch as the Holy Spirit works the Word into calcified parts of our lives. Unused ligaments begin to moan and complain as they are stretched for the first time. Nevertheless, the benefits are worth it.

As the Word gets to work on us we become fitter, more supple, more agile, with fewer 'ailments'. Couch potato Christians become athletes for Jesus. Bitter and twisted believers become sweet and fruitful rivers of life. Depressed and desperate disciples become over-comers with sound minds. Living by the Word is like having your own personal physician, trainer and physiotherapist. Get those shoulders back!

## May 25, 2006: Fit for life

*All Scripture is...profitable...for training in righteousness. (2Timothy 3:16)*

When I was younger I loved playing sports, especially rugby, cricket and football (soccer); I had some natural talent for all of them. I really enjoyed playing the games - but didn't always enjoy the hours of training and practice involved. I tended to rely on my natural skills, which sometimes caught me out. So my dad used to spend hours throwing rugby and cricket balls at me; he wanted me to be able to catch any ball that came at any height or pace. A cricket ball is hard - harder than a baseball - and we don't use gloves/mitts. Sometimes it hurt as the ball smacked into my hand. Eventually I learnt how to catch a ball properly. I can still do it. I was well trained.

The Bible is profitable for training - in righteousness. The Greek word for training means 'to train up and raise a child to adulthood through education and disciplinary correction as a tutor'. Those readers who are familiar with the term pedagogue will identify with that. This is a very interesting facet of the Word of God; it takes us as righteous babes in Christ and works on us and in us to bring us to spiritual adulthood. We don't become more righteous as we grow; we are as righteous in the moment we receive Christ as we are fifty years later. Just as in the natural, where the baby has the same DNA as when he is an old man, so it is in the spiritual. What happens is that the Word of God trains you how to grow in righteousness: to grow in who you are. As you practise righteousness in all the practical out-working that the Bible teaches, it becomes second nature to you. Only it's not second nature! It's growing into the mature son of God that you are by nature in Christ.

This process is nothing to do with age; I know people who have been Christians thirty years and are still children. I know Christians who have been saved just a couple of years and they are maturing fast. It all depends on how we surrender to the discipline of our Trainer.

### May 30, 2006: Grow up
*...so that the man of God...(2Timothy 3:17)*

In this mini series on 2Timothy 3:16-17 we have discovered that the breathed-out-by-God Bible will accumulate gain for us if we allow it to do its work in us. Now we come to the 'so that', the reason why God spoke it. It's so that the man of God: note that carefully - not a baby, nor a child, nor a spotty adolescent, but the man of God.

The Word of God is given to get us to grow up, to become mature, to grow to our fullest potential in Christ. This gets to the very heart of our existence and reason for being on this earth. God created Adam, his son (see Luke 3:38) in order to fill the earth with a people in God's image and likeness. If Adam had grown in his relationship with God he would have matured as a son; but he sinned and became a fool. He acted childishly, wanting to satisfy himself (that's what children do). However, God the Father had always planned, even if Adam had not sinned, that humanity would reach maturity through his Only Son - Jesus.

God's Word - Jesus the Incarnate Word and the Bible, the breathed out written Word - are given for us to grow in our sonship from childhood to manhood. That is why the New Testament writers constantly remind their readers of who they are in Christ - sons of God - who need to leave childish ways behind and become mature, to grow up in all aspects of life, so that we can truly be the sons of God that all creation is standing on tiptoe craning its neck to see (Romans 8:19).

The continued immaturity of the sons of God is totally unacceptable to our heavenly Father. Any father wants his son to grow to be man; a thirty five year old man with the self-centred attitudes of a three-year-old child is an embarrassment to his father. God the Father is no exception; he does not accept immaturity, petulance, and sulking in his sons. He says, 'I have given you my Word, I have spoken to you about who you are and why you're in this world. Now put childishness away and grow up'. Once the Church does that then it is ready to come into the inheritance of our Father.

## June 1, 2006: Men at work
*...for every good work. (2Timothy 3:17)*

These verses about the profitability of the Word of God end in very practical terms. There is work to be done. The Bible is an intensely pragmatic book; God is concerned with principles and concepts, but he is a hands-on God too. Adam was created to work the Garden of Eden; it was only after sin entered that work became hard toil done with the sweat of the brow. The work of God is hard work but it's done in the power of the Holy Spirit and in the joy of the Lord; it's a real delight!

Each one of us has work to do; but it's vital that we do the right work. This is where many Christians trip up; they get involved in so many projects, enterprises and initiatives that they end up chasing the game and achieve very little of eternal value. God does not judge us by our activity but by whether we are doing the work he wants us to do. This was one of the reasons why Jesus was so successful; he knew what the Word of God said he had come to do, and he did only what it said. He did not waste his time in extra-curricular activities; he was the Messiah and did the work of the Messiah and only the work of the Messiah. Each day he listened to his Father's voice and did the Father's will for him, even resisting the 'honourable' pressures and needs of those around him (see Mark 1:35-39 for a potent example of him resisting the emotional blackmail of the disciples).

Christians are great people; they're the best people in the world. Their hearts are servant hearts and they love to get involved in things of the kingdom. But that is also the danger; they can become hyper-active in activity. Each one of us is 'a unique work of art, created in Christ Jesus to do good works, which God prepared in advance for us to do' (Ephesians 2:10). God has work for every one of us that only we can do; and if we don't do it then it doesn't get done or somebody else does it badly. Therefore, I have to cultivate a relationship with the Word of God so that I discover what God's purpose is and what work I have to do in order for that greater purpose to be achieved. That is why I say no to as many things as I say yes to. Having such a sense of focused work will put blinders/blinkers on me so that my work will not be judged as wood, hay or stubble; but as gold, silver and costly stones (1Corinthians 3:12-13).

### June 19, 2006: Diminishing yourself
*There is a 'great' man who makes every man feel small. But the real great man is the man who makes every man feel great. (GK Chesterton)*

When you belittle someone you only end up diminishing yourself. There are too many Christians who are now midgets but who used to be giants, simply because every time they have tried to bring another Christian down, they themselves have shrunk in stature.

### June 22, 2006: A mystery is solved
*I want you to know how much I am struggling for you and for those at Laodicea, and for all who have not met me personally. My purpose is that they may be encouraged in heart and united in love, so that they have the full riches of*

*complete understanding, in order that they may know the mystery of God, namely, Christ, in whom are hidden all the treasures of wisdom and knowledge. (Colossians 2:1-3)*

It is only in knowing Christ that everything else makes any sense at all. Nothing has full meaning outside of knowing him. Christ is the mystery of God. A biblical mystery is something that once was concealed but has now been revealed. God the Father has revealed Christ and has revealed himself in and through Christ, so we can know him, Father, Son and Holy Spirit. That is the only real knowledge, the most important thing any person can know. Paul warns his readers against any accepting false notions of true knowledge that exclude or reduce this fact; they are fine sounding arguments and philosophies which are ultimately deceptive.

We must know Christ in all his fullness, who he really is. He is much, much more than the Saviour of the world. He is that, but he was the eternal God long before he died on the Cross as our Saviour. The essence of Christ's existence is not merely to save us from our sins. In fact the reason for his existence is not primarily for us at all; he exists for himself. Furthermore, all things exist for him, including mankind. Christ's being Saviour of the world lies within his existing for himself as God. We must never make Christ less than he is by understanding him only through our own filter of sinful creatures that have been made saints. We have to know him by the Spirit of sonship, the Spirit of adoption, who conforms us to the image of the Son, which is the reason why we were created. We were not created to be saved; we were created to be sons just like Christ; our salvation is the means by which we become what we were created to be. I don't mean we become gods; not at all. We are creatures and always will be. But knowing who Christ is and knowing him as he is must make me aware of who I am in him.

If Christ remains only a little saviour to us, looking after our little lives while we remain the centre of our little universe, then we don't know him in his fullness. He did not die to run a kindergarten; he died to reap a family of mature sons.

### July 4, 2006: In good company

*Tax collectors and other notorious sinners often came to listen to Jesus. This made the Pharisees and teachers of religious law complain that he was associating with such despicable people - even eating with them! (Luke 15:1-2)*

I find it amazing and rather delightful that Jesus, the Holy and Righteous One, should attract such notorious sinners, the worst kind of people. You would think that he would repulse them, by his purity and goodness. Or else they would mock him for his moral uprightness; but they didn't. They loved being with him; they seemed drawn to him like some invisible yet irresistible divine magnet.

It was the religious people who were repulsed by Jesus; they found him revolting and distasteful. They could not stand being near him. They thought he was the scum of the earth. But sinners loved being with Jesus. There was something about him that drew them. They knew he was one of them and yet not one of them. Jesus was always totally uncompromising towards such sinners: he was brutally honest with them about their sinfulness; but he always had a redemptive attitude towards them that gave them hope beyond their sinful state. Jesus loved them so much that he always told them the truth about themselves, yet never condemned them. He showed them what they could become. That is a fine balance to walk: loving the sinner while hating their sin. If we get the balance wrong we become Pharisees and the world will walk away and listen to other voices.

124

## July 5, 2006: God is not grey – neither is his church

*By him [Jesus] all things were created: things in heaven and on earth...all things were created by him and for him...he is the Head of the body, the church. (Colossians 1:16)*

Jesus brought everything that exists into being; he is the Creator God. Not only is he the Creator; Jesus is the pattern of creation. He created all things for himself, not for us. As the Designer of the creation, so it reflects him and reminds us of him, tells us things about him, just like a building speaks to us about its architect. The creation is not Jesus; he exists apart from it and is greater than it; nevertheless it really and truly reveals him. What might seem strange to us in the creation - a giraffe or some of the odder looking sea creatures found in the depths of the great oceans - are actually there for him. Jesus designed them that way; he is the God of supreme variety and imagination. The creation is not a dull grey, and neither is its Creator. The creation pulses with an abundance of variety and surprise. It should cause us to be in awe and wonder. It sometimes even puzzles us: why a hippopotamus? The creation is designed to lead us beyond ourselves to discover its Creator. It is a signpost to God.

In the same way, the church, the body of Jesus Christ on earth, portrays and displays that same creative genius of its Head. It is full of variety, colour and wonder. It should never be dull and grey. The church, even more than the creation, should be the manifestation of the God who designed this beautiful world to express himself. This amazing body of Christ is designed to take away the breath of the world far more than the most beautiful sight the natural eye can see. Why? Because when you look at the church you see Jesus.

### July 18, 2006: Get plugged in

*You will receive power when the Holy Spirit comes on you. (Acts 1:8)*

I did a silly thing this morning. I decided to wash the car and needed to use an extension cable to connect the power washer. I set up everything correctly, or so I thought. I had all that I needed at hand; but when I turned the washer on, nothing happened. There was no power. Puzzled, I went to the power source and discovered I hadn't plugged the extension cable into the wall socket; I had plugged it into itself!

Naturally, it was an opportunity for the Holy Spirit to bring me a powerful reminder that my power source has to be him, or else nothing will work. I might have all the 'equipment' but without his life flowing through me nothing at all is going to happen. I cannot plug into myself or into anybody else in order to live as a Christian; only the Spirit can live the life of Christ in me. And when I get filled with the power, the dynamite of the Holy Spirit, I am the most powerful person on the planet. The very One who created the universe and raised Jesus from the dead is pouring through me with all his divine energy and ability.

### September 5, 2006: Go west

*He has removed our rebellious acts as far away from us as the east is from the west. (Psalm 103:12)*

There is an old saying: *East is east and west is west, and ne'er the twain shall meet.* I thought about that when I read this Scripture this morning. I am so glad the verse does not say that God has removed our sins as far away from us as far as north is from south, otherwise we would be in trouble.

If you stand on the North Pole and walk in a straight line, eventually you will arrive at the South Pole. So if your sins were only separated from you like that then you could come across them again; they would not have really gone away. But if you stand on the equator and start walking west, you will always head west and never east. You would have to turn around and go the other way to head east. So no matter how long or far you walk you will never go east. That is how far away God has removed your sins: they are gone forever.

## September 13, 2006: Sow to another

*The one who sows to please the flesh will from the flesh reap destruction. The one who sows to please the Spirit, from the Spirit will reap eternal life. (Galatians 6:8)*

It is important that you always sow outside of yourself: that is the essence of what sowing is. If you reap to the flesh - that self-gratifying aspect of your natural desires – you are not really sowing in the Bible way. All you are doing is feeding and indulging yourself. When you sow to yourself you are building the bigger barns like that fool in the parable: and he ended up dead. But when you sow to the Spirit you are sowing outside of yourself. In fact every proper act of sowing is toward God, even though humans may be the beneficiaries of your sowing. And when you sow to the Spirit you sow to Another; and the 'Another' is the great Rewarder. He always reaps back to you far more than you ever sow to him.

## September 26, 2006: The Word is still flesh

*The Word became flesh and dwelt among us. (John 1:14)*

This verse is one of the most profound in Scripture. It expresses one of the most significant events in all history: that the Creator God became one of us. In the Person of God the Son - Jesus - God became, and still is, a man. Many Christians miss this amazing truth: that Jesus is still a man now in heaven. He did not un-become a man when he left the earth in his ascension; he remains a man now as he sits at the right hand of God the Father.

Just as significant is the fact that the God-made-flesh sitting in heaven is incarnate now in his Body on the earth - the church. When you see the church you see nothing less than the glorious God/Man who is reigning over all things from his throne. Therefore, the church's calling is a high one indeed: to manifest the God-Man in the same manner and even in a greater manifestation than when he walked the earth in his humanity. Although we hold this treasure in earthen vessels it remains a true treasure. And the one who finds that treasure finds everything.

### September 27, 2006: I am what I am
*I am not...I am. (John the Baptist, in John 1:19-29)*

It is just as important to know what you are not as what you are. John the Baptist was bombarded with identity questions: 'Are you the Messiah? Are you Elijah?' He emphatically denied being both. But when asked who he was John was quick to respond: 'I am the voice.'

Many people labour under misapprehensions of who they are and never achieve what they could if only they would acknowledge what God has called them to be. Some think that they are the greatest preachers the world has ever seen; but they cannot string two words together. Some have prophecies over their lives from well-intentioned friends about reaching the nations; but they are afraid even to get on a plane.

Did you know that the only thing that counts with God is what you are anointed to do by the Holy Spirit? There sometimes seems to be an over emphasis of sticking labels on people: I know it is important we recognise people's gifts, but it seems that far too many of the saints are trying to get a title without having any gift. John was very simple and very clear in his self-understanding, but he achieved his destiny.

## October 5, 2006: Call on me

*When the wine was gone, Jesus' mother said to him, 'They have no more wine.' (John 2:3)*

I admire the actions of Jesus' mother Mary in this story at the wedding in Cana. The very moment she became aware of that the wine had run out, she immediately involved Jesus. She calmly and coolly went to the source who could resolve the problem. She did not beat about the bush with banal platitudes or religious hogwash; she just stated the reality of what was going on – 'there's no more wine.' Jesus knew the implications: embarrassment for the host; thirst for the guests. Having placed her request before her son and having heard his response (which was not a rebuff but a warm remark), she set off to prepare the administrators of the miracle: 'Do whatever he tells you.'

How many of us, when faced with situations and crises, act like this? Or do we head off in a blind rush, full of anguish, fear and panic? If you are facing something right now, go to Jesus and involve him: then do whatever he tells you. That is how you will receive your miracle.

## October 10, 2006: The man without guile

*When Jesus saw Nathanael approaching he said of him, 'Here is a true Israelite in whom there is no guile.' (John 1:47)*

Jesus gave a marvellous testimony about Nathanael: he was a man without guile; there was nothing false in him. He was a genuinely good man. In this country we have a saying about such people: 'they have no side.' With such people what you see is what you get. Nathanael was devoid of selfish ambition and hypocrisy; he never played the political game beloved of so many Christians. He did not see being associated with Jesus as the way to the highest rung on the ladder, over which he could climb above his friends. I know people like Nathanael; in fact I could fill this page with names.

I also appreciate the fact that Nathanael did not refuse Jesus' assessment of his character. He said, 'How did you know?' He did not come back at Jesus with some mock humility; he knew himself and that this man Jesus had just looked right inside his life. That was the thing that amazed him. It is always wise to accept Jesus' analysis of who you are; he is pretty good at it.

### October 12, 2006: I'm coming in
*He had to go through Samaria. (John 4:4)*

Many times I have heard evangelists use the story of the Samaritan woman: how Jesus had to go through Samaria to reach her and bring her the Good News. That is true; but there is also another reason why he had to go through that area.

For centuries Samaria had been a no go area for Jews. Religious, racial and cultural hatred meant that they had nothing to do with each other. They ventured into each other's territory sometimes at great personal risk. Jesus was having none of that. He was the God who made the world; every inch of it was, and is, his. Nobody was going to tell him where he could and could not venture. No one could put up any sign forbidding him entry. He had to go through Samaria just because they said he couldn't.

The same is true in our lives: we cannot put up a No Entry sign to the Holy Spirit of Jesus. It is impossible to have a 'Private' sign on any door of our lives. He ignores such attempts at independence and strides right in. He is God: that is what he does.

## October 13, 2006: Accentuate the positive
*Nicodemus...came to Jesus (John 3:2)*

I have a particular empathy for the unsung heroes in the Bible. People castigate the Pharisee Nicodemus because he came to Jesus at night rather in the light of day. They mock him for his fear. But I admire him that he came at all. He had a lot to lose and was putting his whole reputation at risk by being seen with Jesus; that he was willing to take the risk speaks much of his courage. And Jesus was willing to see him.

We must never write people off because of where they are at right now. Some are on a pilgrimage of discovery and are treading warily but steadily. Nevertheless, they are moving in the right direction. Of course, their moment of reckoning will come. For Nicodemus it was at the Cross; John 20:39 tells us that when Jesus had died and nearly all his disciples had fled, it was Joseph and Nicodemus who courageously took his body down from the Cross and buried it. At the crunch time this man showed his true colours. That is when it counts.

## October 19, 2006: A house for God
*Zeal for your house will consume me. (John 2:17)*

Jesus had a zeal for the house of God that ate him up. Of course, he was not ultimately concerned about a physical building: we as the church are the house of God (Ephesians 2:19-22). But as I looked again at this story I was interested to see what Jesus focussed on when he made his whip that day. He drove out the sheep and cattle; he overturned the money tables. These were the very things that the people needed for their sacrifices and their worship (they had to exchange their money so they could buy them).

The tools of their worship had become the focus of activity rather than a means to an end. These people had got caught up in the business of worship rather than worship itself. They were concentrating on the mechanics instead of the reason and purpose for which they were there: to present these animals to God in sacrificial worship.

Sometimes we have to look at what we are involved in. Do we care more for the trappings than the essentials? Is more effort given to the peripherals than the Presence? If so, it is time to make a whip.

### October 25, 2006: No fear

*Jesus called out to his disciples, 'I am here! Don't be afraid.' (John 6:20)*

Jesus does not co-habit with fear. The reason why the disciples were frightened during the storm was because Jesus was not there. When they saw him walking on the water towards them they freaked out even more. But fear cannot exist where he is present because his perfect love casts out fear. Jesus is not frightened of anything; he has no phobias and does not sleep with the light on at night.

When you fear something or someone it means that object of your fear has control over you; it exercises power over your life. It determines your thoughts and actions; it directs you as to where you can and cannot go, what you can and cannot do. Fear is the enemy of faith. Since nothing can do that to Jesus, he has no fear. And wherever he is in control fear is banished. So, let him get into your boat.

### October 26, 2006: Look back in faith

*LORD, I have heard of your fame; I stand in awe of your deeds, O LORD. Renew them in our day, in our time make them known; in wrath remember mercy. (Habakkuk 3:2)*

It is very important how we look back at the past. I am not referring to our sinful past, our life before we met Jesus: that has all gone and forgotten. I am talking about the past things that God has done, the acts of fame that Habakkuk was calling to mind. When he realised that God was still in sovereign control and was about to act in his day, Habakkuk reminded himself of the wonderful things that God had done for his people throughout their history. He used these reminders to build his faith for the future.

It is when the past becomes a means of nostalgia that we have to exercise caution. We have to use it to spur us on to the future, and not to sit on our porches in our rocking chairs talking about the good old days. If we see all the acts of God in our past as means of us achieving our destiny in his purpose we will always keep our focus on the future, while using the past to remind us of the faithfulness of God to us so far. The past will thus spur us on in the adventure of faith.

### October 30, 2006: The Turbocharger

*They were three or four miles out when they saw Jesus walking on the water toward the boat. They were terrified, but he called out to them, 'I am here! Don't be afraid.' Then they were eager to let him in, and immediately the boat arrived at their destination! (John 6:19-21, NLT)*

This story of Jesus walking on the water has so many things in it. Elsewhere [see October 25, 2006] I have mentioned that when Jesus gets in the boat of your life all fears go. But the end of the story also has a fascinating twist. The boat was about four miles out from the shore when Jesus got in it. The next thing they knew that boat was on dry land! That fishing boat suddenly became a speedboat, and a very fast one indeed. In fact, it was more like a supersonic jet. Imagine the faces of these hardened fishermen who knew these waters.

One minute they were out in the depths in a fierce storm; the very next moment they were putting ashore!

It is amazing the radical difference Jesus makes to our lives and situations. The supernatural power of the Holy Spirit can take us in a moment from the depths of despair to the height of faith. In an instant he can turn impossibility into reality. He can transform a lost cause into a glorious triumph. All we have to do is to be eager to let him in and let him be who he is.

### November 8, 2006: That's a bit strong

In this 'avoid controversy of any kind' age of political correctness, in which we are encouraged to bend over backwards so as not to cause anybody offence, I am encouraged by what the Bible says. It ignores such ridiculous notions. For example, when God condemned the priests who were dishonouring him during the time of Malachi, he said to them:

*'I will rebuke your descendants and splatter your faces with the dung of your festival sacrifices, and I will add you to the dung heap.' (Malachi 2:3)*

The prophet Amos said to the self-indulgent, bling-obsessed women of his society:

*'Listen to me, you "fat cows" of Samaria, you women who oppress the poor and crush the needy and who are always asking your husbands for another drink!' (Amos 4:1)*

Even the apostle Paul got in on the act. He called his life before he met Jesus *'human excrement'* (Philippians 3:8). Unfortunately, the NIV sanitises it to 'rubbish.' Praise God for a straight-talking Bible.

### November 20, 2006: God's bookends

*It is good to proclaim your unfailing love in the morning, your faithfulness in the evening. (Psalm 92:2)*

Bookends are handy things. They stop your books toppling over. For them to work properly you need a pair. God has given us a pair of 'bookends' for each day: one for the beginning of the day and one for the end. We need to use them both, otherwise our day can be lopsided or we may end up toppling over. These two bookends both involve expressing something to God. In the morning we are to proclaim his unfailing love. That is his dogmatic unchanging attitude of covenant love that never varies, no matter what we do say or do. It is always good to start each day by thanking God that no matter what happens he is good and his love towards you will never vary.

The second bookend is to end the day by thanking God for all his faithfulness to you during that day. He kept all his promises. All he said he would be to you, he was. He never left your side for a second; he never glanced away from you. He remained faithful each moment of the day and in each circumstance. When you put your head on the pillow tonight thank God for his faithfulness during today; and when you wake in the morning thank him for his love. The days will be different.

## December 7, 2006: The eternal suntan

*And we, who with unveiled faces all reflect the Lord's glory, are being transformed into his likeness with ever increasing glory, which comes from the Lord, who is the Spirit. (2Corinthians 4:18)*

You can always tell when someone returns from a vacation in the sun. They are either nut brown, lobster red or a big freckle. The only problem is that after a few weeks the glory has faded and they have usually returned to pasty white.

Something like this used to happen to Moses. If you read Second Corinthians chapter three you will see that whenever he went into the presence of the Lord his face would begin to shine. When he came out he would have to put a veil over his face until it stopped shining and returned to normal. Moses reflected the glory of the Lord in his face. In the new covenant something far greater than that has happened to us. The Holy Spirit, the Spirit of glory, now resides within us so that we believers actually radiate the glory of God from within us. The glory never fades away; in fact its intensity increases. Romans 8:30 says we are not only justified (put right with God), we are also glorified. God actually exhibits his glory through us. Jesus is the glory of God (see John 1); so when people see us they see him. This does not just happen occasionally, the Holy Spirit so fills us that our very faces constantly shine with the glory of Jesus. It is nothing to do with how handsome or beautiful we are: our whole being pulsates with the glory of God.

That is why the church is so important. It is only as we express that life corporately that the world can see God in totality. The church is designed to shine with the glory of God. It cries out: 'Here is your God!'

### December 22, 2006: To be a pilgrim

Here in Wales it is about three in the afternoon, on a cold but dry winter's day. As I write, thousands of travellers are stranded at various airports around the country as fog continues to envelop the nation. Let's hope they all get home for Christmas. As I watch the individual dramas unfold on the news, each one desperate to get on a plane to be home with their loved ones, I am reminded again of Joseph and Mary, who had to make that long and arduous trip from Nazareth to Bethlehem. There is something inherent in the people of God that makes us pilgrims, always on the move to our final destination.

Mary and Joseph were driven by the demands of the Roman occupiers, but more so by the eternal Word of God

136

which had declared the Messiah must be born in their home town. As I look back on another year and look forward to 2007, that same Word of God drives me on to fulfil the purpose for which God brought me into the world: *the earth will be filled with the knowledge of the LORD as the waters cover the sea.* (Habakkuk 2:14)

### January 4, 2007: I'll make it easy for you

*This will be a sign to you: You will find a baby wrapped in cloths and lying in a manger. (Luke 2:12)*

It might seem strange to make my first entry of a new year about a 'Christmas' verse, but this one has been with me ever since Christmas Eve. When the angel met the shepherds on the night Jesus was born, he made it very easy for them to find Jesus. He would be in a manger. That was something they understood; they would discover him in a feeding trough. They knew where mangers would be: they were shepherds; it would be easy to track down this baby in such a small place as Bethlehem. Here was a Jesus they could get to. As I enter the New Year that is something I want to do for people: make it easy for them to get to Jesus. He is not far away from anybody; they just don't know it yet.

### January 8, 2007: The grim reaper

*Don't delude yourself: you reap whatever you sow. (Galatians 6:7)*

You always reap what you sow. It is a law that God put into his creation and it always works. Even when we choose to sow nothing, that is what we are sowing: nothing, no-thing. We make a conscious decision to sow nothing; it is what we have decided to sow. And that is what we reap: no-thing. In fact, because we always reap more than we sow, when we sow nothing we reap back less-than-nothing. We actually suffer loss when we choose not to sow. So I will always be a 'some-thing' sower, never a 'no-thing' sower.

### February 5, 2007: The Separating Spirit

*Jesus…who through the Spirit of holiness was declared with power to be the Son of God. (Romans 1:4)*

The word 'holy' comes from a word meaning to cut or separate, like when you cut a piece of paper in two. Each part becomes 'holy' - it is separate, apart from, the other. That is what the Spirit of holiness does in us: he separates us from whatever keeps us from God. Many times I have heard holiness described as religious activity, something to be done. Holy people are often described as austere or ascetic. But the Holy Spirit is the Spirit of Jesus, the Spirit of Life, and the Spirit of Joy. When he comes to dwell in us he cuts us away from us all that is nothing to do with God. He is the separating Spirit.

While he is the separating Spirit, that act of separation brings me into unity with all my brothers and sisters in Christ. He cuts away independence and arrogance; he tears me apart from loneliness and individualism; he scythes away self-pity and isolationism. The separating Spirit is the Spirit of unity. He cuts me so that I may belong.

### February 12, 2007: The act of courage

*We get knocked down, but we get up again and keep going. (2Corinthians 4:9 NLT)*

What sets the courageous apart is not that they are willing to be knocked down. Neither is it that they get up again after hitting the ground. What sets the courageous apart is that after being knocked down and having stood again to their feet, they keep going. They don't walk from the arena of life; they don't stand still, with bowed heads, in defeat; they don't take a step to the side or turn and run. They keep going in the same direction with the same commitment, with the same determination, with the same passion. Sometimes the true act of courage is the first step forward after getting up.

## February 21, 2007: 'The Spirit told me'

I was in conversation recently with a friend of mine who is also a church leader. We were talking about some of the crazy things Christians sometimes say to justify their actions. He mentioned somebody who had recently left his church after some difficulties. When my friend had gone to see this person they told him, 'The Holy Spirit has told me to stop reading the Bible.' My friend said, 'Whatever spirit told you that, it certainly was not the Holy Spirit.' He was correct.

There are certain things the Holy Spirit will never do; he always acts according to his nature as God and as the third Person in the Trinity who is now the executive agent of God on earth. He will never tell somebody to stop reading the very Word he wrote. He will never tell anybody that they don't need to belong to the church (I meet this one too often). Some claim that they don't have to belong to a church: all they need is the Holy Spirit or their para-church organisation. But the Spirit's role is to produce the Body of Christ; he is not going to tell some people that they are excluded from this plan. It is plain ridiculous to claim otherwise.

Rule of thumb: always check what people say the Spirit is telling them by the nature and function of the Spirit and by the Scripture he has written down for us. He is not here to be used as the justifier of our own whims and flights of fancy. Let's dispel that notion once and for all.

## February 27, 2007: The Spirit within

*Whoever believes in me, as the Scripture has said, streams of living water will flow from within him. (John 7:38)*

*If the Spirit of him who raised Jesus from the dead is living in you...(Romans 8:11)*

I am sometimes a little dumbfounded when I hear certain believers talk about the ministry of the Holy Spirit. They talk about being filled with him as if he were constantly coming upon them from the outside; but that has already happened in the new birth. When we are born again the Spirit in all his fullness enters us; from that moment on he is always within us. The baptism in the Holy Spirit is the explosion of the Spirit beginning to flow out through and from us like the powerful rivers of living water Jesus talked about in John 7:37.

So many Christians get frightened of the Spirit; they try to lock the doors of their lives to keep him from gaining access to them. But it is too late: he is already on the inside! We who have the privilege of ministering in the Spirit have the responsibility to help our brothers and sisters in this. The Spirit's activity in the life of a believer is from the inside out; he does not keep coming in and leaving and coming in and leaving as if he is going through a revolving door. He indwells us permanently as the dynamic ability of almighty God in us, as the never-ending, fast flowing river of life. It is certainly true that he also exists in equal fullness outside of us; but he truly is a permanent resident inside us in the same fullness. The important thing for us is to let the Spirit be the Spirit within us. If we do so, then the flow of the river will constantly increase.

Just think: the eternal God indwells you. The One who raised Christ from the dead lives in you. The same Spirit who hovered over the waters in creation has come to live inside you. And he is not leaving.

## March 8, 2007: First or Third?

When we talk about the Trinity we often number the distinct Persons: the Father is first, the Son is second and the Spirit is third. It is quite acceptable to do so; the Father is the head of the Trinity and all things come back to him. But we have to be careful when we use such language that we don't demote or relegate the Spirit to third place, like the winner of a bronze medal. That is not what it means. In fact, in some ways, we could say that the Spirit is first. Not that he is Head above the Father, or takes the name above all names from Jesus; but that he plays a continual first role in our lives.

For example, the Spirit is the first Person of the Trinity that we encounter; he introduces us to the Father and the Son. It is only through the Spirit that we can know the Father and Son. Only the Spirit can make the Bible understood to us; we have to read it with the aid of the Spirit. It does not make sense any other way. It is the Spirit who makes us understand the creation and its purpose. It is only through the Spirit we know who we really are. If we want to know anything of true value, we can only discover what is of eternal value and worth through the Spirit. So while we use the term third Person, we must always remember that the Spirit is not the junior partner of the Trinity: he is God the Spirit.

## March 9, 2007: Like peas in a pod

*Their idols are merely things...shaped by human hands...those who make them are just like them...(Psalm 135:15-18)*

The other day I saw a man walking down the street with an Afghan hound. The only way I could tell them apart was that the man was walking on two legs and the dog on four.

It is often said that we become like the things we love. In fact, the Psalm quoted above says so: those who fashion and form idols become just like them. You can tell what someone loves, adores, even worships by the way they look and behave. Take a sports fan for example: he will drape himself in the colours of his team. He will sometimes even dye his hair the colour of the team or have their badge tattooed on his body. I once read of a man who named his son after the eleven members of his favourite football team. It only follows that we who are the true worshippers of the Lord Jesus, become like him. We look like him, speak like him, think like him and act like him. Everybody knows that we are besotted with and consumed by him. It is just as if Jesus and us are like peas in a pod.

### March 12, 2007: Best seats in the house
*Above him were seraphs...they were calling to one another...'the whole earth is full of his glory.' (Isaiah 6:2-3)*

The best seats in the house offer the best views. For the seraphs that is certainly true. These angelic beings (seraph means 'burning one') seem to have one function. This is the only occasion they are mentioned in the Bible and we find them declaring the holiness of God and that from their perspective the whole earth is already full of the glory of God. Other passages in the Old Testament declare that the earth *will* be filled with the knowledge of the glory of the LORD (for example, Habakkuk 2:14). Because of the place these beings occupy in the heavenly realms they are able to see the earth already filled: their perspective is the eternal one.

Since we as sons of God are also seated in heavenly realms in Christ (Ephesians 1:3; 2:6), then our perspective is the same as the seraphs. We view everything not from our natural eyes or any of our natural senses; we see things from heaven's viewpoint, from God's eyes. From where he sits all things are under the feet of Christ; the nations are his inheritance; the church is restored; the bride is ready. If we keep that perspective then we do not lose heart when things seem to militate against the plan of God. We don't worry about the raging of the nations; God laughs at them. We carry on working out on earth what is already perfected in heaven. Perhaps some of us need to move to a different seat.

## April 6, 2007: Step forward

*Jesus fully realised all that was going to happen to him. Stepping forward to meet them, he asked, 'Whom are you looking for?' (John 18:4)*

Jesus knew exactly what awaited him that fateful evening in Gethsemane and the following day; nothing about it would take him by surprise. He had known about this moment from all eternity; he had planned the Cross in the council of the Godhead together with the Father and the Spirit. It was the reason why he had come into this world thirty-three years earlier. Those who had come for Jesus that night would not have to drag him kicking and screaming to his fate. He would not even resist passively as an advocate of non-violence. This was his moment, the time when the plan of the Father to sow his Son and reap a family of sons (Isaiah 53:10) was about to come to its climax. For the joy that was set before him he was willing to endure the appalling physical agony and degradation that was heading his way. He was prepared for death itself and separation from his beloved Father. And he knew that on the other side, three days later, he would stand victoriously and gloriously alive! So Jesus stepped forward.

## April 11, 2007: Step forward (2)

*He stepped forward and took the scroll from the right hand of the one sitting on the throne. (Revelation 5:7)*

There was another occasion when Jesus stepped forward. This time he was not going as a lamb to the slaughter; he was the Lamb that had been slain. John heard him described as the Lion of the tribe of Judah and then saw him in vision form as the living Lamb who had been killed. But now Jesus was on the other side of the Cross as the only one in the entire universe worthy to break the seals on the scroll. Because of all that he was and all he had done he uniquely was worthy to take it from his Father's right hand. And as he did the whole creation - the four living creatures, the twenty-four elders, the entire heavenly host, and every creature exploded in worship and praise before him!

As the Easter weekend passes and you get back to work and the humdrum of everyday life, don't let the miracle of what you have just celebrated leave you. Jesus is not only alive, he is ascended and ruling and reigning at his Father's right hand. He is the supreme Lord of all things; there is nothing in this universe that is not subject to his Lordship. Jesus is Lord!

### April 24, 2007: More than words

*They spoke a single language and used the same words. (Genesis 11:1)*

This incident at Babel was the greatest threat to the purpose of God in Genesis. The builders of Babylon put into effect a God-given principle to such an extent that God himself had to step in and confuse their language so that they could no longer use it.

They not only spoke the same language: they used the same words. They knew what they meant by those words: that was the key. It is important that we know what we mean a word to mean when we use it. If I use the words 'covenant', 'baptism' or 'church' I have a whole sense of what I am conveying when I use those words. Someone else might use the same words but not mean the same thing. It is not only the words that matter; it is also what we mean by those words. Helpfully, we have a dictionary that defines and gives those words their power and meaning: the Bible.

Let's be careful always to use a word in the same way the Bible uses it. If we do then we will discover more and more that we will unlock the same principle as those early Babylonians did: nothing will be impossible for us together in unity.

## April 30, 2007: Get Back
*'Get back to where you once belonged.' (The Beatles)*

This line from that Beatles classic was going through my head when I read about Abraham's two visits to Bethel in Genesis 12:8 and Genesis 13:3. In between those two events things did not go well for Abraham: he went to Egypt and convinced Sarah to join him in an act of deceit and lies to protect himself from Pharaoh, who took Sarah into his palace as his wife. But disease came upon Pharaoh's house because of this; eventually he found out that Abraham had been lying to him. This was not an auspicious time for our forefather in the faith.

When Abraham returned to Canaan he headed straight back to Bethel. This was important: this was the place where it had last been right with him and God. From here he had gone into a season of fear, of sin (he lied), and of failure. He had to get back to the place where he had left the path of faith. Note that he did not have to go all the way back to Ur, nor to Haran. He only needed to get back to the place from which he wandered off. This was no retreat; it was a time repentance and restoration. From here he could move on.

Sometimes we stupidly leave the path God wants us to walk on because of our fear or through plain disobedience.

When we come to our senses we have to get back to the place we left the path, not right back at the beginning of our walk with God or further on down the road. Once we get back, then we can move on.

### May 2, 2007: The vultures

*Some vultures came down to eat the carcasses, but Abram chased them away. (Genesis 15:11)*

Isn't it typical of the enemy to try and destroy or disrupt our walk with God at those crucially important times in our life? This is what happened to Abram, just as he and God were about to enter into a covenant concerning all the things God had promised to achieve through Abram. In those days, if two people were making a covenant, they would kill animals, cut them in two and lay them out so that a path was formed between them. Then the two people making the covenant would walk together along that path between the dead animals, signifying that if either of them broke the covenant then what had happened to the animals would happen to them. God did not ask Abram to walk along the path; God was going to do it to show that he was faithful to his promise. Abram had to believe God and obey him.

Just before the Lord began to move along the path, those vultures tried to spoil it all by eating the animals. That is what vultures do: it is their nature as carrion. But Abram would not allow that to happen; nothing was going to get in between him and the God of covenant. Sometimes we have to fight off and scare away those 'vultures' that try to destroy our faith walk with our covenant-keeping God. Don't let vultures of fear, doubt, cynicism, unforgiveness, pride, peer pressure, religious tradition or fierce opposition stop you inheriting all that God has promised you. Chase them away.

## May 9, 2007: The ripple effect

*'I'll draw water for your camels too.' (Genesis 24:19)*

I doubt very much if Rebekah knew the repercussions that those words would have for her destiny. She was merely blessing a stranger, responding to his request for a drink of water. Being the kind of woman she was, Rebekah performed an act of kindness; she blessed the stranger by offering to water his camels as well. Little did she realise that this man was Abraham's servant, sent to find a wife for Isaac. The servant had prayed to God that the right woman would say these very words; his prayer was answered. But Rebekah was just being kind.

However, that act of kindness started a ripple. Within twenty-four hours she would leave home, travel many miles to meet her new husband and take her place within the great eternal purpose of God that was promised to Abraham - that his offspring would fill the whole earth.

Nothing we do for God or others is small or trivial. The road to greatness is often a series of steps in which we are doing the right thing at the right time unto the Lord. Then sometimes the moment arrives in which all that we have sown is reaped back to us and we find ourselves launched into the next phase of the life of God. But we never stop doing the right thing at the right time unto the Lord. That is why Jesus said that the way to be great is to be the servant of all, just like he was.

## May 22, 2007: Praise Him!

*O God, praise is waiting for you in Zion. (Psalm 65:1)*

*I will not offer to the Lord that which cost me nothing. (2Samuel 24:24)*

Praise and worship does something to God; he is affected by it. It does not change his nature or make him feel better; it does not make him feel more accepted by us and more acceptable to us. Nevertheless, it does affect him; never forget that.

Our worship and praise pleases God; it causes him genuine pleasure. That alone is sufficient reason to praise and worship him. He loves to receive our adoration; it is one of the reasons he created us. That might sound incredibly selfish of him; well, yes, it is selfish. God lives for himself, not for us. He is the centre and circumference of everything, not us. He doesn't only look at our hearts when we praise and worship, he looks at all of us. That is why he asks us to lift our hands, dance, bow, kneel, clap our hands, laugh, cry, shout, run, sit and wave things before him as expressions of our love for him. We praise and worship with everything we are and have. If he wants us to lift our hands, that is what we do. It is not enough to say, 'The Lord sees my heart;' he wants to see your hands raised to him as well. If you have a heart for praise and worship your body will show it. My rule of thumb in praise and worship is simple: I will offer the Lord whatever he requires. Just to know it pleases him is enough.

### May 25, 2007: We don't need another Pentecost...

...We just need to live in the reality of the original one. This weekend is Pentecost and we at All Nations Church are celebrating it. As I have been preparing for the weekend I have been reminded that we cannot re-enact Pentecost: we don't need to. The Holy Spirit has come and is now living within all who have faith in Christ (Romans 8:11). So for us there will be no looking back with nostalgia or envy. Nevertheless, our experience of the Holy Spirit cannot be any less than that of the one hundred and twenty, in the same manner and in the same measure. Their experience that morning is not out of our reach or remains a one-off act of

God in history. The promise made to them that day is made to us: the gift of the Holy Spirit is for all whom the Lord our God will call (Acts 2:39). Anything less than what they experienced is less than Pentecost; and there is no way that we should view Pentecost as the high point of the church's experience of the Holy Spirit.

We must not be nostalgic; we must be in faith. We may not experience literal wind and fire, but there again, why not? Nevertheless, we must experience the Holy Spirit as wind and as fire in just the same dynamic measure as the one hundred and twenty did. The Holy Spirit is the same yesterday, today and forever, just as Jesus is.

So when we gather together this weekend my expectation is nothing less than a divine visitation. The Holy Spirit within me and the same Holy Spirit who is not confined within me is going to manifest himself, and the church will never be the same again.

### May 31, 2007: A marked man

*The sun rose as Jacob left Peniel, and he was limping because of his hip. (Genesis 32:31)*

*By faith, Jacob, when he was old and dying, blessed each of Joseph's sons and bowed in worship as he leaned on his staff. (Hebrews 11:21)*

God always leaves his mark on a man or woman of God. The night Jacob wrestled with God at Peniel, which means 'face of God', was a turning point in his life. It was the night he had to finally acknowledge who he was: Jacob the deceiver, the twister. In looking into the face of God he saw what he was really like in comparison; and it was not good. But God in his grace changed his name that night to Israel: 'the one who contends with God' or 'the Prince of God'. The vow that Jacob had made God years before when he fled from

Esau - that if God looked after him then Jacob would one day serve him - was called in that night at Peniel by the sovereign God.

Just before he let him go, God touched Jacob; he touched him so powerfully in his hip that for the rest of his life Jacob walked with a limp. In his old age, as he prepared to die, he leant on his staff and worshipped. There was a vulnerability about Jacob after that encounter with God. There was the mark of God about him. Gone was the old deceiver, the man constantly living in self-preservation, the man who grasped at anything he could to further his own ends. He had met with God face to face and could not remain the same. Every step he took for the rest of his life was a reminder that he had encountered the living God; it caused him to walk humbly in worship before God. When the hand of God touches a person, that person is never the same again.

### June 8, 2007: Reactions and responses

*Amazed and perplexed, they asked one another, 'What does this mean?' Some, however, made fun of them and said, 'They're drunk.' (Acts 2:12-13)*

We should never be surprised that the activities of the Holy Spirit will usually cause both a positive response and a negative reaction. It is something I have learned to deal with over the years. No matter how powerful the manifestation of the Spirit has been and the tangible results of that manifestation are so evident, many times there is a competing negative reaction of mockery, cynicism or arrogant criticism. At such times it is not necessary to enter a self-justifying debate. All that is needed is to point to Jesus, as Peter did. He did not attempt to explain the manifestation itself; he used it to talk about Jesus.

I care nothing if people fall over, stand still like rocks, laugh or cry, shake, rattle or roll. The question is: did they encounter the living Christ? I do know this: when he manifests himself in the anointing power and presence of the Holy Wind and Fire of the Spirit, we will know it; and people will be amazed and transformed.

## June 20, 2007: The Overplus

> *Jacob said to Joseph, 'I never thought that I would see you again, but now God has let me see your children, too'. (Genesis 48:11)*

I find this episode in the lives of Jacob and Joseph quite emotional. Here was Jacob on his deathbed, with his children and grandchildren around him. Joseph had brought his two sons, Ephraim and Manasseh, to see their grandfather before he died. Jacob was so grateful to God: the son he thought he would never see again had been back in his life for seventeen years since Jacob had left Canaan and moved to Egypt to escape the famine. But much more than that had happened to Jacob: God had also given him grandchildren whom he never knew existed and therefore never expected to see.

This is the biblical principle of restoration at work. Usually when we use the word it means returning something back to its original state, like restoring furniture or houses. But that is not biblical restoration: it always has another element to it. Biblical restoration returns what was lost but then adds what I call the overplus: something that was never there before. That is what Jacob received: he not only received his son back, his overplus was the grandchildren. He received back more than he lost.

This same principle holds true in our salvation. We don't only have our sins forgiven, as marvellous as that is. No, we also receive something we never had in the first place: complete and utter righteousness. We are not forgiven sinners: we are restored saints.

When Jesus returns, he will come again when all is restored (Acts 3:19-21). He is not coming back for the church of Acts chapter two or the church of the New Testament. He is coming back for a church that is restored to his original intention; for the church that the world has yet to see.

### July 3, 2007: Basic ingredient

The encounters of Moses and Aaron with Pharaoh and his magicians in Exodus chapters seven to twelve are hallmarked by supernatural manifestations and demonstrations. The interesting thing is that it was not only Moses and Aaron who were able to do these signs, so were the Egyptians. Their staffs also turned into snakes; they could turn water into blood; they caused frogs to invade the land. It was only with the formation of the plague of gnats from the dust of the earth that the magicians failed to replicate the sign.

The point of this is that Christianity without the supernatural does not stand a chance in today's world. In fact, the supernatural is the very essence of Christianity. God is spirit, and the Holy Spirit is the Spirit who lives and works only supernaturally. The early church was characterised by believers who were at home in signs and wonders, in miraculous signs, in healings, and in angelic interaction. For them the supernatural was not the icing on the cake: it was a basic ingredient.

The church will not survive on agendas, campaigns, committees, methodologies and doctrines that deny the place of the supernatural. The devil laughs at such strategies and beliefs. However, when people take hold of the Holy Spirit, he comes with all the accompanying signs and wonders which belong to the Gospel. When was the last time your jaw dropped in amazement, awe and wonder at the moving of the Spirit? Or is it getting all too predictable?

## July 9, 2007: All mouth and trousers

*All the forces in Pharaoh's army - all his horses, chariots, and charioteers - were used in the chase. The Egyptians caught up with the people of Israel. (Exodus 14:9)*

My dad used to have a special way of describing people who were so full of themselves and who constantly talked a good talk but who could never deliver the goods. He said such people were 'all mouth and trousers.' I have no idea where that saying originated, but I was reminded of it when I was reading how Pharaoh came chasing after the Israelites when they left Egypt. The noise of those chariots, horses and soldiers must have been frightening. The sight would be terrifying: dust flying, whips flailing, horses racing. It was an experience to chill the marrow.

But it was all mouth and trousers. God had already defeated Pharaoh: his nation had been utterly decimated by the plagues. The Passover had brought death to every home. Even when the Egyptians finally caught up with the Israelites the cloud of God's presence prevented them from even being able to find where the Israelites were. They groped around in the dark, unable to locate their prey.

The final blow came when the Red Sea, which is a picture of water baptism, opened up, and the Israelites walked through on dry land to the other side. When the Egyptians tried to chase them the Lord dismantled their chariots by causing the wheels to fall off, and the water closed over them. They all lay dead on the riverbank.

No matter how hard Satan tries to scare you, lie to you, suggest to you that he can still get you, he is all mouth and trousers. Through your faith in Jesus and your water baptism all his power has gone. He cannot touch you. No matter how loud he shouts, no matter how many forces he tries to throw at you, no matter how scary he tries to be; the power of the

Gospel of Jesus Christ has delivered you from his dominion and transferred you into the Kingdom of the Son.

### July 10, 2007: Time is of the essence

*During the forty days after the crucifixion Jesus appeared to the apostles from time to time...on these occasions he talked to them about the Kingdom of God. (Acts 1:3)*

Louis Armstrong's song, 'We have all the time in the world' is a classic. It is a great song to chill out to. Unfortunately, the words are not true; we don't have all the time in the world. We only have a certain, fixed amount of time. And once we stop breathing, time is up for us all. You cannot grab one more second than your allotted time.

The same was true for Jesus. He only had forty days after his resurrection, and no more, in which to impart to the apostles all he could before he had to go away. So he did not waste any time. Each moment was spent instructing them about the Kingdom of God. Even when they were eating, he took the opportunity to teach them. Even when they tried to distract him by asking about the nation of Israel being restored, Jesus brushed the question aside to press on with his instructions. Time was of the essence to him.

Each one of us is given exactly the same amount of hours, minutes and seconds each day. What we do with them determines our effectiveness. As Ecclesiastes 3:1 says, there is a time for everything; but we have to do the right thing at the right time. The time to plant is not the time to harvest.

In recent times I have learned to appreciate much more the time I have been granted by God, even the time to rest and relax. Covet and guard your time; each second is an entrustment from God.

## September 4 2007: Sin makes you stupid

*Israel was reduced to starvation by the Midianites. Then the Israelites cried out to the Lord for help. (Judges 6:6)*

I am amazed how stupidly the Israelites sometimes behaved. They had turned away from God and, as he had warned them, they became subject to their enemies. On this occasion it was the Midianites, who for seven long years stole their crops and destroyed their property. But it was only when the Israelites were finally starving that they called out to God for help. That is stupid.

If only they had come to their senses and repented the moment they began to get into trouble, then God would have graciously helped them and delivered them. But they refused to turn away from their sin and serve him, preferring to have a life of defeat and hunger. Whichever way you look at it that is pretty idiotic. The amazing thing about God is that as soon as we turn to him he acts. Why do people insist on going their own wicked ways and reaping the consequences when all they have to do is repent? Sin makes you stupid.

## September 5 2007: It's personal

*Micah ordained the Levite as his personal priest, and he lived in Micah's house. (Judges 17:13)*

At the end of the book of Judges is a collection of incidents that summarises the theme of the book: *'in those days Israel had no king; everybody did whatever seemed right in their own eyes.'* One of these stories involves a man called Micah who made an idol out of silver with which to worship God. Then he installed his own son as his priest; then a wandering Levite was hired to become Micah's own personal priest.

As I read this story I was struck once again by the incredible things that the so-called people of God do when proper order is absent or removed. What is even more incredible is that they do these things thinking it is acceptable. This man actually thought that God would be pleased, because he had made an idol and installed his own personal priest. Yet the man had violated many of God's principles and broken at least two of the Ten Commandments in his actions. Proper authority and headship are of paramount importance for the church to function according to the Word of God. It is no use saying, 'Well, Micah had good intentions; we should look at his heart.' That is ridiculous: this man knew better. He was part of the covenant community of God which collectively had abandoned their Lord. They had the word of God, which made it very clear to them: so do we. They chose not to obey. The result was anarchic chaos.

If all we do is value good intentions and fail to establish the proper ordering of things then we end up with pseudo-Christianity, which is no Christianity at all.

### September 6, 2007: The Singer

Tributes are being paid today to Luciano Pavarotti, who has died from cancer at the age of seventy-one. There is no doubt that he was the greatest operatic tenor of the past fifty years. Even if you are not a classical music fan, his rendition of 'Nessun Dorma', the theme for the 1990 football World Cup, was a worldwide hit. Pavarotti could move you in your soul with his beautiful voice. I loved to listen to him.

A couple of weeks ago I spoke at the funeral of my friend Bob John, who also died of cancer aged seventy. Bob was a big man with a beard, just like the Italian maestro. And Bob could sing too; he was no Pavarotti, but he did have a wonderful tenor voice. His funeral was marked with an abundance of singing: his favourite hymns and the worship songs and choruses he would often break into during our times of praise and worship. Bob was known as a man who loved to worship God with singing.

As I thought about Bob and Pavarotti this morning, I realised what the difference between them was. While Pavarotti could move me in the soul and stir my emotion, Bob moved me in my spirit and led me into the very presence of God. Pavarotti could not do that: he sang for himself and his audience. There is nothing wrong with that at all. But Bob sang to his Saviour out of the depths of a sanctified spirit and a grateful heart. No amount of natural skill or years of operatic training can ever do that for you. Only a love of Jesus can make us worship him.

### September 20, 2007: We're all sowers
*The LORD was gracious to Hannah; she conceived and gave birth to three sons and two daughters. (1Samuel 2:21)*
*...Hophni and Phineas will both die on the same day. (1Samuel 2:34)*

We have to remember that everything we say or do is an act of sowing; it is not only to do with finances, even though the law of sowing and reaping certainly includes that aspect. All our actions and words sow something, and we always reap back in greater dimension than what we sow. This is true in the natural and the spiritual: if I reaped only one potato from my seed potato I should be very disappointed.

This principle of sowing and reaping is highlighted in the examples of Hannah and of the two sons of Eli: Hophni and Phineas. Hannah had previously sown her firstborn son, Samuel, to the Lord. It cost her dearly to do so; she had waited many years for a child. But she was so grateful to God for what he had done, her gratitude overflowed in an act of worship. God duly reaped back to her five more children. Hannah sowed blessing and she reaped it.

On the other hand, Hophni and Phineas lived a life of sowing to their own desires: they were morally and spiritually corrupt. The Bible tells us they had no regard for God. This was compounded by the fact that they were priests, who should have led the people in the example of sowing and reaping. Such was their evil sowing that they reaped something back that was terribly severe: they died.

This is what Galatians 6:7 means when it says, 'We reap whatever we sow.' Life is not a game of chance; it is meant to be lived by obeying God's spiritual laws. That is why I tithe, am generous in giving offerings, will speak only good things to and of people, and will do only good to others. Everything is to do with sowing and reaping.

### September 24, 2007: The real deal
*As he is, so are we in this world. (1John 4:17)*

I heard the other day that there are over eighty five thousand official Elvis Presley impersonators in the world. Thirty of the best have recently gathered in London for a competition to find the Greatest Elvis. As good as these entertainers are it is very clear that they are impersonators: there are Irish Elvises, Chinese Elvises and Nigerian Elvises. You can tell they are not the real deal, besides the fact of course that Elvis is dead!

Some people think that our relationship to Jesus is one of impersonation or imitation; we try to live like him to the best of our ability. But the Bible says that as he **is**, so **are** we. That is more than impersonation. It does not say as he **was**, so are we. Jesus' life is not confined to those thirty-three years when he lived on earth as the God/Man. No, as he is, so are we. We should not ask, 'what **would** Jesus do?' or say, 'if Jesus **were** here today'. He **is** here today. As he is, so are we. Let me make it quite clear: we are not Christ. There is only one Christ. But in saying that as he is, so are we, the Bible means that it is Jesus himself being who he is, living and expressing his life in us and through us by the Person of the Holy Spirit who now lives within us. In encountering us people actually encounter none other than Christ himself. Christ lives his life on earth through us.

## September 25, 2007: As he is in status

*You disowned the Holy and Righteous One and asked that a murderer be released to you. You killed the author of life, but God raised him from the dead. (Acts 3:14-15)*

*You were taught, with regard to your former way of life, to put off your old self, which is being corrupted by its deceitful desires; to be made new in the attitude of your minds; and to put on the new self, created to be like God in true righteousness and holiness. (Ephesians 4:22-24)*

When we become Christians, we become the righteousness of God (2Corinthians 5:21). A divine transaction takes place in which we become righteous and holy, just as Christ is righteous and holy. Let me emphasise again: we are not Christ, but we are as righteous and as holy as he is. In that sense we share the same status; we are as holy and righteous as he is. We are no longer sinners but saints; righteous and holy sons of God just like our older brother (Hebrews 2:11). Jesus is proud that we are just like him. To deny who we are in Christ is to slander and libel God. Therefore we no longer live with any sin consciousness. There is no condemnation for us (Romans 8:1); in Christ we are designed and empowered to live righteously. It is no longer our nature to sin. If we do sin it is only because we choose to, not because of the tug of a sinful nature – that has gone. Neither do we live with any sense of unworthiness. We must never think of ourselves as just making up the numbers or as not belonging, or as unimportant. Christ never thinks of himself that way; and as he is so are we. The Father predestined us to be just like him.

## October 2, 2007: As he is in position

*The Son is the radiance of God's glory and the exact representation of his being, sustaining all things by his powerful word. After he had provided purification for sins, he sat down at the right hand of the Majesty in heaven. (Hebrews 1:3)*

*God raised us up with Christ and seated us with him in the heavenly realms in Christ Jesus. (Ephesians 2:6)*

Not only are we as Christ is in status, we also share his position. Right now he sits in the heavenly realms at the right hand of the Father. Jesus is in complete peace; he is sitting down, not running around like a headless chicken in panic or worry. As he sits, all his enemies are being made a footstool for his feet: he is ruling and reigning. Jesus lives victoriously from a heavenly perspective.

We as sons of God also sit in the heavenly realms, even though we live on earth. Our life is not earthly but heavenly. There is not a great chasm between us and God, in which we live far away from him here on earth. No, we actually live from the same heavenly perspective; we have the same view of everything that Jesus has. We don't sit on his throne; that is his sole right as the Son of God. But we do sit with him; the Bible is very clear on that. Therefore, like Jesus, we are in peace; we don't panic and worry; we rule and reign. We rule over ourselves, and over our circumstances. We rule our minds and our emotions; we rule our spirits. We overcome difficulties and reign through times of tragedy and hardship. We live by faith because our eyes are fixed on Jesus. We don't have to gaze up into the heavens to see him; we merely have to turn our heads to see who is sitting close to us on his throne.

## October 8, 2007: Mea culpa

In this age of wrongdoer-as-victim it was refreshing to read of Olympic Champion Marion Jones' open admission of her guilt. Jones, who won five medals at the Sydney Games in 2000, had long denied any involvement in performance-enhancing drug taking, despite strong evidence to the contrary. She had even made statements to Federal investigators asserting her innocence and ignorance of shady business dealings by her associates.

Last Friday, Jones stood on the steps of the court after being convicted of lying to the investigators. She had pleaded guilty to the charges. Facing the reality of being stripped of her Olympic medals and the possibility of a jail term, she blamed nobody but herself for her actions; it was a case of *mea culpa*: I am responsible. Apologising to her family, friends and fans she said:

> *'I am responsible fully for my actions. I have no-one to blame but myself for what I've done...I want to ask you for forgiveness for my actions, and I hope that you can find it in your heart to forgive me...I have asked Almighty God for forgiveness...'*

Jones' career is over; she announced her retirement in the statement. Her wealth will be greatly diminished. But for Marion Jones the person, the road to recovery has begun. She did what King David did when he was caught out in sin: she came clean. Instead of squirming, denying, negotiating, or blaming others, she took it on the chin and said, 'Yes, I am guilty'. When someone reaches that place they are ready to receive the mercy and grace of God. And there is an abundance of mercy and grace available to the contrite.

## October 15, 2007: As he is in attitude

> *Your attitude should be the same as that of Christ Jesus. (Philippians 2:5)*

A couple of weeks ago we were looking at the topic 'As he is so are we in this world' (1John 4:17). We discovered that we are as Christ is in status and in position. We are also the same as him in attitude. Philippians chapter two tells us that Jesus had an attitude that flowed from his nature: he had the nature of a servant. Note that: he did not merely serve; he served because it was his nature to do so. Has a waiter who is not a servant ever served you in a restaurant? Their attitude spills all over the table, doesn't it?

Jesus is still a servant. When he got back to heaven he did not heave a great sigh of relief that now he had his throne his serving days were over. He did not say, 'Well I'm glad that's all done with. Washing feet, especially those dirty fishermen's feet, was not fitting for me. You'll never catch me doing that again!' No, the throne that Jesus occupies is that of a Servant King, a Servant Son. He lives to serve his Father.

Jesus told us the way to greatness. One day the mother of James and John asked Jesus to give her two sons the top two places in the Kingdom. The other ten disciples were angry with her, but not because she had asked such a thing. They were angry she had got in before them! They wanted it too. Jesus nailed that ungodly lust for power:

*Whoever wants to be great among you must be your servant, and whoever wants to be first must be your slave - just as I did not come to be served but to serve and give my life as a ransom for many. (Matthew 20:26-28)*

Jesus gave us the recipe for greatness. He did not condemn us for wanting to be great; he just told us how to do it. Greatness is achieved by being a servant; not merely doing acts of service, but actually being a servant by nature. It is that attitude which marks out the truly great in the Kingdom. Such people never grasp for their place; they don't tread on others to advance themselves; they don't hold others back to keep themselves in position; they don't become jealous of those who advance beyond them. They rejoice in the promotion and success of others. And they serve.

### November 1, 2007: Perfect soil
*You reap whatever you sow. (Galatians 6:7)*

The other day Dianne and I were sitting under a sycamore maple tree. We were waiting for somebody, and as it was a lovely sunny day we were enjoying the autumn colours of the trees around us. As I looked at the ground I saw literally thousands of sycamore seeds all around us; they had come from the tree we were sitting under. What struck me was that few if any of those seeds had any chance of producing another tree. They were lying on the concrete pavement; they were on top of each other; there was not enough soil to support them in their attempts to germinate. They would be blown away by the wind.

The Holy Spirit spoke to me as I looked; he reminded me that, unlike the sycamore seeds, every seed sown into God is guaranteed to produce fruit. No seed sown to God is wasted. He is the perfect soil for whatever we sow to him: finance, worship, faith, service, whatever. Even when we sow to others we are sowing to God, if that other person is also 'good soil'. Just giving to any old cause does not mean we are sowing to God. I never give an offering under spiritual blackmail; I give out of faith. That is why we must take care what, how and where we sow.

### November 5, 2007: Face the fact
*Abraham faced the fact that his body was as good as dead. (Romans 4:19)*

Faith always demands that we face the facts; it never asks us to live in unreality. When we exercise faith in God we don't stick our heads in the sand or stick our fingers in our

163

ears in an attempt to ignore the issue we need to exercise our faith in God over. Once we have heard the voice of God and taken it into our hearts in faith, the next step is often the crucial one for us. It is in that moment when we face the fact - the issue we need faith concerning - that we have to hold fast to what we have heard and believed. We have to trust completely and solely in the integrity and ability of God to do what he has promised. His word must be the controlling factor. The fact we are facing must never loom larger than the promise of God. The dominating fact in moving in faith is the promise and ability of God. Don't constantly put out fleeces like Gideon did, or trust in your natural senses. Trust only in God and his Word. Then turn your attention away from the fact and confess the word and act on it. Let that word become the focus of your attention. And the creative force of your spoken agreement with God will bring the resolution.

### November 12, 2007: A good investment
*Store up for yourselves treasures in heaven. (Matthew 6:20)*

Yesterday I had the opportunity to have lunch with my friends Per and Bjorg Kristing. As we caught up with each other we spoke of our families. Bjorg is an excellent watercolour artist; their home is festooned with many of her creations. I asked her if she is currently painting; her answer blew me away. She said, 'Well I do paint when I can, but now I spend lots of time with the grandchildren. I want to invest as much as I can in what I can take to heaven.' I thought that was a brilliant reply from a lady who has learnt the true value of things. Bjorg and Per pour the life of Christ into their family, knowing that in doing so they are storing up treasure not only for themselves but also for those coming after them. That is true wisdom.

## November 21, 2007: All I want for Christmas

*What I want is your true thanks...I want you to fulfil your vows...I want you to trust me. (Psalm 50:14-15)*

I managed to hold out quite well this year; but I have to admit I have finally succumbed and finally bought some Christmas presents. This is the time when heavy hints are dropped about what we would all like for Christmas. The Marks & Spencer brochure is strategically placed; the perfume bottle is shaken ostentatiously to show it is almost empty; 'I want one of those' is heard during every commercial break on TV.

I came across this verse in Psalm 50 this morning and discovered that there are things that God wants too: not for Christmas, but all the time. He doesn't need them; the verses just before these tell us that. God makes it very clear that he has no need of us, or our things. But he has desires; he wants things from us.

The first thing he wants from us is true thanks. Later in the Psalm, in verse 23, God says that giving thanks is a sacrifice we make that truly honours him. Therefore it is something we should do all the time. 1Thessalonians 5:18 says we must give him thanks in all circumstances. No matter what happens to us, good or bad, we should be thankful to God. We don't thank him **for** every circumstance, but we thank him **in** every circumstance; we give God something when we give him thanks. We are giving him of and from ourselves. We are the most grateful people on the planet. If you haven't given God true thanks yet today, take time to do it now. You can thank him for anything: your sight; the food in your stomach; the family or friends who are with you now; Jesus; your health or that he is helping through recover from illness; anything at all. Try it: God requires it; it will also do you good and God will accept it as a sacrifice that honours him.

### November 22, 2007: All I want for Christmas (2)
*I want you to fulfil your vows to me. (Psalm 50:14)*

The second thing God wants from us is that we fulfil our vows to him. Words are very important to God; his own word is creative. He brought everything into being in the first place by speaking. Every word God speaks can be trusted; he never tells lies or goes back on a promise. God and his word are one; this is the foundation stone for our faith in him. Every word he speaks demands we believe him: and because he is trustworthy and fulfils all his promises or vows, we can have faith in him that he will do all he promises to do.

God also demands the same of us. We expect him to be faithful to his word; he expects the same from us. We take him at his word; he takes us at our word. It cannot be one-way traffic: we cannot demand of God that he keep his word to us and then fail to keep our own to him. It does not work that way. When God hears us make promises to him through our affirmations of faith, our agreements with him, our prayers and the songs we sing to him, he believes us and expects us to do what we promise him. Jacob discovered this facet of God. When he left home after deceiving Isaac and Esau he had his first major encounter with God at Bethel. The Bible tells us that:

> *Jacob made this vow: 'If God will be with me and protect me on this journey and give me food and clothing, and if he will bring me back safely to my father, then I will make Yahweh my God'. (Genesis 28:20-21)*

God heard that vow. Many years later, when Jacob was on his way home to his father, God met him again, at Peniel. On this night of struggle, blessing and change in which Jacob became Israel, God called in Jacob's earlier vow. On that night God became Jacob's God; and Jacob would never be the same again. God treats us the same; we cannot say to him, 'Lord, I didn't really mean it', or 'Lord, I've changed my mind'.

That just doesn't wash with God. If you have made God a promise then you are honour bound to keep it. God wants a people whose word is their bond; and it starts by keeping the vows we have made him.

### November 23, 2007: All I want for Christmas (3)

*I want you to trust me in your times of trouble. (Psalm 50:15)*

We have been looking at Psalm 50:14-15, discovering what God wants of us. We have seen he wants our thanks, that we fulfil our vows, and finally in this passage, he wants us to trust him in our times of trouble. Troublesome times are part and parcel of life. Jesus told us that while we are in the world there will be occasions when we have trials, difficulties and sorrows (John 16:33). However, in those times he also said we will have peace, because he has overcome the world. Life is not one long struggle after another; we are designed and destined to enjoy life, to prosper and to be blessed. Life is wonderful! Often we look at Job and think that his suffering was for most of his life, but it wasn't. If you read the story you will find that he lived the vast majority of his long life full of blessing, wealth and joy. His suffering was a comparatively short but intense and severe period.

How should we respond when troublesome times come? God wants us to trust him, to believe him, to put our faith in him. In fact, these times are often the means by which our faith is tested to see if it is genuine, 'strong and pure' as 1Peter 1:7 says. Troubled times are the fire that tests our faith in God, that demonstrate whether we have a faith that is only theory or a faith that works. You only have to read any one of the stories of the men and women mentioned in Hebrews chapter eleven to see that their faith was proved in conflict, setbacks, failure and endurance, sometimes over long periods. Such faith is overcoming faith; it is a faith that wins the prize.

It produces faith-fulness, stickability, and is characterised by genuine joy and peace. It also pleases God.

### November 28, 2007: I'm an atheist
*The fool says in his heart, 'There is no God'. (Psalm 53:1)*

The forthcoming release of the movie *The Golden Compass* caused me to think about this verse and a conversation I had with an atheist a long time ago. The movie is based on the book of the same name (in the UK it is called *Northern Lights*). It is written by the avowed anti-Christian and fundamentalist atheist Philip Pullman, and is the first book in his trilogy *His Dark Materials*. The movie has been toned down so as not to offend certain religious groups in the USA. Pullman is no passive unbeliever; he is on record as stating that one of his aims in writing is to 'kill God in the minds of children'.

I happened to be reading Psalm 53 yesterday, which opens with a comment about atheists. The Bible is quite dismissive of them; several times this phrase appears and it is quite curt: such people are fools. God doesn't seem to be setting out to win them over by proofs of his existence; he just says, 'They don't believe I'm here. How foolish'.

I have never tried to prove the existence of God to an atheist. I get on very well with most of the ones I have met over the years. But trying to prove the existence of God to a closed mind is not worth it. The most interesting conversation I had with an atheist was many years ago; he was my boss. I liked him very much and we often would sit and chat about many things. When it came to Christianity and the existence of God there was, naturally, a chasm between us. My boss had been raised in a strict Welsh religious home, which he hated.

One day as we were talking I felt prompted to ask him what seemed to be a strange question: 'Bill, what kind of a God don't you believe in?' He looked at me with a puzzled expression: 'What do you mean?' he replied. I said, 'Well, somewhere along the line you must have had some idea of what God was like and then decided you didn't believe in that God.' Bill said, 'That's right; I did.' I then asked him to describe to me the kind of God he didn't believe in. As he did I couldn't recognise the God of the Bible at all. The god Bill was describing was some harsh, vindictive, remote being who bore no resemblance to the living God. When he had finished I sat there for a moment and then said, 'Bill, I'm an atheist too.' His eyes almost popped out of his head! Before he could respond I explained. 'I don't believe in the god you've just described either. That god doesn't exist; he's a god you made up from what you were told when you were young and from the way your parents used God against you. Since I don't believe in that god you've just described, I'm an atheist too.'

## December 13, 2007: Kingdom paradoxes
*'My Kingdom is not of this world.' (Jesus, in John 18:36)*

The kingdom of God is like no other kingdom; in fact, it is the very opposite of the 'kingdoms of this world'. In the kingdom of God:

- Your greatness is measured by your servant-hood;
- You gain your life by giving it away;
- You love your enemies;
- You are freed from slavery to sin to become a slave of God;
- You are well fed but always hungry;
- You are full of joy but always dissatisfied;
- You have all things but count nothing as your own;
- You keep on giving but always have more than enough;
- Partial obedience is complete disobedience;

- When you are walking through the valley of the shadow you are also sitting down at the table of the Lord;
- Childlike faith is the path to maturity;
- Singing can defeat an army;
- Bread and wine can heal you;
- Nobodies become somebodies;
- Orphans become sons;
- Enemies become friends.

### December 20, 2007: The Hall of Fame

During the past few days I, like millions of other believers, have been reading the opening chapters of Matthew and Luke. While I have once again been moved by the wonder of God becoming one of us in the Person of Jesus, the character of Mary has also affected me. To a large extent she has been ignored by Protestantism, as a reaction to her elevation to near deity in Roman Catholicism. However, I fear we have thrown the baby out with the bath water. Trying to get inside the mind of this young lady has been a fascinating exercise.

Mary was an incredibly brave woman. Firstly, she was willing to wave her reputation goodbye so that God could fulfil his purpose for her and the world. The moment Mary said yes to God she was prepared to be misunderstood, branded an adulteress or even worse, and to lose any good name she might have had. For a righteous, virtuous young woman to be prepared for that makes her something special.

Furthermore, in saying yes to God's plan she put herself in very real physical danger. In parts of Iraq today, young Muslim women who refuse to wear a veil are being murdered. Mary faced the same fate; she could have been stoned to death for getting pregnant outside of marriage. But she went ahead, so that the Saviour of the world could be born.

Mary was also prepared to lose the love of her life, her fiancé Joseph. He had every right to break off their engagement after discovering she was pregnant. In fact, he could have led the stoning. Even though she loved this young man with every fibre of her being, there was a prior love: she loved God with all her heart too. Mary was ready to let go of what she valued the most for the sake of her Lord. Mary was no insignificant player in the history of God's people of faith: she belongs in the Hall of Fame.

## January 17, 2008: Faith and understanding
*By faith we understand. (Hebrews 11:3)*

Understanding does not give you faith; faith gives you understanding. Faith does not originate in our minds or in our ability to reason and understand. In fact, faith is irrational to the natural mind; that is why so many people live with an 'I'll believe it when I see it' pattern of behaviour. Faith comes from hearing God speak. And whenever God speaks it will demand a response of faith; then understanding will follow.

## January 28, 2008: The source
*I will rebuke the devourer for you. (Malachi 3:11)*

Recession. Sub prime. Higher energy bills. Increased insurance premiums. Inflation. Falling stock markets. Weak dollar. Tighten the belt. Less money. Hard times ahead. These scary words dominate headlines all over the world. Many in the financial sectors are forecasting a gloomy 2008 for all of us. They tell us to batten down the hatches, cut our costs and forget the holiday. It is going to be a tough year.

It costs me more now to fill my car with fuel; my mortgage has gone way up in the past year; I heat my home with gas that has spiralled in price. But I refuse to submit to the forecasters when they tell me that as far as finance is concerned I am going to be worse off this year. I live by different financial laws from them. I live by God's financial laws of sowing and reaping, of bringing God the whole tithe and being generous in my offerings.

God promises to look after us if we live by his principles. He says that he will rebuke the devourer and ensure that our children never beg bread. God is the source of our life and he has many resources by which he cares for us. If we make the mistake of seeing our jobs as our source then we will panic if we lose them. If we view our investments as our source then we will worry when the stock market dips and falls. But if we understand that God is our source, then we have no worries. When one resource ends or dries up he opens another one for us.

Now is not the time to stop tithing - God forbid. I will never do that: it keeps the windows of heaven open to me. Neither will I cut back on my giving to the Lord. These are the days in which the church has a glorious opportunity to demonstrate to the world that the laws of the Kingdom of God really work.

### February 6, 2008: Defining moments

Today is the fiftieth anniversary of the Munich air crash in which twenty-three people, including eight Manchester United footballers died. They were known as the Busby Babes (Matt Busby, the manager, survived the crash), and their average age was just twenty-two. They were regarded at the time as the best club team in the world. The loss of the majority of the team was the equivalent of losing around seventy five percent of the best players in a team in just one day. The disaster was a tragedy that is still remembered. In fact, commemorations are being held today in Manchester.

Listening to the survivors, it is clear that Munich was the defining moment of their life. It affected them in so many ways that even now, fifty years later, they still define themselves in the light of that occasion. It is a common thing to do; in fact we all do it. Some would point to Martin Luther King's 'I have a dream' speech or the death of John Kennedy, or the release of Nelson Mandela as the defining moment of their life.

We all have these defining moments in our lives: experiences that have such an impact on us they determine the way we live. They shape us and make us what we are. They might well be difficult ones, or even life and death ones. It is what we do in and with those moments and experiences, how we use them and move on from them that determines how they define us.

### February 7, 2008: Life in six words

Ernest Hemingway once bet that he could write a complete story in six words. He wrote, 'For Sale: baby shoes, never worn.' He won his bet. Now the online magazine *Smith* is asking its readers to sum up their own lives in just six words. Could you sum up your life in six words?

### February 14, 2008: Take responsibility

I heard a story on the news this morning that highlights again our ludicrous 'blame-others' culture. Graham Calvert is suing the bookmakers William Hill for £2 million. Calvert, a self confessed gambling addict, claims that this is the amount he lost on bets after asking the bookmaker not to let him bet again. Calvert would often place bets of £25,000 with the bookmaker. They agreed to bar him. But then he registered a new account with the firm in a new name and subsequently lost more than £2 million. Now he is suing for negligence.

This incident is so typical of a society where we blame everybody else for our own mistakes or folly, but are so reluctant to take responsibility for our own lives and actions.

It goes all the way back to the Garden of Eden: when God challenged Adam over sin, Adam said to God, 'It was the woman you gave me. Don't blame me.' Eve blamed the devil; neither of them would face up to their own wilful acts. The moment we take responsibility for ourselves, when we face up to the fact that we got ourselves into the mess in the first place, when we stop blaming others, including God, for our own mistakes, that is the first step on the road to repentance and change.

### February 21, 2008: Be careful what you ask for
*God gave them what they asked for, but he sent a wasting disease along with it. (Psalm 106:15)*

Not everything we get is good for us. The Israelites in the desert were fed up with the manna that God miraculously provided for them. They insisted on having meat. They did not want what God's desire for them was, so God gave them the desire of their sinful, rebellious hearts. But he also sent leanness to their souls.

We should not equate the blessing of God on our lives solely in terms of our material wealth, or whether we have everything we want. Material wealth can certainly be a sign of God's blessing: the biblical law of sowing and reaping demonstrates that. Poverty is not a spiritual virtue. When we tithe and give offerings we should expect to prosper. But merely having lots of things and then claiming that they are proof of God's blessing must be accompanied by the evidence of the rest of our lives: are we living in obedience to his will? I know many people who have material wealth, but they are far from God. They are also some of the most miserable and sad people I have met. True riches are obtained by doing the will of God.

## February 28, 2008: Keep flowing

*If anyone is thirsty, let him come to me and drink. Whoever believes in me, as the Scripture has said, streams of living water will flow from within him. (John 7:37-38)*

This morning I sat at my desk and picked up my fountain pen to write a friend of mine a note. It had been a few days since I last used it, perhaps a whole week. The pen had remained in full view all that time, but I had chosen other ways to write in the previous days. As I put the pen to the paper nothing happened. I scratched it around on another piece of paper but it only gave out a rather pathetic scrawled line. I ran it back and forth trying to get the ink to flow; but the nib had dried out and was stopping the flow of ink, of which there was plenty in the chamber.

As I thought about that my mind was drawn to the passage in John where Jesus talked about the life of the Holy Spirit flowing from within us in a never-ending stream of living water. We cannot afford to leave the Holy Spirit unused in our lives for even one day, not even one moment. We have to keep the 'nib' of life open all the time and not drying out. We do that by actively allowing the Holy Spirit to flow from within us with his divine life each and every second of the day. And when we live that way we write a best seller.

## March 20, 2008: That's torn it

*Jesus shouted again, and he gave up his spirit. At that moment the curtain in the Temple was torn in two, from top to bottom. (Matthew 27:50-51)*

In the moment that Jesus died on the Cross, about a mile away from Golgotha something incredible occurred in the Temple in Jerusalem. The curtain that separated the Most Holy Place from the rest of the world was ripped apart, but not by any human hand. This curtain was sixty feet high and over four inches thick. It was reputed that two teams of horses tied to either end could not tear it. In the moment that Jesus died, God the Father took hold of the curtain and tore it from top to bottom.

God had insisted that the curtain be installed when he designed the tabernacle in the time of Moses. It was a constant reminder to the people that they were separated from a holy God because of their sin. Once a year the High Priest would go behind the curtain into the very presence of God with shed blood to atone for the sins of the people and himself (see Leviticus chapter sixteen). But on this day at Golgotha, the Son of God, the real Great High Priest, had entered the true Most Holy Place by his own blood and dealt with the problem of our sin once and for all. That was good enough for God the Father, who reached down from heaven and tore apart the curtain, signifying that the way was now open for us to come to him. God the Father flung his arms open wide and declared, 'COME ON IN!'

### March 25, 2008: The unconfined Christ

While reading the four gospel accounts of Jesus' death and resurrection over Easter, I came across a pattern that I had never noticed before. Everyone who came into contact with Jesus from the moment of his death and through that first day after he rose again either tried to confine Jesus or were themselves confined by something that hindered their response to the fact that he was alive. Over the next few entries I am going to mention some of them.

Today I want to draw your attention to the religious leaders who orchestrated Jesus' murder. If you read the various accounts, especially from Matthew 27:62-66, you will see that they were men who were confined by their religious conceptions. The Pharisees were legalistic control freaks who were terrified of anything beyond their control. They were proud and arrogant, just like their father the devil. The other religious group, the Sadducees, didn't believe in anything supernatural: no angels, and certainly no resurrection of the dead. Once they had Jesus in the tomb they thought they could keep him there by putting a seal over the stone and posting a guard of soldiers to stop the disciples stealing the body. How pathetic.

That is what religion does: it tries to confine Jesus so that he becomes manageable. The seal was their sign of authority. Religion claims to represent God. Religion tries to get God to settle down, to become respectable. It attempts desperately to entomb God. Religion keeps God at arm's length. There is no life of God in religion. Jesus did not come to give us religion. He came to give us life: and life in all its fullness.

## March 26, 2008: The unconfined Christ (2)

Today's confiners are Joseph of Arimathea and Nicodemus (you can read about them in Matthew 27:57-61 and John 19:38-42). Strange choices, you may think, and at one level you would be right. After all, when all the other disciples had deserted Jesus, these brave men were the only two left. They boldly went to Pilate and asked for the body of Jesus. They took him down from the cross and buried him. That is where they fell into the trap of confinement.

Joseph and Nicodemus were confined by their good intentions. They allowed their sentiments and desire to do the right thing for Jesus to override what he had said: that he was going to rise from the dead after three days. The immediacy of what they regarded as a tragic occasion shut out the greater reality: phase one of Jesus' plan was complete. Joseph and Nicodemus failed to see that. So they covered him in seventy-five pounds (thirty four kilos) of myrrh and aloes and then wrapped him up tightly in a burial cloth. They had no faith expectation that Jesus would rise from the dead. They confined him to the grave. Then they rolled the heavy round stone into its rut and left him. Jesus was not the one confined: they were.

### March 28, 2008: The unconfined Christ (3)

You might be surprised at the next person who tried to confine Jesus: Mary Magdalene. Now I must admit that of all the characters involved that day Mary comes out quite well; but we will get to that in a moment.

Mary features in all the Gospel accounts of the resurrection; she was right in the middle of the action. We have to say that at the beginning of the day she was in exactly the same position as everybody else: she had no faith that Jesus would keep his promise and rise from the dead. She had come with spices to complete what Joseph and Nicodemus had begun. John 20:10-18 tells how she stood outside the tomb crying her eyes out in grief and mourning, not only because Jesus was dead but also that his body had been taken away. Or so she thought. She even spoke to the risen Jesus, thinking he was the gardener. She asked him if he knew where Jesus had been hidden so she could recover the body.

It was only when she heard Jesus call her name that she realised Jesus was alive. Her grief gave way to uncontrollable joy and she grabbed him and held on to him. Mary was not going to let Jesus go, not again. Not her Jesus; not her Lord. She had been through so much and she was going to hang on to him with all her might. She would make this moment last forever. She was confining him to her own little moment in her own little world. What was Jesus' response? He told Mary, 'Don't cling on to me. I have things to be getting on with. Come on, get up, I have things for you to do. I have work for you. Go and tell the disciples I'm alive. Stop clinging on to me and get up. Move beyond yourself and your own little world.'

Now here is where Mary gets the credit. She moved beyond her own situation: she let go of Jesus and obeyed him.

That lady could run! She flew like a bullet from a gun with the news that the world was waiting to hear: 'I have seen the Lord: he's alive!'

## April 1, 2008: The unconfined Christ (4)

Today's examples are the two disciples on the road to Emmaus. You can read about them in Luke 24:13-35. They were really depressed; their faces were downcast (verse 17). They were in such a state that they had even left the scene of the action in Jerusalem. They were walking away from where they should have been; and that was their first mistake. If they had had any faith they would have hung around. What was worse: they had decided to leave town even after hearing the news from the women that Jesus was alive! Why on earth were they heading in the opposite direction to where they should have been? Once bitten and twice shy, perhaps? Their clear disappointment and dashed hopes had now confined them.

But Jesus was so gracious; he went after them. Luke tells us how Jesus got alongside them and played along for a while. It really is quite a funny story. But Jesus came with a purpose to them: he opened up the Scriptures and explained everything to them. That had been their other confinement: they were ignorant of the Word of God and what it had to say. That is such a big issue today: so many Christians have little or no idea of what the Bible has to say about God, his purpose, who we are in Christ, and the Kingdom of God. Biblical illiteracy today is staggering. I am not talking about owning a Bible; I am talking about reading it, believing it, obeying it, living by it. If you want to be free and unconfined, then let the Word of God get to work on you.

## April 4, 2008: The unconfined Christ (5)

For our final part of this series we turn our attention to the disciples. Each of the Gospels gives various information on what happened to them from the night when Jesus was betrayed all the way through to his ascension. One thing they all had in common was this: they were in fear of their lives. They all deserted Jesus in Gethsemane, although John was brave enough to be present at the Cross. But after Jesus died they locked themselves together in a room because they were afraid of what the Jews were going to do to them (John 20:19). They thought they were next on the religious leaders' hit list and their days were numbered. They were confined by their fear.

So Jesus, the unconfined Christ, just appeared in the room where they were. He knew there was no way they would open the door, so he ignored it and barged right into their house of fear. Mark 16:14 tells us that instead of rejoicing with them that he was alive, Jesus rebuked them because of their lack of faith and their continued stubborn refusal to believe what they had been told all day by Mary and the others: that he was alive. Jesus had no sympathy for the disciples that night; he would not let them wallow in their fear. There was no reason for it; he had told them plainly that this would be the day he would rise again. Their unbelief had locked them behind closed doors in dread and fear. Jesus had to get them out of that room: after all, they were destined to go into the entire world.

### April 24, 2008: God's masterpiece

*We are God's workmanship, created in Christ Jesus to do good works, which God prepared in advance for us to so. (Ephesians 2:10)*

Several years ago my family and I had the opportunity to have a holiday in Rome. During our stay we went to the Vatican. There we saw what is regarded as a true masterpiece: Michelangelo's *La Pieta*. Carved from marble it looks as fine as high quality paper. My eyes could not pull themselves away from this magnificent piece of art. Then I thought of the one who created it: Michelangelo truly was an artistic genius to fashion something like *La Pieta.*

We are God's masterpieces, we are magnificent works of art. That is what the word 'workmanship' means in this verse: a masterpiece. God sees us exactly like that; he created us in Christ to be like just like Christ. We truly are amazing pieces of artwork.

The point of that is so that the genius who created us will get all the credit and honour. Michelangelo received honour, wealth and glory for his creations. Just imagine the honour, wealth and glory our Heavenly Artist deserves for making something so wonderful as you.

### April 29, 2008: Odious and So Touchy
*I plead with Euodia and Syntyche: because you belong to the Lord, settle your disagreement. (Philippians 4:2)*

I admire the way Paul dealt with these two ladies in the church at Philippi. A friend of mine used to call them Odious and So Touchy. Obviously nearly everybody in the church was aware of what was going on between them; and if they were not aware, they were about to be. Paul decided to take the direct route: 'stop it!' He didn't send them for counsel or blame therapy. He appealed to who they were in Christ: 'You belong to the Lord and this is totally unacceptable behaviour for such people'. Furthermore, note that Paul dealt with them publicly: he raised the matter before the whole church. He brought the matter into the forum of the whole body because the whole body was being affected by the sinful attitudes of two people who belonged to the body. Paul's revelation of the Body of Christ allowed him to act in such a way. The testimony of Jesus was far more important to him than the sensitivities and reputations of two stubborn women.

### May 1, 2008: Whatever happened to Jesus?

*Jesus was taken up before their very eyes, and a cloud hid him from their sight. (Acts 1:8)*

Today is one of the most important days in the Christian calendar, yet it is one of the most ignored. It is Ascension Day, when we remember that, forty days after rising from the dead, Jesus ascended into heaven. Many Christians never give it a thought; maybe because it is always on a Thursday, when most of us are working.

The Ascension is important because Jesus could not only rise from the dead and stay on the earth. He had to ascend so he could take his place ruling and reigning as King of Kings and Lord of Lords at the right hand of the Father. That is what he is doing in heaven right now: all his enemies are being made a footstool for his feet. He had to ascend to the heavenly realms because when we get saved we are raised up there with him too, even though we are living on the earth.

Furthermore, if Jesus had not ascended then he could not have sent the Holy Spirit at Pentecost, ten days later. The coming of the Spirit is the proof that Jesus is where he said he would be. And right now his ascended power and glory is unleashed on the earth through the Holy Spirit, living in his people.

### May 6, 2008: See it my way

*One day I went into the sanctuary, O God, and I thought about the destiny of the wicked. (Psalm 73:17)*

Until the moment Asaph, who wrote this Psalm, went into the presence of God, he was a troubled man. Like many of us in the years since he wrote these words, he was perturbed by, even envious of, the wicked people who totally ignore God all their lives, yet still seem to prosper. They have everything they could possibly need or want; they seem to

182

have no troubles, have great health and wealth; yet they continue to ignore God, even glorying in the fact that they don't need him. At the same time the righteous suffer, they go without things, work hard, are in pain and have difficult times with constant trouble. How can that be right?

It was only when Asaph entered into the presence of God that he understood; you can read about it all in Psalm 73. He began to understand everything from God's perspective; he saw things God's way. It was this that brought him peace. The biggest thing he learned in it all was about himself: 'I realised how bitter I had become' (verse 21). Sometimes things happen or don't happen to teach us about ourselves. Have you ever been overlooked for a promotion that should have been yours? Did somebody else get the credit for what you did? Did your non-Christian neighbour just pay cash for that car you have been saving long and hard for? Did that lazy colleague get the promotion that should have been yours? It is interesting what you learn about yourself at those times.

## May 19, 2008: All together now

*Sing a new song to the LORD! Let the whole earth sing to the LORD! Sing to the LORD; bless his name. (Psalm 96:1-2)*

God is musical; he loves a good tune. That shouldn't surprise us: after all, he created music. God loves to hear his people sing to him. In fact, to him the whole earth is one massed choir of praising singers, each one singing out their songs of adoration. I am so glad that the Psalmist didn't say, 'All those who can sing in tune, sing to the Lord'. I am relieved he didn't limit those allowed to sing praises to those with voices like Andrea Bocelli, Celine Dion or Frank Sinatra. He said to us all, 'Sing! Sing! Sing!' God is not concerned with the tunefulness of the voice; he can sort out the niceties of the notes when they reach his ears. All you need is a voice, a song of praise and a thankful heart. All together now...

### May 22, 2008: Famous last words

*It was by faith that Joseph, when he was about to die, confidently spoke of God's bringing the people of Israel out of Egypt. He was so sure of it he commanded them to carry his bones with them when he left! (Hebrews 11:22)*

I wonder what you would like your last words to be? Joseph's were really good, because they were words of faith. He spoke not only about his own future but also about that of his descendants. He went out with a bang, not a whimper. So powerful were these last words that, over four hundred years later, they were obeyed. Exodus 13:19 says that Moses made sure that the departing Israelites left Egypt with Joseph's bones. Even though this man was long dead, his words of faith about the future destiny of his people were still living. I think I'd like my last words to be: 'Look! Here comes Jesus!'

### June 5, 2008: The ancient power

Today I have been with my brother, David. He has not been well recently, but happily is now recovering and enjoying the hand of God on his life. He has been taking time to go through our family history, collecting photographs, letters, and information on our ancestors.

David has uncovered a letter written in March 1908 to our grandfather, Jim Griffiths, by his brother, Tom, who was a seaman. Tom had a remarkable conversion to Christ: at one time he was infamous in the pubs of Cardiff as a drunkard who would fight anybody. He would stand with his back to the bar and take on all comers. One night, however, he met God. Tom was standing at the bar and reached out his hand to pick up his drink when the Holy Spirit came upon him. Tom could not physically lift the glass; such was the power of God on him in conviction of his sin. Right there and then, Tom received Christ. He was a changed man, who became known for his gentleness and kindness.

The letter I held in my hand was written by this man of God, still a seaman, but now transformed by the love of Jesus. He was writing from Norfolk, Virginia, to his brother Jim, about the goodness of God and how much Tom loved his Saviour. The last sentence of the letter reads: 'His touch still has its ancient power.' As I read these words out loud to my own brother, written by our ancestor one hundred years ago, I was moved in my spirit by their power. I felt something of the eternal nature of almighty God, how down the ages the touch of his hand that Tom had experienced is the same today. Both my brother and I have known the ancient power of Jesus' touch. Then I thought about the Scriptures. Even though my Bible is fairly new, having been purchased just a few weeks ago, it is an eternal book, written by the Ancient of Days. It has an ancient power, and that power is as alive and potent today as when the inspired writers first wrote the words.

When the eternal God touches you with his ancient power, you can never be the same again.

## July 15, 2008: A wise investment
*Don't store up treasures here on earth, where moths eat them and rust destroys them, and where thieves break in and steal. Store your treasures in heaven, where moths and rust cannot destroy, and thieves do not break in and steal. Wherever your treasure is, there the desires of your heart will also be. (Matthew 6:19-21)*

One of the ways in which we can store up treasures in heaven is by using our earthly treasures in heavenly ways and for the advancement of the kingdom of God. Take money, for example: even though it's only paper or metal, it represents something spiritual. Jesus taught more about money than many other subjects. He understood its power. Jesus never preached a gospel of poverty; he taught us how to control and use our wealth. The way we handle our money demonstrates where we have stored it. That is why we bring our tithe to God and also give him generous offerings; and why we are generous with our finances; and why we handle it with integrity and honesty. If we have stored it in heaven then heaven's King has ownership and control of it. If God has your wallet he has you.

### September 17, 2008: Prosper in the credit crunch

The credit crunch continues unabated across many if not most of the world's economies. In the United States, Lehman Brothers, the massive investment back, has gone bust. And AIG, one of America's largest insurance companies, has been bailed out by the US Federal Reserve to the tune of $85 billion. In the UK, the FTSE dipped below 5000 yesterday, while HBOS and Lloyds TSB are planning to merge. Everyday life is affected: petrol continues to be expensive and food prices have soared. UK inflation is officially at 4.7%, the highest for a number of years. Essential items, such as milk, bread and meat, have risen by up to 20%.

For Christians, this is a golden opportunity to demonstrate how the financial laws of the kingdom of God differ from the systems of the world. We are not immune to what goes on in the world: we have to eat and clothe ourselves. We have to drive our cars and travel to work, just like everybody else. Nevertheless, I believe that certain things we practise help us avoid the crippling effects of recession. For me there are three things that I must maintain, not only in credit crunch times, but also as a lifestyle.

The first is to always bring God my tithe. It belongs to him and I must never rob him of what is his. Therefore, no matter what, I will always tithe, with thanksgiving and faith, and in the fear of the Lord. If I bring God his tithe, he has promised to open the windows of heaven and bless me. The second is that I will continue to give offerings generously. 2Corinthians 8 and 9 tell me how to do it; I may not be able to give as much as I want, but I will always give. It's only in my giving that I begin to sow out of what is mine. The tithe belongs to the Lord, so it's not mine to sow. But my offerings are my seed to sow. The third thing is to live according to my means. Many people are paying the price of living way beyond their means and are now suffering for it. It's biblical common sense to budget, to save up to buy something and not stick it on a credit card knowing you can't pay it off. Jesus told us to count the cost before we embark on a building venture; the same principle holds true in all areas of finance.

In the kingdom of God, everything is of the Holy Spirit, including its finance. When we put into practice the financial laws of the kingdom, God will move miraculously in our finances. Put it to the test and see what happens.

## October 28, 2008: The self-destructive power of jealousy

*Anger is cruel and fury overwhelming, but who can stand before jealousy? (Proverbs 27:3)*

Jealousy has a potency that is not present in anger and fury. Anger and fury are themselves wrong (there is a righteous anger and God gets angry, but they are altogether different things). But jealousy stands in a place of its own. It possesses a destructive, cancerous quality that eats away at the heart of a person. Anger and fury can flare up and then disappear, but jealousy lingers, it seeps deeper and deeper into you and rots you. It desires what it doesn't own and covets what it cannot have. Jealousy is spiritual robbery: it's theft in the mind. At its root, jealousy is self-centredness: it craves what it doesn't own and wants it for itself.

### October 30, 2008: Pay attention

*We must pay more careful attention to what we have heard,*
*so that we do not drift away. (Hebrews 2:1)*

We must pay more careful attention to what we *have*
heard, not only to what we are hearing now. It's vitally
important that we do not forget or neglect what we have
heard from God in the past, because we continually build our
faith on what we hear. One of the ways our faith perseveres
and grows is by remembering how God acted in the past; how
he was faithful to what he promised. Even when we are still
awaiting the fulfilment of his word now we have to keep alive
what we have heard; don't let it slip away, or faith can drain
away. You keep reminding yourself of God's track record and
the reliability of his word. In paying attention to what we
have heard we're in a much better position to keep hearing
God in the present.

### November 3, 2008: The heavenly light

*Your word, O LORD, is eternal; it stands firm in the*
*heavens...Your word is a lamp to my feet and a light to my*
*path. (Psalm 119:89, 105)*

God's word created the heavens. Every word God
speaks has heavenly DNA in it. Therefore, God's spoken word
written down - the Bible - will always lead you heavenwards.
It will always lift you up from the earthly, natural and
worldly way of living and thinking, to the realm of God: the
eternal, heavenly realm. A true encounter with the Word of
God will never leave you earthbound.

Because the word of God is eternal and heavenly, it
'shines with a heavenly light', so to speak. It acts as a lamp
and a light to guide you in your walk with God. It guides
your feet, lighting the way it wants you to go. If you are
finding right now that the path is dark or you've lost your

way, it could be because you're on the wrong one. God will always lead you on the right, brightly lit path of his will as revealed in his heavenly word. You may not know all the steps you have to take and can't see the whole of the path. After all, you're walking by faith. Nevertheless, you should be able to see the next step that you have to take: the light of the heavenly word is showing you the way.

### November 27, 2008: Garlic or God

> *The Israelites started wailing and said, 'If only we had meat to eat! We remember the fish we ate in Egypt at no cost - also the cucumbers, melons, leeks, onions and garlic. But now we have lost our appetite; we never see anything but this manna!' (Numbers 11:5-6)*

Garlic is popular in the Aubrey household; it adds that lovely zip to certain dishes and it's very healthy. I try to avoid it before meeting lots of people, although it can be handy if you want to avoid certain people!

The Israelites decided that they preferred garlic to God. Every day in the desert he provided miracle food for them - manna. It was the food of angels. He had brought them out of slavery and deprivation and was guiding them to their own land, which flowed with 'milk and honey.' But these people were an ungrateful, unbelieving, complaining and rebellious bunch. Such was their state of unbelief and ingratitude to God that they now lived with a distorted, even false sense of reality. They looked back to a time that did not exist: they had not enjoyed these delights in Egypt - at no cost. They were slaves who had cried out to God to deliver them from their plight and he had graciously responded and delivered them. In rejecting his provision they rejected him. They were in complete unreality. An absence of faith and the Holy Spirit will always result in a distortion of reality.

### December 12, 2008: Easily pleased

*Without faith it is impossible to please God, because anyone who comes to him must believe that he exists and that he rewards those who earnestly seek him. (Hebrews 11:6)*

It's not difficult to please God; in fact it's very easy. All you need to do is have faith. Some people read this verse and miss the point completely; they think that it's so hard to please God, but it isn't. He is good and kind, full of love and grace. His mercies are new every morning. He created us so we would know him, and faith is the means by which we know him. God never makes it hard for us to please him; he just tells us the way to do it. And because he is so good, and because he knows we need faith, he gives it to us. How good is that?

### December 18, 2008: The same but different

*As you come to him the living stone - rejected by men but chosen by God and precious to him - you also, like living stones, are being built into a spiritual house...(1Peter 2:4-5)*

The house that the Holy Spirit builds - the church - is a house of living stones. Each one is uniquely different from all the others; we are stones not bricks, which are man made and all look the same. Stones are all different from each other; they all have their own distinct shape and facets. Each believer is a one off work of art (Ephesians 2:10).

At the same time, each living stone is exactly the same as every other living stone, because every one of us is just like the Living Stone - Jesus. It is Jesus who makes the difference. He makes us like him, so that we are all the same. The Holy Spirit is building a Jesus House; and he uses stones that are just like Jesus to build it.

## January 7, 2009: Stop horsing around

*The king must not make the people return to Egypt to get more horses, for the LORD has told you, 'You are not to go back that way again'. (Deuteronomy 17:16)*

Egypt - their old life - held nothing of value for Israel in their new life in Canaan, even something as valuable and useful as a horse. This is a picture in which God tells us about our old lives before we came to Christ. We must never hanker after the things that once held value for us, or even try and retrieve them, spruce them up a bit and introduce them into the new life in Christ. We must not even hanker after them. Whatever was in Egypt was buried in the Sea. Your old life was buried in the waters of baptism. Nothing of your old life can assist you in the new one. Nothing of the old life has any place in the new one. Nothing of the old makes any positive contribution to the new. Old things are passed away; all things have become new.

## January 27, 2009: Don't cave in

The superscription at the beginning of Psalm 57 reads: *For the director of music. To the tune of 'Do not Destroy'. Of David. A miktam. When he had fled from Saul into the cave.*

I don't think I've ever written here about the title of a Psalm before. These summaries about the Psalm that follows give valuable insight into what was happening to David at the time and how he responded. This particular Psalm was written when David was on the run from Saul and found himself trapped in a cave. If you read the Psalm you will discover how David handled the situation.

First, he took time, right in the middle of a life-threatening situation, to write a song about it! In the midst of his trouble he lifted his spirit in praise to God. Even though he was in a cave he took refuge in the Lord. Second, he didn't cave in; he reached out to the God of the heavens and brought the reality of heaven into his earthly situation (verses 2-3). Therefore, he could say, 'My heart is steadfast, O God, my heart is steadfast' (verse 5).

If you find yourself trapped in a cave by an enemy, don't cave in. Call on the God of the heavens to deliver you.

### February 16, 2009: The end is nigh?

*He must remain in heaven until the restoration of all things spoken by the prophets. (Acts 3:21)*

I woke up this morning thinking of the end of the world. I know it's Monday, but that is not the reason why I thought of such a thing; in fact, there was no overwhelming reason at all. I just thought about it.

As I thought, this verse came to me again; it's a verse that guides my life, my theology and doctrine; and is the focus of what I do. One day this world will end, but it will not be through global warming, environmental meltdown or nuclear disaster. Now let me say quickly that Christians should be concerned about the environment and have a clear stance on ecology and political matters. Too many believers live in ignorance of the world we live in and the issues facing it.

The end will come when God says so; and the end will come when all things spoken by the prophets are restored. Integral to this restoration is the condition of the church, because the church has yet to be restored to God's original intention for it, not merely trying to replicate or return to the church of Acts chapter 2. The church that Jesus will return for is not ready to receive him yet; but once it is ready - restored to what God always had in mind for it - the heavens will open and he will come again in glory. That's why I thought about the end of the world this morning.

## February 26, 2009: Come back and finish what you started

In John chapter 5, we read the story of Jesus healing the man who had been crippled for 38 years. This man couldn't get into the water fast enough when it was stirred. Jesus' question to him seems a strange one: 'Do you want to get healed?' You'd think that was obvious; but Jesus never takes anything for granted. The man needed to say what was in his heart. Accordingly, Jesus healed him and then slipped away in the crowd.

However, Jesus wasn't finished with this person. Later on he tracked him down and warned him to stop sinning so that something worse didn't happen to him. Jesus didn't intend for him only to be well in his body; he wanted him to be well in spirit and soul. This man had issues in his life and he had to get right with God.

Jesus always finishes what he starts in you. He never leaves a job half done; he is not satisfied with incompletion. This principle works in every area of life. If we give up on ourselves he never will. If we think that we can partly obey, thinking that will satisfy him, we are in for a rude awakening. Jesus only sees us as the finished article and works in us to achieve it. He will not settle for anything less. Depending on the condition of your heart that will be a blessing or an unwelcome piece of news. Whatever, he will finish what he starts.

## March 3, 2009: Why love is greater than faith

*And now these three remain: faith, hope and love. But the greatest of these is love. (1Corinthians 13:13)*

Faith is indispensable; without we can't know God or please him. It's only by faith we can be saved. We live by faith and not by what we see with our natural eyes. For all that, love is greater than faith. There are many reasons why that is so, but one of the reasons is that love creates the atmosphere for faith to flourish.

Perfect love casts out fear. Fear is the enemy of faith: it neutralises faith. Fear will paralyse the believer, making faith difficult to function. But where there is love, faith will flourish. When you know that God loves and accepts you and that love and acceptance is present in the church, faith will flow freely. Love has no fear of failure or rejection, or of making mistakes. Love brings a freedom for people to move in faith, knowing that God and his people are with them and behind them. And if they make a mistake (for example, mistiming a prophecy in a meeting), nobody is going to write them off as a failure. At least they had a go. Somebody once said that the person who never made a mistake never made anything.

A few weeks ago a lady was healed by Jesus in our Sunday meeting; one of the other ladies prayed for her in a time of ministry. When the lady who prayed gave testimony she said that she got the words all wrong, but she had faith - and the other lady was healed. I appreciated that testimony; not just that someone was healed, but that the one who prayed felt no condemnation because she got the words wrong! She acted in an atmosphere and attitude of love and acceptance and her faith worked. That's the power of love.

### March 4, 2009: Listen to the question

*Jesus said to Philip, 'Where shall we buy bread for these people to eat?'...Philip answered him, 'Eight months' wages would not buy enough bread for each one to have a bite!'* (John 6:5,7)

This was a fascinating conversation, carried on two different levels. Jesus asked Philip a faith question: 'We're going to feed these people. Where shall we get the bread from? How shall we do this?' But Philip's answer was from another planet; all he could think was, 'We have no money to buy bread, let alone feed over five thousand men!' Jesus didn't mention money; his question was: how shall we perform the miracle? Philip couldn't see any opportunity for a miracle, because he wasn't listening to the question. He wasn't tuned in to the faith question; all he saw was an impossible situation. Had he listened to the question, he would have had the answer. He would have heard that a miracle was about to take place and he had a part in it ('where shall we buy bread?').

You have to listen carefully when Jesus asks you a question like this. And if he hasn't yet, you can guarantee that he will. His questions are very specific and aimed at moving us on in faith. He has all the resources to perform the miracle; he wants us to be involved in them and do them. So, listen to the question.

## March 11, 2009: The wrong shoes

Recently I was listening to a lecture given by the musician and conductor Benjamin Zander on his passion for classical music. He finished his lecture with a quote from a lady who survived Auschwitz. As a young girl this lady had been transported to the death camp with her younger brother and parents. Unaware of the terrible fate that awaited them they arrived on those trains expecting life to carry on. As they were about to get off, the lady looked down at her brother's feet and scolded him: 'You are wearing the wrong shoes.' Sure enough, the young lad was wearing odd shoes. They were the last words she ever said to her brother: she never saw him again.

Such an experience is bound to have a profound effect on anybody. This lady, now an old woman, lives by this statement: 'I will never say anything that could not stand as the last thing I ever say.'

### March 25, 2009: What's in your house?
*Elisha asked the widow, "What do you have in your house?"*
*(2Kings 4:2)*

So often the answer to our situation lies within us. The God of all resource, who is more than enough to meet all the needs of all his people all the time, is living his life as God within us. When we look within ourselves we don't see our own resources - we have none outside of the Holy Spirit. But when we look within and see the eternal God living in us by the all-powerful Holy Spirit, then we understand - 'I can do all things through him who gives me strength.'

### April 14, 2009: The tools of faith
*Abraham...carried the fire and the knife. (Genesis 22:6)*

Abraham needed two things in order to obey God's command concerning Isaac. God had told him to sacrifice his son and burn him. Abraham obeyed without question, because he knew that God would reconstitute Isaac and raise him again from the dead. God had promised Abraham that through Isaac all the earth would be blessed; and a dead man could not fulfill that promise. In his hands Abraham carried the tools he would need to obey God in faith.

God always gives you the tools of faith: whatever you need to obey him he will give you. He doesn't hang you out to dry or leave you to your own devices. God equips you with exact things you need to do what he asks. If you need to sow finance, he will give you enough finance to sow. If you need to lay hands on a sick person, you will have all the measure of faith and anointing to see that person healed. God's toolbox of faith is packed with every kind of tool you'll ever need to move in faith.

## April 20, 2009: Bringing is not giving

It's important for us in our stewarding of finances that we always remember that there's a difference between bringing and giving. The Bible teaches that we should tithe to the Lord; we do so because it belongs to him. When I tithe I do not give God anything: I am only bringing him what already belongs to him. I haven't given God anything in my tithe. It's only when I consider what my offering will be that I move into the realm of giving to the Lord.

Because I love God and want to express that love in every area of my life, I am going to be a generous giver. I won't be stingy towards God because he is not stingy towards me. I won't give God my small change because he doesn't act towards me in a 'small change' way. When I give to God in my offering I have to consider how good he has been to me. True: I could give him every penny and that would not express his generosity to me. Furthermore, I have to live on my income and calculate out of my finances what I am able to give. Nevertheless, if I understand that my giving to the Lord begins only after I have brought him my tithe, then surely my giving will be generous. I have discovered that in my bringing and giving God is so generous that he reaps back to me. That's the kind of God he is.

## April 24, 2009: Rocks into pools

*Tremble, O earth, at the presence of the Lord, at the presence of the God of Jacob, who turned the rock into a pool, and hard rock into springs of water. (Psalm 114:7-8)*

The presence of the Lord is miraculous; it turns 'rocks' into 'pools'. First of all this is a reference to the water that gushed from the rock in the desert when Moses struck it with his staff (Exodus 17). That rock was Christ himself (1Corinthians 10:4). Living water gushed forth from him to satisfy the thirst of the people. Everything to do with Jesus

Christ is miraculous; he specialises in the impossible. He can change the unchangeable.

The Holy Spirit within us is the Spirit of Christ; he is that personal presence of the God of Jacob in us. As such, he is able to change the 'rocks' that we face into 'pools': he has the same ability to do the miraculous in us, for us and through us. Whatever 'rock' you face, trust in the God of Jacob and he will make it a 'pool'.

### April 28, 2009: The uprising

Whenever I read Numbers chapter 16 it chills me to the bone. It reveals an interesting but unsurprising fact: rebellious leaders are always in it for themselves. It may not be obvious at the beginning; but eventually the un-crucified heart will rise up against rightful, God-appointed leadership. (It's significant that when Moses was challenged here by these men that he fell facedown, not in fear but in humility). That uprising may take many forms, often plausible to the natural person. But it is an uprising, nevertheless.

Korah, Dathan and Abiram were leaders of the people; but they were so only because they had been ordained by those over them in the Lord. That's what makes any church leader's authority authentic: who appointed him? Eldership is an entrustment from an apostle; and if an eldership is no longer willing to work under that apostle they should step down and hand the church back to the apostle. It's not the elders' church.

Sadly, that very rarely happens. In this instance in Numbers we see the heart of such 'leaders': they were not standing for a principle at all. They wanted what was not theirs to have. In my experience over many years I have never known a rebellious leader stand for a principle in which he was prepared to lose everything - the building, the money, his position. They have never just walked away with empty hands and humble hearts. There is no self-sacrifice in a rebellious leader. Only the crucified leader holds everything lightly, because he knows that nothing belongs to him. Moses was such a man; that's why he was faithful in God's house (Hebrews 3:2). That is a basic biblical principle; Jesus said:

*If you have not been trustworthy with someone else's property, who will give you property of your own? (Luke 16:12)*

Another version says, 'If you've not been faithful in another's house...' Today there are far too many cases of leaders violating this principle. They reap what they sow. Someone will take from them what they have taken from another. That's just the way it is.

### April 30, 2009: Real or Replica?

I have an interest in watches; one of my favourites is the Patek Philippe Calatrava. It currently retails for about £12,000 for an entry-level model. Before you ask: no, I don't own one! However, I could buy one for a fraction of the price: excellent quality and looking exactly the same on the outside. The cost? About £200. That's because it's a replica, not the real thing. Unless you were a watch expert you wouldn't be able to tell the difference. But the moment someone who really knows about Calatravas looked at it and held it, he'd know I was wearing a fake.

It's easy to build something that looks like church without the aid of the Holy Spirit. A leader can have natural gifts and methods that make him attractive to natural people. Indeed, he can even have a large degree of success and build a supposedly marvelous ministry and church that can last a considerable period of time. What he builds looks exactly like the real thing. But when you look closely there's something missing. When you examine it closely it begins to be exposed for what it really is: a replica.

Many people are happy with replica church: it looks good and satisfies the natural person. But those of the Spirit are satisfied only with the genuine. Once you open up a real Calatrava you see what makes it so valuable: the quality of the mainspring, the gears and the levers; the number and quality of jewels; all testimony to the skill of the watchmaker. It's the same with the church: The spiritual person is looking for the authenticity and quality of the Spirit. It's only what is of the Spirit that makes church genuine.

Patek have a motto: *'You never actually own a Patek Philippe watch; you merely look after it for the next generation.'* The genuine lasts and is handed from generation to generation. The replica doesn't; it's not built to last. Do you belong to the genuine or to the replica? Have you given your life for something that lasts for a moment or for eternity?

### June 3, 2009: Faith is not positive thinking
*Have faith in God. (John 14:1)*

Once faith is removed from its root in the nature of God it becomes mere positive thinking. It's true that faith will make you think positively, and it's good to have positive thoughts. But positive thinking in itself is not faith. Faith must have a basis, a root. That basis is God. He is what makes faith possible. Never remove faith from God; don't have faith in faith or just have faith for something. Have faith in God.

### June 19, 2009: Prophetic essence
*David was a prophet...Seeing what was ahead he spoke... (Acts 2:30-31)*

This is the essence of the prophetic. David was a prophet; he saw what was ahead. He spoke what he saw. The prophet sees what is ahead, what is yet to come. What he or she sees in the future he or she speaks of in the present. In doing so the prophet creates faith in his or her hearers for the future, even if that future is only a minute away. The prophet's word creates faith.

A prophetic word that doesn't create faith is not prophecy. Even a prophecy of judgement will have faith in it; everything God speaks demands faith of us. The prophet speaks only what he sees or hears from God. God has already spoken his word to the prophet and the prophet must have faith that what he has seen or heard is from God. The prophet brings the future into the present, because faith is always active in the present. Therefore, every prophet must see what is ahead.

### June 23, 2009: Right from the start
*Get up and go into the city, and you will be told what to do. (Acts 9:6)*

Jesus started with Paul the way he would carry on the rest of Paul's life: he told him what to do. There was no appeal to Paul to submit and follow, only a command. The issue of the Lordship of Jesus was settled in Paul the moment he heard the voice and fell to the ground under the power of God on the road to Damascus.

That's why God achieved so much in Paul: there were no wasted years waiting for Paul's will to become one with God's. In a moment, in one encounter with the living Jesus, an independent, arrogant, cruel, self-willed, religious bigot became clay in the Potter's hands.

### June 25, 2009: Forty day training sessions
The forty days between the resurrection and ascension of Jesus were important in his training of the disciples for their future. Acts 1:1-2 says that Jesus instructed them through the Holy Spirit; this was the difference between how Jesus had trained them over the previous three years. After he had risen from the dead, and having his resurrection body, he breathed

on them and they received the Spirit (John 20:22). That was the moment they were 'born again.' At Pentecost they would receive the baptism in the Holy Spirit. But for Jesus to instruct them through the Spirit logically means that they now had received the Spirit.

Now the disciples had to learn to relate to Jesus in a new way: not through their natural senses, because he was going to leave them, and would come to them again in the Person of the Spirit at Pentecost. Therefore, Jesus spent as much time as possible preparing them for their new way of relating to him. This is vital for us: it demonstrates that none of us can know Jesus through our natural senses. We too can only know him through the Holy Spirit. That's why Jesus makes no sense to the natural person - the person without the Spirit.

### June 26, 2009: When icons die

Yesterday saw the deaths of two icons: one expected, the other a total shock to many. Farrah Fawcett, an original *Charlie's Angel* who later became an accomplished actress, died after a long battle with cancer, aged 62. Michael Jackson, self-styled king of pop, died suddenly at the age of 50. I happened to be watching the news last night as the story of Jackson's collapse and death unfolded. Then I turned to Twitter; it was amazing to see literally thousands of messages each few minutes popping up on the screen. Fawcett's death had been reported earlier in the day with measured and prepared tributes. Jackson's passing seemed to be a media event: helicopters over his house; footage of the ambulance leaving the home; his sister and other members of the family caught on camera in their moment of grief. Even in death he had no privacy.

While one is naturally saddened by these deaths, especially since both Fawcett and Jackson were relatively young, such events make us think of our values and hopes. I can remember that in the 70s every girl wanted Fawcett's hair and teeth; we all thought that we could dance like Jackson! I can remember him as a young boy with the Jackson 5 singing 'I want you back': just great pop music. But values and hopes must have more substance than that, because icons die. Their memories live on, but they are gone. It's true they leave us values, but the fact that they are no longer here leaves a terrible chasm in the heart of their followers.

That's why for Christians, all ultimate values and hopes can be placed only in Jesus Christ. He is not an historical, popular, dead icon, but a living person. Many people confine him to the pages of the New Testament as a man who lived and died two thousand years ago. Jesus is the Eternal God who became a man, and still is one today. Christians should never look back with nostalgia to history and a past life, as fans of Fawcett and Jackson will have to. We don't live with the memory of Jesus; we live with him. He is alive today.

## July 28, 2009: The ever-growing kingdom

The parables of the kingdom in Mark chapter four teach us that everything to do with the kingdom of God will always grow and never decline and pass away. There is something inherent in the genetic nature of the kingdom that ensures its growth: a growth of life, power, influence, health, numbers and dominance. It is the only kingdom that does this. All other kingdoms have a life span and then pass away; even if they last hundreds of years.

The genetic nature which makes the kingdom of God unique in this aspect is none other than Jesus Christ himself: he is the kingdom. The kingdom is righteousness, peace and joy in the Holy Spirit (Romans 14:17), and the Holy Spirit is the Spirit of Jesus Christ. That's why Isaiah could say in chapter nine: 'Of the increase of his government [kingdom reign] there will be no end'. It's not just that the kingdom of

God lasts forever: because Christ is the infinite - unlimited, unending God - then his kingdom by its very nature will always continue to grow, to increase.

The church, as the agent and instrument of the kingdom, has to manifest this nature of the kingdom on earth. Not in political machination, religious activity and ungodly domination, but as it allows the life of the Spirit of Jesus to be expressed in fullness. Where a church says no to the Spirit, it ceases to express the kingdom, and it dies. It may well continue to limp along as an institution for centuries, but it is dead all the same.

### July 29, 2009: Hupernikao – my new favourite word

Today I have been preparing to speak at All Nations Church this coming Sunday. I will be ministering on Faith that Overcomes. As part of the preparation I have been studying again the words for overcoming and victory in the New Testament: John 16:33; 1John 4:4; 1John 5:4-5; 1Corinthians 15:57, for example. The word means success, victory, supremacy, conquer. That in itself is a great study.

For Paul in Romans 8:37, however, the word is not strong enough. So he adds the word *huper* to it; the only time it occurs in the New Testament. In doing so the meaning of the term is heightened significantly (that's what *huper* does). It means not only to overcome or conquer, it means that through Christ we are more than conquerors; we over-conquer; we overwhelmingly overcome; we over-conquer; we thoroughly vanquish; we go beyond conquest.

The key for all this overwhelming overcoming is that it comes 'through him who loves us' (verse 37). Jesus said in John 16:33 that he has overcome the world. He said this before he went to the Cross. Now he sits enthroned in heaven as the Glorious Overcomer and we sit with him in the heavenly realms. Whatever we face, we already have over-conquered it, even though we may have to walk through the valley of the shadow.

## September 2, 2009: Church is people not preachers

*Now you are the body of Christ, and everyone of you is a part of it. (1Corinthians 12:27)*

Something that has come home to me again in recent days has been the concept of church that so many Christians have. I can't help but notice how often I read or hear people describe their Sunday experience of church as 'going to hear such and such' or 'really looking forward to having "brother so and so" to preach today'. Church becomes something or somewhere that is gone to in order to hear someone speak. I am sure that many of these preachers are fine men and women of God; and I believe in the necessity of preaching and teaching as part of our meeting together. The ministry of the Word of God is vital.

But it's not the be all and end all of why we come together. Church is people not a preacher. It's not having a minister or pastor do it all for you while you sit passively in your seat. It's not attending a church. Church is people. It's being the church; and the church involves everybody. 'When you come together everyone has' (1Corinthians 14:26). Therefore, everything that happens in a church meeting is not the precursor to the preacher; the Word must serve the purpose of our gathering together. One of the ways we have to tackle the passivity of so many believers is by dismantling the notion of the preacher being the climax or purpose of the church's meeting. Spirit-led thanksgiving; praise; gifts of the Spirit; testimonies; revelations; prayer: all these should be manifested too, by the body itself. The church then becomes a body functioning in wholeness rather than only one voice, no matter how fine the Word is.

Let me reiterate: I am not calling for an end to preaching and teaching of the Word - far from it. Neither do I advocate the current trend in which church is almost indefinable (*organic* is a popular term which seems to be a synonym for chaos): it has structure and form. The church is not organic, it's spiritual. My appeal is that we consider carefully what church is all about. It cannot be a one-man band in which the majority of the time spent is listening to one voice.

### September 3, 2009: The day war broke out

Today is the 70th anniversary of Britain declaring war on Nazi Germany, two days after the Germans had invaded Poland. It was the beginning of a war that would cost over 60 million lives during the next six years and change the face of Europe, indeed the world. After World War II, nothing would be the same.

As I thought about this special anniversary this morning, my mind turned not to the great battles and events of the war; I thought about my parents, who lived through those years. Mum and dad were engaged to be married when war broke out; dad was 22, mum was 23. They got married in 1940, the day the Battle of Britain started (something they would mention if they ever argued!) They were just ordinary people, planning to be together the rest of their lives, never expecting their world to be torn apart. They were typical of nearly everybody else they knew. The war changed all that.

Dad was in what was called a reserved occupation. His job meant that he would not be conscripted into the forces, because he was needed at home. However, in late 1941 he volunteered and joined the Royal Engineers. My mum was mad with him; but she knew it was the right thing to do. In 1944 he was due to take part in the D Day landings, but broke his leg playing football for his battalion a few weeks before. I used to feel sorry for him that he had missed such a great adventure, until I grew up to realise the full horror he was spared, especially when I visited the Normandy beaches and cemeteries a couple of years ago. He ended up in the Far East and didn't see my mum and sister for over two years. But they survived, unlike some of their friends. My mum grew up with a lad called Jacky Hart, who lived next door. He volunteered as a tail gunner in a Lancaster bomber and was killed in his early twenties.

It's strange to think what my parents, like all parents of my generation, went through. And when it was all over, mum and dad got on with their lives. They appreciated life, because they had to fight for it, and didn't take anything for granted. They lived without bitterness and rancour; life was too short and meant to be enjoyed. They discovered that when the going gets tough, the tough really have to get going. They were always grateful to those of their generation who never came home, people like Jacky hart. They never looked back in anger, but got on with their future. That's how they taught my sisters, my brother and me how to live. And that's why I think of my parents today.

## September 21, 2009: If you only knew

*Jacob set up an altar and called it El Elohe Israel. (Genesis 33:20)*

*If you knew...who it is that asks you for a drink... (John 4:10)*

These two incidents in the Bible have a vital link: they occurred in the same place, though separated by some 1,700 years or more. The first reference recounts how Jacob, after his life-changing encounter with God at Peniel ('face of God') moved on and met his estranged brother Esau. When he arrived at Shechem he bought a plot of land with a well; he named it 'God, the God of Israel.' It was a place of significance, with a powerful name. All who came to draw water knew its name. Time passed, and its significance waned.

All those years later a Samaritan woman came to the same well; she did it every day, as was her habit. There was nothing special about the place anymore, just a well with water to meet her natural needs.

This particular day, something special was about to happen at that well, something even Jacob had not experienced. That day, God, the God of Israel, Jesus, was sitting there, waiting for the woman and about to invite her to drink Eternal Water! But she had no idea who was speaking to her. This well, 'El Elohe Israel', had been reduced to 'Jacob's well' (verse 6). But the supernatural God of Heaven was about to invade her natural life; she would never be the same again.

If we only knew whom we are dealing with when we encounter Jesus Christ, our lives would be drastically different. He is the God who made the universe, the One who brought the vast star fields into being with one word from his mouth. He is the God of Abraham, Isaac and Jacob; the One who appeared to Moses in a burning bush; the One who walked in the fire with Shadrach, Meshach and Abednego. He is the holy God whom Isaiah saw.

Never reduce God, the God of Israel, to anything less than he really is, to the mundane and the natural. Don't let your Christianity become a life of tedium and habit, of God-in-a-box. Never let God have to say to you: 'If you only knew who is speaking to you.'

### October 1, 2009: A life worth living
*I consider my life worth nothing to me. (Acts 20:24)*

Paul uttered these words in Miletus as he bade farewell to the Ephesian elders. He knew what was facing him: arrest and persecution. However, this was no abandoning of purpose or resignation to his fate: far from it.

Paul knew his life was worth nothing - to him. He did not devalue his life; he knew it had great worth. It just wasn't worth anything in his own hands, making his own plans, with him as the master of his destiny. His life would be worth nothing if he lived only for himself and fulfilled his own self-centred ambitions. Paul's life had worth because he had surrendered that life many years previously into the hands and plans of God. It's the same for all of us: our lives only yield their true worth and value when handed over to the One who made us. God created us for his purpose; when we submit our lives to him through the Lordship of Jesus our lives express the worth that we were created for. Our lives have worth when we discover not what we can make of them, but what God can make of them.

## October 6, 2009: The Spirit is given when Jesus is glorified

*The Spirit had not been given, since Jesus had not yet been glorified. (John 7:39)*

This verse reveals an important principle, even though it specifically refers to the ascension of Jesus and his subsequent sending of the Spirit at Pentecost. It was only when Jesus was glorified - enthroned in heaven as King of Kings and Lord of lords - that he gave the Spirit. The Spirit came when Jesus was glorified.

In a sense that is what happens today, even though the Spirit has come once and for all and indwells all who believe. If we desire the increased sense of the Spirit's presence among us, we must glorify Jesus. That is what the Spirit has come to do: he makes Jesus known. In a kind of complimentary act of mutual love Jesus responds to the Spirit's activity of glorifying him by increasing our sense of the Spirit's presence. When people leave a meeting expressing their love of Jesus and are more keenly aware of the Spirit's presence, rather than dissecting a sermon or being enchanted with the preacher, you know that God has been at work. That is why more and more I take interest in what people talk about after the church meeting and in the following hours. If their talk is of Jesus and the Spirit then I am doing something right. If their conversation is about my skill (or lack of it) at teaching and preaching, then something is amiss. A glorified Jesus will give the Spirit; and the Spirit will glorify Jesus.

### October 8, 2009: Perfect timing

*No-one seized him, because his time had not yet come. (John 8:20)*

That phrase, 'his time had not yet come', appears a few times in John's gospel in reference to Jesus. For Jesus, it was not only the case that he did the right thing; he did the right thing at the right time. For him, timing was everything.

To do the right thing at the wrong time is to do the wrong thing. What may have been the right thing to do becomes the wrong thing because it's done at the wrong time. I'm not talking about objective truth here: I am saying that things have their time. Ecclesiastes tells us so: there's a time to love, a time to hate, a time of war and a time of peace, for example.

We don't only have to know what to do and how to do it: we also have to know when to do it.

### October 13, 2009: In God's Louvre

*We are God's works of art, newly created in Jesus Christ to do good works, which God planned and prepared a long time ago for us to do. (Ephesians 2:10)*

The Mona Lisa is probably the world's most famous work of art. Created by Leonardo da Vinci, it hangs in pride of place in the Louvre in Paris. Those who gaze on it marvel at its beauty and multi-faceted originality. It is testimony to the genius who painted it. People stare at it for hours; academic papers by the truckload are written about it; it's the most recognisable and most valuable work of art in the world. When the Mona Lisa is discussed, conversation always returns to Leonardo: praise and adoration are heaped on him for creating such a masterpiece.

The Bible tells us that we believers are God's works of art. Our genius God has created billions of 'Mona Lisas': breathtaking, beautiful, original, beyond value, multi-faceted masterpieces. That's who we are; Christians are not cheap, tacky, mass manufactured prints. Each one of us is a unique work of exquisite art, created by the most creative Artist of all: our Father. What makes us such works of art is that we have been re-created in God's image, to be just like him.

Just as when people view the Mona Lisa their breath is taken away by Leonardo da Vinci's evident genius, so when people see us they marvel at the Artist who made us - they give praise and adoration to God.

### December 3, 2009: That tastes good!
*Like newborn babies, crave pure spiritual milk, so that by it you may grow up in your salvation, now that you have tasted that the Lord is good. (1Peter 2:2-3)*

My late mother used to make the best bread pudding in the world. Don't confuse bread pudding with bread and butter pudding; they're quite different. Mum's bread pudding, fresh and warm out of the oven, was one of the great pleasures of life. Cold out of the fridge it was a slab of sheer delight. I sometimes ate other bread puddings; none of them compared to mum's. I'd tasted the best, and nothing else held a candle to it. Eventually I refused to eat any bread pudding but my mum's.

Then mum suddenly died. In one of those weird moments when my siblings and I were clearing out the house, we began to search for mum's bread pudding recipe, but to no avail. We realised that the recipe was in her head, which was no use to us! She got the recipe from her mother; it had been handed down by word of mouth and demonstration. You can imagine the awful feeling we had: not only was mum gone but so was the best bread pudding in the world. I began a quest and searched high and low for a decent bread pudding: shop bought ones, friends who tried to make it, grannies of friends, I tried everything. All failed. I had tasted the best.

As I read this passage of Scripture I was reminded of my bread pudding experience. Once I had tasted the best, nothing else could compare or satisfy me. It's the same with the Lord: once we have tasted him, once we have encountered him and he becomes our very life, nothing can remotely compare with him. We are spoiled. Some of the puddings I tasted came close to mum's; but with the Lord nothing comes close, nothing at all. There is nothing like knowing Jesus. If you've tasted how good God is, don't waste your life trying to fill it with something else, something that will substitute for him. You've tasted the best, ignore the rest.

*(My bread pudding quest had a happy ending. One day I came home and my wife had made me a bread pudding. She had seen my mum's and knew what it should look like. So she made me one. It was just like eating mum's!)*

### December 9, 2009: Same words: different voices
*'Let all who are simple come in here.' (Proverbs 9:4 and 16)*

This invitation occurs twice in Proverbs chapter 9. It's an invitation to participate in two contradictory ways of life. The first invitation comes from Wisdom - the life of God; the second comes from Folly - the life of the devil. Both use the same words, but the voices that speak those words are diametrically opposed to each other. The consequences of following the voices are different too: life or death.

Don't listen only to words; ask 'who is the source of those words?' Ask 'who is speaking those words?' This is important when listening to preachers or teachers. Whenever somebody gets up to speak you're not only opening yourself to the words they speak but the spirit by which they speak those words. The devil can speak the Word of God: he used it to tempt Jesus to abandon the Father's will and worship him. It's possible for believers to use the Word of God for anything. Just because somebody quotes the Bible at you doesn't mean that God is speaking to you. You have to know the voice behind the words. That's why you need to be filled with the Holy Spirit: so that you may discern who is speaking the Word of God to you. Anybody can use the Bible; only God uses it correctly.

## December 21, 2009: Consequences of faith

Sometimes we are in danger of making the Christmas story nothing more than a sentimental fairy tale. This is especially true of Mary, the mother of Jesus. Mary plays a higher role in Roman Catholicism than Protestantism, where she is regarded as an incidental player in salvation history. Catholics have all but deified her. Both extremes are wrong. The truth is she was an ordinary woman who said yes to God's will and purpose.

Mary was about sixteen or seventeen when Gabriel visited her in Nazareth. We know from Jewish tradition of the time that girls were betrothed around this age and Mary was already betrothed to Joseph before the angel's visit. She was a wholesome, ordinary young lady with her whole life ahead of her, living in a small town in northern Israel, marrying the man she loved, and raising their children. Then God turned up.

Mary's response to God's plan was an emphatic 'yes', unlike Zechariah earlier in the story, who in effect said to God, 'Do you seriously expect me to believe that?' All Mary wanted to know was how God was going to do it: how was she going to have a baby since she was a virgin?

Mary's 'yes' to God brought massive consequences to her life; these are often ignored or overlooked by us when reading the Christmas story. The first consequence was the Mary kissed her reputation goodbye. She lived in a small town which was noted for its religious fervour. She would be well known in such a place. In saying 'yes' to God she knew what would come her way: misunderstanding, abuse, gossip, ostracism, and shame, even though she was blameless. Mary was prepared to go through all that because God spoke to her about her life and destiny, which meant far more to her than her good name and reputation.

God is not interested in a respectable Christianity that never rocks the boat. Our faith starts at the Cross of Jesus, the ultimate place of ostracism. Christ does not call us to a life of respectability. When he says, 'Believe in me', he says, 'Come and lose your reputation.'

### December 22, 2009: Consequences of faith (Part Two)

Another consequence of Mary's faith was that she put herself in mortal danger. Not only would she lose her reputation, she could have lost her life. Imagine it: she was pregnant but not married. She could have been stoned to death for that. Or she could have been convicted of adultery, another capital offence at the time. The religious leaders would be ready for her.

Once again, Mary's faith in God and her obedience to his word put her directly in the firing line, where her very life was at stake. Nevertheless, she said 'yes' to God. Her faith and confidence in God to fulfill his promise remained unflinching, regardless of her personal safety. She had true grit. A steel rod of faith ran right through her.

Whenever I read Hebrews 11, I see this same characteristic in all the heroes and heroines of the faith. Their unswerving faith and hope in God's ability to deliver on his promise frequently gave them a total disregard for their own welfare. They were not mindless idiots; they counted the cost, they realised what they were doing, but still did what God told them.

We may not have to face physical danger and mortal threat (although many of our brothers and sisters in certain parts of the world have to), but real faith gives you the courage to stand up against any threat and adversary. Real faith makes you stand up under intense pressure without crumbling. Real faith brings you through impossible circumstances with overwhelming victory, because, as Gabriel said to Mary, 'Nothing is impossible with God.'

## December 23, 2009: Consequences of faith (Part Three)

A third consequence of Mary's 'yes' to God concerning Jesus was that she faced the certainty of losing the love of her life: Joseph. She weighed up everything very carefully, knowing that her response in faith to God's word and will might mean the end of her relationship to him. Joseph had the right to 'divorce' Mary because of this (under Jewish custom of the time couples were regarded as semi-married when they were betrothed). We know from the Gospels that Joseph had considered doing so, until God spoke to him in a dream. Furthermore, Joseph could have been the one to stone her to death, if he so wished.

Mary's life was never to be the same again after saying 'yes' to God. Even though she loved Joseph and wanted, more than anything else, to spend the rest of her life with him, she was prepared to lose him for the sake of God's purpose. Mary had a greater love in her life: she loved God with all her heart, and any other love would have to find its place within that greater love. Her faith was an act of love for God.

This is often the big one for us. When God invades our lives his question is always, 'do you love me more than anything else?' He doesn't need our love; he is not lonely and desperate for love. We were created to love him; and life only makes sense and has the right perspectives when we love him more than anything else. It was Jim Elliot who said, 'he is no fool who gives what he cannot keep to gain what he cannot lose.' In Philippians chapter 3 Paul regarded everything as excrement compared to knowing and loving God. Faith works out of a love relationship with God. Faith sees the true value of God.

Of course, the great thing about Mary's life was that God blessed her faith and obedience. She didn't lose Joseph after all; she actually gave birth to and raised the Saviour of the world; she and Joseph had at least six more children; and she was one of the 120 at Pentecost. Mary was filled with the Holy Spirit that day, spoke in new tongues and ended up in the street, praising God and being mistaken for a drunk! She who had carried the Creator of the world in her womb was indwelt by the Spirit of that Creator God. She had quite a life, don't you think?

### January 21, 2010: My Mini Cooper S and the Holy Spirit

Last night at our church Life Group we talked about our favourite Christmas present and something the Holy Spirit showed us about it. I chose my Mini Cooper S moneybox. Dianne bought it for me. I won't go into the whole story why (just before Christmas a good friend had one to sell; great price; really fancied it; Dianne said no; she saw an old lady driving one next day; told me even more reason not to buy one; didn't buy car; got moneybox instead).

Anyway, the reason why I chose it as a Holy Spirit reminder is very simple. Minis are very small cars. Last year we had a friend live with us before she got married who is also rather small (five feet and a couple of hairs). She drove a small car with the seat right up against the steering wheel. One day she'd parked behind me on the drive and I had to move her car so I could get out. I'm not the tallest man in the world: 5 feet 9 inches when I'm upright. But when I tried to get into that car I felt like a giant. It was all I could do to squeeze myself into the thing: my head was almost touching the windscreen. I couldn't move my legs to find the pedals; my arms were too long to turn the wheel. I could hardly move: it was very uncomfortable.

Then came the Holy Spirit moment. He said to me: 'This car's too small for you isn't it?' Rather obvious, I thought, even for the Spirit. But I knew he had something important to tell me. He continued: 'You're used to a bigger car; and you can't fit inside this one. That's what it's like in your relationship with me: never go from one experience with me to a lesser or smaller one. Never confine yourself or grow smaller in your experience of me. Always grow and stretch into bigger and larger dimensions of me. Don't put yourself into tiny, safe situations when I want you to grow and enlarge. You were born to grow in me, not shrink.'

Every time I look at the moneybox I am reminded of what the Spirit said to me while I was hunched up inside that tiny car. And each time I ask myself: Have I grown in the Spirit today?

### February 2, 2010: The Gift

*Wait for the gift my Father promised. (Acts 1:4)*

Always remember that the Holy Spirit is the promised gift of the Father, poured out by Jesus. Why would anybody be afraid of the Spirit, if they understood that he is the promised gift of God? Nobody in their right mind would refuse the gift that God promises. God doesn't give cheap gifts; when he gives gifts they're always incredibly generous, because God gives himself.

If we keep in mind that the Holy Spirit is the gift of God, we will always live with the awareness that everything to do with the Spirit belongs to the Spirit. We can't earn the Spirit or own him. We have no ownership rights on the anointing or the gifts of the Spirit. We cannot control or manage the Holy Spirit; we cannot determine his plan or permit him freedom.

While the Spirit is the gift of God, he is the gift *of God*. God gives him to us for himself. That is a paradox of the kingdom. The Spirit is given by the Father for the purpose of the Father. The gift owns us.

### February 3, 2010: The Gift (2)
*Wait for the gift. (Acts 1:4)*

The Holy Spirit is *the* gift of God; not *a* gift of God. That is not a matter of semantics; it's the very essence of what God is all about when it comes to the Holy Spirit and us. In a sense, God has nothing left to give us: in giving us the gift of the Holy Spirit he invested all of himself, his plan and his purpose. God has no plan or purpose for us outside the Holy Spirit. He doesn't offer us the option of choosing between the Holy Spirit and something or someone else. Pentecost was all about God's sole option and offer: the Holy Spirit or nothing.

That's why we must never make the Holy Spirit optional for Christians, even when it comes down to basic foundational things like the baptism in the Spirit and speaking in tongues and the gifts of the Spirit. God says to us: 'Here's my gift to you. He's called the Holy Spirit. Take him in all his fullness on his agenda or leave him. I have nothing else to give you.'

### February 10, 2010: No half measures
*When the Day of Pentecost had fully come, they were all together in one place. (Acts 2:1)*

There's a little word missing in the NIV text of this verse that it is in the Greek text: 'fully'. It means to fill up completely, to fulfill, to be swamped.

It's an important part of the text, because it tells us something about this day. The Day of Pentecost was like no other day before it; it was a day of fulfillment, of fullness. The day came in all its fullness. God was about to fulfill something on this day that he had never done before: the believers were going to be immersed in the Holy Spirit, to demonstrate that all who are subsequently baptised in the Spirit also experience that same fullness. In the Baptism in the Spirit something significant happens to us; something is fulfilled in us. It's a moment of fullness, in which the same Spirit that raised Jesus from the dead is released like a never ending river from within us in that explosive moment we speak in tongues for the first time. All the ability of God is made available to us; the *dunamis* – the dynamic ability – the power of God is unleashed. The Baptism in the Spirit should make a significant impact on us and difference to us. It's a moment when something 'fully comes'.

## February 16, 2010: Causing a disturbance

*They were greatly disturbed because the apostles were teaching the people and proclaiming in Jesus the resurrection of the dead. (Acts 4:2)*

The preaching of the resurrection, and the fact of the resurrection of Jesus, always disturbs the establishment: religious, political, social. That should not surprise us; rather, it should be an encouragement to us that we are doing something right. The resurrection means that Jesus has overcome all his enemies and anything or anybody who would seek to rule him and control him. His subsequent ascension to the throne of heaven means that he is King of kings and Lord of lords. Practically that means he is enthroned over the 'authority' and 'control' of the establishment: those institutions and entities that exalt themselves over him. Their authority is but a puff of air.

You can always test what is of Christ and what is not: is he enthroned over it or does it attempt to make him less than he is? If it is the former then Christ is in it. If the latter, then somehow or other it will seek to dethrone him, often by trying to keep him dead in the ground.

### February 18, 2010: The Candidate

If you were planning an evangelistic campaign into a new area, or seeking to outreach with the Gospel into a nation, who would you look for as the people to reach first? Business people? Political leaders? Celebrities? Youth? Eunuchs? Eunuchs! That's what I said! Hardly the first choice on most evangelists' agendas; but the Holy Spirit doesn't work to our agendas.

That's what happened in Acts chapter 8. The Spirit had been speaking to a eunuch from Ethiopia for some time. He had been in Jerusalem worshipping God, and was now going home, without finding what he was looking for. He pored over the Scriptures, eagerly searching for the Jesus he had not yet met. He was a candidate for the grace and love of God; so the Holy Spirit engineered for him to hear the gospel of Jesus.

I know the eunuch was an important person in his society; but hardly respected by many. Yet God loved this man so much he wanted his story recorded for all time, so that we could see and understand that God is no respecter of persons. He sees beyond the natural into the heart, no matter who we are. His love is greater than our prejudice. His grace is more powerful than our derision. His mercy is greater than our judgementalism.

## March 2, 2010: Accepted

*God, who knows the heart, showed that he accepted them by giving them the Holy Spirit. (Acts 15:8)*

The Council of Jerusalem was a watershed for the early church. The heretical faction of the Pharisees that had risen in the church had insisted that in addition to faith in Jesus, the Gentile believers also had to be circumcised. Only then would the church accept them as genuine believers. No wonder Paul and Barnabas, the apostles to the Gentile world, opposed this demonic doctrine.

It was Peter, who had had his own struggles with God over the Gentile question (see Acts 10), who encapsulated the matter. Looking back at his own previous experience in the home of the Cornelius, when the Holy Spirit had come on all the Gentiles in the house, he observed that since God had accepted them, how could the church refuse them? The proof that they were accepted was simple: God had given them the Holy Spirit.

We Christians must never question whether God has accepted us: the fact that the Holy Spirit indwells us is ample and sufficient proof that our Heavenly Father has gladly accepted us and welcomed us into his family. Furthermore, since he has accepted us, we must also accept ourselves and our brothers and sisters in Christ.

## March 4, 2010: Leave grace alone

*We believe it is through the grace of the Lord Jesus we are saved, just as they are. (Acts 15:11)*

The Jerusalem Council was faced with the vital question of the nature of the gospel. The pressure from those advocating grace plus circumcision for salvation was intense. Even the Twelve had struggled with it. Peter's argument with the Lord in Acts chapter 10 demonstrated that he had not yet understood the nature of the gospel: that it is for everybody by grace alone. Happily, the Council came to the right conclusion, condemning those who insisted on circumcision for the Gentiles to make them 'real Christians'. Paul faced the same heresy in Galatia.

This tendency to add to grace is a major feature of religious legalism. It cannot accept the power of the grace of God, always wanting to add something to it. 'Receive grace, but then do something to make you more acceptable to God.' This attitude diminishes and even nullifies the power of grace in the life of the believer, so that we are always doing things in the hope that God will accept us more. But grace is nothing to do with us, with what we do or what we don't do. It's not dependent on religious observance of special days; it's not gauged by our success or failure. It's God's willing and loving acceptance of us.

This doesn't mean we stay the same or abuse God's grace by living unrighteously; the grace of God changes us as it works with his mercy. In his grace God gives us what we don't deserve; in his mercy he doesn't give us what we do deserve. Grace and mercy are the love of God in action. He doesn't need anything from us to love us like that. Leave grace alone; it's powerful enough.

### March 30, 2010: Simplicity

The book of Acts opens and closes with Jesus. Luke begins his account of the early church with a summary of his Gospel; 'everything that Jesus began to do and teach.' It's as if the Gospel is but the prelude to the next act. Luke concludes his account with Paul in Rome many years later teaching about the kingdom of God and the Lord Jesus Christ. The intervening chapters recount the adventures, challenges, victories and failures of the early believers. In it all, Luke comes back to the simple fact of Jesus and the reason for his coming: to establish the kingdom of God.

As one reads Acts one can't but be affected by the difficulties the church often faced, not only from without but more importantly from within. Luke paints a 'warts and all' picture of the church: disagreement, deceit, hypocrisy, racism, nationalism, peer pressure, creeping institutionalised religion, legalism, are all present at various stages. This is what happens when people who do not have Jesus as the beginning and end get involved in God's purpose. If Jesus is not the focal point, and the Holy Spirit is edged out (these two things always go together), the church will fail to function as it should and its identity as the Body of Christ on earth is lost. The tragedy is that the world suffers because it then identifies Christ with what purports to be his church but which is in fact a denial of it.

I met this situation just a few days ago at a wedding. At the reception I was placed next to a delightful couple who were members of the groom's family (the groom is a member of All Nations Church). They had many excellent questions about what they had experienced at the wedding ceremony and concerning their relative, who, as they confirmed, is a totally different person since he became a Christian about ten years ago. They could not gainsay the change in him was genuine; but their problem was their concept of church. This was compounded by the recent revelations seeping out about the appallingly evil things done to children by paedophile Roman Catholic priests, and the attempted cover up by the Vatican. This couple couldn't get beyond that something which claimed to represent God acted in a way totally contradictory to what they rightly thought God was like. They couldn't get to the Jesus they were looking for, and that they had seen in their relative because of all that passes for Christianity today, but is in fact no Christianity at all.

Just because something claims to represent God, that does not make it so. Institutionalised religion has nothing to do with the simplicity of Jesus Christ. 'Churches' which deny his deity, reject the truth of the Bible, forbid the reality of the Holy Spirit in practice, who emphasise and 'deify' their pastors, cannot make valid claims to represent God. They just can't. This is what the apostles and early church faced in Acts; they knew that the authentic is easily replaced with the replica. Zion can act like Babylon. The word *babel* literally means 'gate of God', and that is its danger. It says, 'If you want to find God, come in here'. But when you do look in you don't find him; you discover something quite the opposite.

This is Easter week. We remember a simple yet world changing event: Jesus of Nazareth, the God/Man, died on a Cross for the sin of the world. Three days later he physically rose from the dead and is alive today. And that is the simple fact. Let's not confuse the world; God loves it too much.

### April 22, 2010: Honour the humble
*Humility comes before honour. (Proverbs 15:33)*

Never honour a proud person; all you are doing is feeding his ungodly, devilish, selfish ambition. Pride originated within Satan, and it was the cause of his rebellion against God. When you honour a proud person you're sowing the wind; rest assured you'll reap the whirlwind.

Honour the humble person; he knows where any honour that comes his way truly belongs: to Jesus. The humble person can handle honour; it doesn't go to his head or cause him to become arrogant. He understands that it's the Lord who has done something in him that others recognise and they are really giving honour to God. That's why a humble person can receive honour: he knows that in his honouring comes honour of God.

### April 28, 2010: The shame of dishonour
Recently I read an online article about a well-known Christian man whom I knew back in the '70s. In the article this

man was giving an interview, which included his account of how and when he became a Christian. I read his account with interest, which soon turned to sadness, dismay and a degree of anger. He described the crusade meeting, the music, the participants and especially the preacher in derogatory and mocking tones, apologizing that he had been saved in such circumstances.

I was at that meeting; an evangelist took our church youth group, which included me and this young man, to hear this preacher, who was an old man by then and had served God in ministry for many years. I remember vividly this young man responding to the preacher's appeal and receiving Jesus as his Lord. Now, many years later he was deriding and insulting the ministry and memory of a servant of God. That's what made me angry and upset. He had also forgotten the grace and mercy of God; that God had planned before time that he would be saved in that way in that meeting through that preacher. Yet he showed no gratitude, only a pompous arrogance.

I was saved through a preacher in a church that did not baptise in water or believe in the baptism in the Holy Spirit. It was a 'hymn sandwich' service, which used to bore me to death. But it was the means through which God saved me from my sin. While that particular preacher today is far from me on many things theologically, I will always honour him as the vehicle that God used to deliver me from hell and save me. He is still alive and now a very old man; but whenever I think of him or his name is mentioned, I always thank God for him, that he preached the Gospel to me that night and through his preaching Jesus saved me.

King David understood the importance of honour. When Saul, his enemy died, David refused to besmirch his memory. Even in death, Saul was not dishonoured by David. He spoke well of him, refusing to slander the Lord's anointed. I hope that the man I have talked about here today one day remembers with honour the servant of God, who was anointed to preach to him the Gospel.

### June 8, 2010: What lies within

Last Wednesday, the tranquility of west Cumbria here in the UK was brutally scarred by local resident Derrick Bird. In the course of a few hours on a beautiful summer day, Bird murdered twelve people, including his own brother, before killing himself. The killings were the worst case of mass murder in the UK since the 1996 Dunblane massacre. In the days since, a picture has emerged of Bird, who on the surface was an ordinary chap - a taxi driver. He was under intense pressure; the tax authorities were investigating him; he had long standing grudges against people; he had nursed bitterness and hatred. What is becoming more evident is that Bird planned his killing spree well beforehand. Then he exploded, murdering and wounding total strangers and those he had selected as his targets. Finally, he blasted himself into eternity with his own gun. Cumbria is still reeling.

The immediate question: what caused Derrick Bird to do such a thing? I have listened to the various answers offered by psychologists, criminologists, social commentators, even religious leaders. They have all made interesting and in some instances, perceptive comments. But nobody has talked about the heart of Derrick Bird: what lay within him. We are appalled when such horrific acts are done by so called normal people. But normal people do the most horrific things: you only have to look at Rwanda, the Balkans, the Final Solution, My Lai.... the list is unending.

There is something about the heart of mankind that is rotten; the Bible calls it sin. The first recorded sin after the fall of Adam and Eve was the murder of Abel by his brother Cain. The heart of sinful mankind showed what it is really capable of right there.

I'm not saying we're all potential mass murderers. But let's wake up and smell the coffee. Mankind was made in the image of God to belong to God, to love God, to serve God, to be like God. Mankind without God is an aberration, potentially capable of acting like Cain, in attitude as well as action. Cain hated his brother before he killed him. He was jealous of his own flesh and blood before he snuffed out Abel's life.

Jesus came to give us a new heart, his heart, the heart of love. Only in Christ can the old nature that hates and kills be done away with and replaced by the heart of God. Derrick Bird never had the change of heart.

### July 13, 2010: Assume the position

*Elijah said to Ahab, 'Go, eat and drink, for there is the sound of a heavy rain'...Elijah...bent down and put his face between his knees. (1Kings 18:41-42)*

Why did Elijah put his face between his knees? He had just made a prophetic statement to Ahab: 'there is the sound of a heavy rain.' But it wasn't raining. There wasn't a cloud in the sky. There wasn't even the far off sound of thunder or a light drizzle. No rain.

However, for Elijah it was already raining; he lived in the dimension of faith, he lived in the presence of Almighty God. So, once he had spoken his word he shut out all physical and natural distraction and influence: having his head between his knees meant he could not hear anything or see anything. He was not burying his head in the sand: he wasn't going to let any natural thing turn him from what he had heard from God - it's raining.

Sometimes we have to put our heads between our knees. God has spoken to us - and faith always brings the future hope of eventual good into a present reality - faith is always now. But circumstances, opposition, fear, doubt, unchanging situations, conspire to sap our faith. At those times we may have our physical eyes and ears open, but we need to put our 'faces' between our knees: we have to shut out anything that runs contrary to what we have heard God say. We might even have to literally assume the position and put our face between our knees. It might not be very attractive. Just do whatever it takes!

### August 12, 2010: All about me

*The eyes of both [Adam and Eve] were opened, and they knew that they were naked. And they sewed fig leaves together and made themselves loincloths. (Genesis 3:7)*

The very first thing that sin does is to turn us away from God and concentrate on ourselves. Adam and Eve discovered this: whereas just a few minutes before they had lived to be in fellowship with God, the moment they ate the fruit their whole centre of existence changed. They became the centre; they were concerned only about themselves, not about God. Their life now revolved around them. This was the fruit of their disobedience. It was only when they heard God's voice calling out for them they realised that their action had affected their relationship with him; so they hid themselves. It was all about them.

Sin always causes us to self-consumed, self-focused, self-possessed, self-seeking, selfishly ambitious. When we come to Christ the centre of our identity changes; we no longer live but Christ lives in us (Galatians 2:20). That's what it means for Jesus to be Lord. It's no longer all about me; neither is it all about Jesus and me; it's all about him.

### September 8, 2010: To burn or not to burn?

The decision of Terry Jones, leader of Dove World Outreach Center in the USA, to burn hundreds of copies of the Koran on the anniversary of 9/11 continues to draw worldwide criticism and condemnation. Jones is well known for condemning Islam and is quoted as saying, "How much do we back down? How many times do we back down? Instead of us backing down, maybe it's to time to stand up. Maybe it's time to send a message to radical Islam that we will not tolerate their behaviour."

I believe Jones is wrong in taking this action: not because of the fear of reprisals, inflaming tensions, endangering lives, or that the Koran is regarded as a holy book. It is wrong because it is nothing to do with the Gospel of the kingdom. Jones claims he is acting on behalf of Jesus; he isn't. Jesus is not in his actions at all on this matter.

The power of Christianity is that the motivating factor of the Gospel is John 3:16 - 'God so loved the world'. We must freely acknowledge that certain forms of Islam violently persecute Christian believers, murder Christian converts, abuse Christian families and destroy Christian places of worship. That is evil and must be condemned. But that is nothing new for Christians: the Roman Empire did the same off and on for three hundred years. Totalitarian regimes throughout the world still do. I agree that Islam and Christianity have nothing in common, not when you get to their roots. Jesus Christ is the uncreated Creator God, the only begotten Son of the Father. The Bible is the unique Word of God. Islam denies that. Christians and Muslims do not worship the same God: it is nonsense to assert otherwise. There is only one God: the God of the Bible. The God of the Koran does not exist.

Having said that, the Gospel of the kingdom is a gospel of the love of God for his world, including Muslims. After all, they are still sinners who need Jesus, just like everybody else. They are no different from or less than a Wall Street Banker, rock star, or postal worker in that regard. Jesus never commanded us to go on crusades of destruction; he gave us the ministry of reconciliation, love and hope. I do not believe the Koran is a holy book; neither is the book of Mormon or the New World Translation of Jehovah's Witnesses. Burning books serves no purpose at all; the Nazis learned that in 1930s Germany. The power of the Gospel of the kingdom is that it doesn't behave like the world does; it doesn't react like its opponents do; its source is completely different from anything else.

Love does not make us the doormats of the world to wipe their feet on as they walk over us. That's not the Gospel either. Christians are not meant to be naïve wimps. You only have to read the Gospels and Acts to see that. But the power of the Gospel will bring a man to his knees and turn a murderous hater into a self-sacrificial lover of sinful humanity. That only happens when a sinner finds himself face to face with the holy God who is also the God of love.

Mr. Jones, if you plan to go ahead with this, please don't do so in the name of the Jesus of the Bible. If you do, you might as well burn the Bible too.

### January 20, 2011: Catch a grip

*I press on to take hold of that for which Christ Jesus took hold of me. (Philippians 3:12)*

All too often we Christians get the wrong end of the stick. We view our faith and life with Christ as something we inititiated and which depends on our self-effort. Nothing could be further from the truth.

Christ Jesus took hold of you; never forget that fact. It was Christ who apprehended you in the first place. True, you had to respond to the demands of his Lordship and you made the decision to surrender to him. Nevertheless, he started it - he began the good work in you. He called and chose you before a star was placed in the universe, long before God called out, 'Light, be!' It was Christ that began it all; he took the initiative; he took hold of you in that loving, all conquering vice-like grip. He planned it; he started it; and he will finish it.

## March 8, 2011: Teamwork

*(Today we have a guest blogger: my wife Dianne.)*

Recently I had the privilege of meeting Rebecca Romero, who won a gold medal in cycling in the last Olympic games. She was part of the most successful British cycling team ever.

I expected her to talk a lot about herself and what she had achieved, but she didn't. She talked mostly about the team she was part of and her part in that team. There were all sorts of people who made up the team; her part was to ride her bike as fast as she could, get the best times, and win championships and medals for the team. To her it wasn't the most important part, it was just her part. She didn't win the gold medal simply for herself but for the team. Whilst she did show us her medal, the photographs and footage that she brought contained images of the whole team and relatively few of her.

Together they succeeded. She was never on her own. When things didn't go well, there was always someone to offer encouragement. When things did go well, there was always someone to celebrate with. Together they agreed a plan and each person knew what they had to do. No one gave up on the way and no one gave anything other than 100%.

To me it sounded like the body of Christ. Romans 12 says: 'For just as each of us has one body with many members, and these members do not all have the same function, so in Christ we, though many, form one body, and each member belongs to all the others. We have different gifts, according to the grace given to each of us. If your gift is prophesying, then prophesy in accordance with your faith; if it is serving, then serve; if it is teaching, then teach; if it is to encourage, then give encouragement; if it is giving, then give generously; if it is to lead, do it diligently; if it is to show mercy, do it cheerfully.'

Each one of us has a unique part to play in the body and if we don't play our part then the whole body suffers. There's no such thing as a passenger in the body of Christ. We have a responsibility to make sure our walk with God is right because it impacts the whole body. If we don't bother to attend church gatherings then there is something missing: us. We need to keep ourselves full of the Holy Spirit and the Word of God so that we can encourage ourselves and one another.

Let's run the race set before us, not being be concerned about ourselves but about one another and the testimony of Jesus. Together we can do it, together we can win, and together we can make a difference.

### March 29, 2011: The joy thief
*"No one will take your joy from you." (Jesus, in John 16:22)*

The only person who can rob you of your joy is you. Jesus said that no one can take our joy from us. God certainly doesn't want to: he gave it to us in the first place. Circumstances, people, the devil, life itself, will all try and grab our joy. But Jesus said no one will take it from us. The only person who can rid you of your joy is you. That is a powerful thought: you actually have the power within you to live in joy in the most tragic circumstance. In fact, the joy of the Lord is your strength and the kingdom of God is hallmarked by joy.

Joy is not happiness. Happiness depends and relies on beneficial and positive situations. Joy is an attitude that is rooted in hope and faith, in righteousness and peace. It is unaffected by externals. If there is no joy in your life, don't blame others. You misplaced it.

## May 23, 2011: Thoughts on a non-Rapture

We are still here. Despite the well-publicised claims of Harold Camping, the California based 'evangelist', Jesus did not return last Saturday. This was Camping's second attempt at predicting the date of Jesus' Second Coming: his first was back in 1994.

Notwithstanding the ridicule such antics and clear anti-biblical behaviour bring to the rest of us Christians, Camping has caused incalculable damage to those gullible enough to take him seriously. People left their jobs, sold homes, said goodbye to loved ones, gave all their money away, on the word of a self-proclaimed Bible expert. He is nothing of the sort. People like Camping have plagued the church since the very early days; even the New Testament speaks of those who falsely claimed Jesus had already returned. A reading of church history reveals the countless sects, cults and individuals who wrongly predicted the end of the world; many of them had several attempts. The tragedy is that they always leave in their wake a whole raft of people who are shaken in their faith or abandon their faith altogether. Furthermore, they do nothing to enhance the reputation of Jesus, which is the biggest crime of all in this matter.

It is important we have a biblical eschatology (doctrine of the end times). The Bible is crystal clear that Jesus will return, but that nobody knows when. It goes out of its way to warn us against such charlatans and deceivers, no matter who they are or how fine sounding their reasons are. The fact that Camping was able to fool and deceive so many people illustrates all too painfully the general biblical illiteracy and ignorance that pervades large areas of the church. We accept too readily the latest fads and theories of anyone brandishing a Bible and a 'ministry' without subjecting them to proper biblical analysis with the aid of the Holy Spirit's guidance and accountability to our brothers and sisters in Christ.

It was said of the Bereans that they received Paul's word with eagerness, but also diligently searched the Scriptures every day to see if what he was teaching them was in line with what the Word said (Acts 17:10-11). If we were to adopt that same Berean attitude then people like Camping would be deprived of the oxygen that feeds their heresies and they would suffocate far quicker.

### June 30, 2011: Starry, starry night

Last night I went outside to catch a glimpse of the International Space Station as it passed over. It appears as a fast moving bright light; the sky was clear and, as the ISS sped off on its orbit, the stars began to come out.

As I looked up I was reminded that four thousand years ago, Abraham also looked up and saw the same sky; he stood outside his tent and he saw real stars. God spoke to him through the reality of what he saw in the reality of his situation. God is the God of reality: he met real people in real places. People like Jacob, Esther, Daniel, Elijah, David, Rahab - they all met God in real, everyday, even humdrum places that are still there today. Paul met Jesus on a real road on the way to a real place - Damascus - a city that is in great crisis at the moment. He is still the same God today.

We don't have to travel to places like Jerusalem, Galilee, Horeb or Mount Carmel to meet God. We can meet him in the real places we are in right now. God will meet you in McDonalds, Starbucks, the hospital, in your school or college. You can meet him sitting in your living room while you sit on the sofa with a cup of tea in your hand. You can meet God wherever you are. He is not a million miles away; you are in his presence at this moment.

### July 14, 2011: The Conductor

Today at All Nations Centre, our church facility, one of the country's leading orchestras is rehearsing for a forthcoming concert at the Proms. Each individual member of the orchestra is highly skilled, able to play to a world class standard.

You would never have guessed that when they started to play. The sound that emanated from the Hall as they began could only be described as a cacophony: each musician was tuning up, playing their scales, or going through a particular section of the score, each seemingly oblivious to any other. Violins played one thing; trumpets another; trombones still another. They all played in tune with themselves, but the whole sound was appalling.

As I write, there is the sound of the most beautiful, melodic music flowing through All Nations. What happened? The conductor of the orchestra went to the podium, raised his baton, and immediately the cacophony ceased. He spoke, instructing the orchestra what they would play and where they would begin. He raised his baton again and at his signal and direction the orchestra played as one from the score in front of them. The contrast was stark - and the sound was so much better! As they continue to play, every so often the conductor stops the orchestra and addresses a particular section, asking them to play louder, softer or with a different emphasis. They respond positively. The baton is raised again, and off the whole orchestra goes again. Sometimes the bassoons are prominent, then the timpani, then the violins. Each part plays to make the whole piece of music sound as good as possible.

The Holy Spirit is a conductor. He takes our individual lives and forms us into a spiritual 'orchestra'. We all have our individuality, our own 'instrument', if you like. But it is only when we become part of the whole 'orchestra' - the Body of Christ, the community of God's people under the Lordship and direction of the Holy Spirit - that our individual lives can make the beautiful music that is the life of the Lord Jesus. The kingdom of God is not a collection of solo artists or one-man bands: it's a massive symphony orchestra, under the baton of the Holy Spirit!

### July 20, 2011: Earth to earth

Yesterday I stood by a grave while a body was lowered into it and committed the body to be buried - 'earth to earth, ashes to ashes, dust to dust'. It was the body of a great friend of mine, Patricia Dibble, who left her body just over two weeks ago. Patricia now lives somewhere else; she is in heaven with Jesus. That is what death means for a Christian.

Every time I conduct the funeral of a Christian, this wonderful reality strikes home again. The Bible says to be absent from the body is to be present with the Lord (2Corinthians 5:8). The spirit of the person we are burying or cremating has long gone from the body. At the moment of death, they are immediately transported by the angels into another realm in which they enjoy fellowship with God, join the great cloud of witnesses, and await the return of Jesus to the earth when they will receive their new immortal resurrection bodies. This is the hope for every believer in Jesus.

At some point in a funeral I always read these words from the Word of God; if you have recently lost a loved one who knew Jesus, or if you yourself are approaching the time to leave this earth, let these words of Scripture encourage you and give you hope:

*Brothers, we do not want you to be ignorant about those who fall asleep, or to grieve like the rest of men, who have no hope. We believe that Jesus died and rose again and so we believe that God will bring with Jesus those who have fallen asleep in him. According to the Lord's own word, we tell you that we who are still alive, who are left till the coming of the Lord, will certainly not precede those who have fallen asleep. For the Lord himself will come down from heaven, with a loud command, with the voice of the archangel and with the*

*trumpet call of God, and the dead in Christ will rise first.
After that, we who are still alive and are left will be caught
up together with them in the clouds to meet the Lord in the
air. And so we will be with the Lord forever. Therefore
encourage each other with these words. (1Thessalonians
4:13-18)*

## August 16, 2011: The great lie

*"You will be like God." (Genesis 3:5)*

Lying is the devil's native language. He is really good
at it. Since he is the father of lies, he is the supreme master of
the carefully crafted lie. His lie to Eve was an object lesson in
deception: 'you will be like God.' Adam and Eve were already
like God! They had been created in the image and likeness of
God; yet Satan managed to convince them they were less than
they really were.

That's what happens when the devil lies to you. He
always tries to make you less than you are, and more
importantly, to make God less than he is. Satan attacks the
truth and integrity of God, attempting in his twisted logic to
make God appear to be the liar.

Any time the devil speaks to you - and he will speak
through many media - he will aim to diminish you and God;
that's how you know it's him. He does that because his motive
is to exalt himself; and he does that effectively when he brings
you and God down. All you have to do is either ignore him or
speak truth back to him, as Jesus did. The devil hates truth,
because Jesus is the truth, and the truth always exposes and
destroys the lie.

## August 31, 2011: Not only, but also

It is dangerous and rather foolish to emphasise one of
God's attributes over and above any or all of his other
attributes. Likewise, it is wrong to diminish or downplay any

attribute of God in order to promote another. We cannot play games with God's nature and character. We must not ignore any attribute we might find uncomfortable, nor speak only of those we find attractive and which suit our current circumstance. All of God's attributes are equally important; he cannot be God without having each of his attributes to the full. As the infinite (unlimited) God he has all his attributes infinitely - without limit, both in quantity and in quality.

God is love; he is also light. He is holy; and he is merciful and gracious. He is faithful; and he is just and righteous. If we over emphasise one of these attributes at the expense of any other, we no longer worship the true God. We cannot know the love of God fully without also knowing and appreciating his holiness and even his wrath, since God's wrath is an expression of both his love and his holiness. The love of God without the wrath of God makes God a sentimental, indulgent sop. The wrath of God without the love of God makes God a hard bitten, short-tempered figure, who can barely think of us with any warmth or affection.

Too often we ask the wrong question: 'what do I think God is like?' The right question is always: 'what is God really like?' It is true that when we need God to express his love to us he will. Nevertheless, that love will always be a holy, righteous love. When God expresses his wrath - as he will - he will always express it in faithfulness, mercy and grace. He does not suspend any attribute to act as God; he does not cease to be holy when he acts in mercy. He does not put aside his love when he expresses his wrath. God is not like us. He always acts in the totality of his being. As the early church fathers used to say: All of God does all that God does.

### November 25, 2011: Check it out

News reports in the UK today are 'exposing' a church that has reportedly told HIV sufferers to stop taking their medication after receiving prayer for healing. Leaders of the

Synagogue Church of All Nations (no connection at all to All Nations Church Cardiff, which I belong to), have been filmed by undercover reporters who pretended to have the HIV virus. There are claims that up to six people have died as a result. If true, that is tragic.

I believe in the God of miracles and healing; I have personally experienced healing by Jesus and I have prayed for thousands of people to be healed in Jesus' name. Many have been healed; some have not. Some receive miracles, others have died. None of those who died did so as a result of my telling them to stop their medication. That is one thing I know, because I never have and never will tell somebody to do so. It's just a practice that I follow and that we ensure in our church. (In fact, I take life-preserving medication every day myself). I have been privileged on many occasions to see Jesus heal people who also take life-preserving medication, after I have prayed for them, my wife has prayed for them, or people in my church have prayed for them. I have even seen people healed when nobody has prayed for them. Nevertheless, I do not feel it is my place to tell somebody to stop their medication. That is not a lack of faith; I believe we have precedent in the Bible. When Jesus healed a leper he told him to go and check his healing with the priest, which was required of anybody who had that terrible disease (Matthew 8:3-5). In being checked out by the priest, the miracle could be independently verified and the man declared cured. Jesus honoured that process, even though he knew the man was healed. It is wise to let the miracle be affirmed; it doesn't lessen it in any way at all. Rather, it brings greater glory to God.

I am sure that the folks in the Synagogue Church of All Nations are sincere in their faith in Jesus, and we should not be swift to condemn them out of hand. It would be interesting to hear some reports of the miracles and healings that do take place among them, as I am sure is the case. Let's not take this opportunity to hang them out to dry, but to ensure that all we do is not only radical, but also wise and responsible.

### December 19, 2011: Well said, but...

British Prime Minister David Cameron's recent comments about the continued value and importance to this country of 'Christian values' has met with varying degrees of approval and rejection. That is only to be expected. Mr. Cameron made his remarks during a speech commemorating the four hundredth anniversary of the King James Version of the Bible.

In his speech the PM said that Christian values were central to Britain and should be 'treasured'. He said that faith gave people a 'moral code' and that the summer riots that shattered several UK cities were evidence of the fact that this country has lost its way. He also said "[Christian values] are also values that speak to us all – to people of every faith and none. Those who oppose this usually make the case for secular neutrality. They argue that by saying we are a Christian country and standing up for Christian values we are somehow doing down other faiths. I think these arguments are profoundly wrong."

I applaud Mr. Cameron's remarks. To hear a modern politician speak of morality and right and wrong is refreshing. (It is interesting that his Liberal Democrat Deputy, Nick Clegg, today embarks on a campaign to stop plans for tax breaks for married couples, citing it as a return to 1950s morality. This despite all the evidence that overwhelmingly proves the benefit of marriage to society). We are right to stand for Christian values; the Bible tells us that righteousness exalts a nation (Proverbs 14:34). The problem in this nation is that there is too much anti Christian legislation; we cannot support Christian values, while passing laws which militate against those values. Therefore, if Mr. Cameron really wishes to see those values restored then somewhere along the line he and his government will have to introduce legislation in line with that desire.

We must face the fact, too, that Britain is not a Christian country. There is no such thing as a Christian country, not even the United States, which has 'In God we Trust' on its money but it's against the law to pray in school (to quote the late Larry Norman). The Gospel of the kingdom does not produce Christian countries, it produces Christian communities (the Church) in countries, which transform and challenge their societies with the love and power of Jesus Christ. One of the biggest disasters to befall the Church was when it became the official religion of the Roman Empire. Christianity's function is not to be such a thing, it cannot be the State Church. When Mr. Cameron directs his comments to the Church of England, he speaks to the wrong body. A state-sponsored and state-controlled religious organisation in which large numbers of its leaders deny the truth of biblical Christianity, cannot speak for Jesus Christ or truly represent him.

Ultimately, the promotion and support of Christian values will not be sufficient. Society is truly changed only when people are changed, for society comprises real people. Acceptance and acknowledgement of a value system is not far enough. The need is not only for legislation which promotes Christian values; the Church - the real Church that is - has to preach a Jesus as Lord, who is alive as Lord, the reality of the miracle of a changed life through new birth, the love and holiness of God, and express that life in the Church and to the world as an invitation, a demonstration, a provocation and a proof that Jesus is the living Lord of all. If the Church incarnates Christ with all his life and 'values' then the nation will sit up and take notice - as it is beginning to do - and acknowledge that the kingdom of God has come.

### January 5, 2012: The Great Liberator

It's impossible to live the resurrection life of Jesus if you have not first died. The Cross of Jesus is the Great Liberator: it is the place where we all have to die to free us from our old sinful self. As Jesus said, "The grain of wheat has to fall into the ground and die" (John 12:24). The Cross liberates you from yourself, it liberates you to become the son of God that God always intended you to be. The Cross enables God to get hold of a dead person and fill them with his own life. His life is eternal life, not a life that just goes on forever. It is a totally different kind of life from anything you have experienced. The God-life is a life lived free from selfish ambition and self-promotion. It knows nothing of self-interest and self absorption. You live by the life of Another. The great paradox of the Great Liberator is that the Cross of Jesus does not set you free to be independent and isolated; it brings you into true servanthood with Jesus as your living Lord. There is an old hymn that says, "Make me a captive Lord, and then I shall be free." You are liberated to be God's captive!

### February 15, 2012: True freedom

When God said no to Adam - 'don't eat of the tree of the knowledge of good and evil' - it aroused in the mind of Adam that he could choose to do so if he wished. Along with that choice came a responsibility for the consequence of his choice - life or death. God did not create an automaton; he created a spiritual being who would relate to God by his own free, loving choice.

This is the only way God creates spirit beings, because God is a covenant; he is the God of relationship. He created the angelic beings this way too, for they also are spirit beings. The power of choice - whether to serve and love the Creator or take one's fate upon oneself - is the responsibility and the privilege of every created being, human and angelic. We live with the consequence of that choice. Such a choice given to us does not put us in the place of God; rather it confirms and affirms the nature of the Creator as the God of relationship. He desires that his created beings, who have been designed specifically and uniquely to relate to him, do so freely. Our freedom to say no to God determines the outcome of that free choice - ultimately we send ourselves to hell. Never blame God for hell; it was not designed for us but for the devil.

Our freedom to say yes to God brings us into the freedom or liberty of the sons of God, expressed in our being owned and controlled by our Heavenly Father. Thus the really free person is the slave son of God; only such a person is truly free. He or she gladly surrenders their sinful independence and thus becomes the true free son of the Father. That is why Jesus' prayer in Gethsemane - 'not my will but yours' - is the perfect example of the free surrendered self to the Father.

### February 23, 2012: You have it all

Each one of us who has received Jesus as Lord has the entire Holy Spirit – all of God himself – living in us. Each one of us is filled with the same Person in all his fullness: he who hovered over the waters in the creation; he who raised Jesus from the dead; he who came from heaven at Pentecost. We all have all of the Spirit. The Spirit lives in us all with the same degree of ability or power: we all have the same ability, the same power, that the Holy Spirit gave to the Church at Pentecost. We all have the same ability that the Spirit used to raise Jesus from the dead. Through the Spirit we all have the same power in us that created the universe. He is exactly the same Spirit with exactly the same nature and ability living in every believer. The Church is not a motley collection of spiritually impotent and impoverished weaklings: it is God's powerhouse, empowered with all the resource of heaven to fill this world with Jesus Christ. Through the Holy Spirit, the Church is full of the kingdom power of its King.

### April 10, 2012: The in-between time

*Jesus appeared to his disciples over a period of forty days and*
*spoke about the kingdom of God. (Acts 1:3)*

The time between his resurrection and ascension was vitally important for Jesus. He didn't sit back, basking in the victory of the moment. He didn't take time out, visiting the family back in Nazareth. He didn't arrange a 'Resurrection' tour ('come and see the miracle man!'). He focused himself on the next step of the great purpose for which he had come. Jesus had only forty days to spend on earth after being raised before he went to heaven. This was a pre-determined time, not a moment longer or shorter (the Old Testament makes that clear; study the various feasts and you'll discover he would ascend forty days after he rose again).

What did Jesus do during this in-between time? He spoke to the disciples about the kingdom of God; that was his priority. Even when they tried to distract and divert him to their way of thinking by asking about restoring the natural kingdom of Israel (which shows they still hadn't understood), Jesus refused to enter into dialogue about secondary or peripheral matters. Nothing would distract him. He concentrated on the important, the vital, the essential. He didn't allocate to the disciples their ministries or titles. He didn't tell them to arrange or attend conferences or instruct them regarding their preaching schedules. His resurrection had launched the next phase of God's eternal purpose, and his ascension would be the prelude to the coming of the Holy Spirit at Pentecost. Jesus had far bigger fish to fry than indulging the whims and personal agendas of the disciples. It was time for them to get in on his plan - so he spoke to them about the kingdom of God.

Now that Easter is over and everybody is filled with chocolate and hot cross buns and sung their resurrection songs, for many the Church tends to slip back into its own sub-resurrection existence in which people live as if Jesus were still in the grave or had never reached the Cross. The world carries on as if nothing of significance has happened. That is because we reduce the resurrection to an event we remember on the calendar instead of living in the power of the Jesus who is alive today and present in us through the Holy Spirit - as he is so are we in this world (1John 4:17). The Spirit who raised Jesus from the dead is living in us (Romans 8:11). Let's not put Easter on the shelf as if it really makes no difference to the way we live. Jesus spent those forty days in intense focused activity in which he knew that he had that small window of time in which he would impart to these apostles their future destiny. He didn't waste it on the trivial things we so often see as the essential - his priority was the kingdom of God. That is why Jesus said: 'Seek first the kingdom of God and his righteousness - make the kingdom of God your priority' (Matthew 6:33).

Any priority that is not the kingdom of God is a complete waste of time and bears no relationship to the purpose of the resurrection of Jesus. I pray that we all focus on Jesus' priority - the kingdom of God.

## May 24, 2012: No contest

*We don't wrestle against flesh and blood...so put on the complete armour of God. (Ephesians 6:12-13)*

In this passage Paul combines two images that his readers would be very familiar with: wrestling, which was a major sport of the time, and a Roman soldier, fully armed and equipped. His readers would realise straight away how ludicrously one-sided such a contest would be: an unarmed man dressed in very little against a tough Roman soldier in all his battle gear. The wrestler wouldn't stand a chance! He would be mincemeat in just a few seconds as the soldier cut him down while being fully protected in his armour.

The Christian life is not a lifelong struggle against an unseen enemy who tries to get us in headlocks or pins us to the ground to get us to submit. It's not a constant grapple with an equally powerful foe. We wrestle as fully armed soldiers against an enemy who is not only at a distinct disadvantage: he has already lost the contest! Our wrestle is not engaging in close quarter holds; it is destroying our opponent's lies with the Word of God while being fully protected by faith, truth and righteousness. Jesus' victory over Satan becomes ours when we are born again into the kingdom of God. It really is an unfair fight; and one we should enjoy winning! That's why every time I read Romans 8:37 - 'in all these things we gloriously overcome as conquerors - I have a little chuckle as I'm reminded that my enemy really doesn't stand a chance!

### June 12, 2012: The never-ending story

*In my former book, Theophilus, I wrote about all that Jesus began to do and to teach until the day he was taken up to heaven. (Acts 1:1)*

The eternal purpose of God, God's story, is a never-ending story. While it is true that 'it is finished' - that Jesus has done it all in dying for our sins and rising from the dead - the reason why Jesus accomplished that was part of the greater unending purpose of God. The administration (I use that word in a spiritual sense) of the kingdom of God, God's eternal plan for his universe, never concludes. Even when this age is complete and Jesus returns we won't all live happily ever after in some heavenly retirement home, singing worship songs and popping into each other's mansions for a cup of tea! In the age to come the kingdom of God will continue to increase and increase and increase (Isaiah 9:7). We as the mature sons of God will have an essential role to play in the administration of that eternal increase. It will be an age free of sin and death and decay, of resurrection bodies, of unbroken fellowship with the triune God and with every perfected saint. It is often said that the church is writing Acts 29 - I like that. But when the age to come is inaugurated at the coming of Jesus we will spend eternity writing a whole new book - of a never-ending story!

### June 19, 2012: Intrusion or instigation?

*When the lame beggar saw Peter and John about to enter the Temple, he asked them for money. (Acts 3:3)*

There is one aspect of this remarkable story in Acts that we often overlook: the miracle took place because, without realising it, the lame beggar instigated the whole thing. He didn't realise what he was about to unleash, or experience; nevertheless it was he who interrupted Peter and John's routine by asking them for money. In doing so he caught their attention. The rest, as they say, is history. Of course, the sovereign hand of God was at work, and Peter and John were alert to that once they tuned in to the Holy Spirit.

That is the key. Something that we might initially regard as an intrusion on our routine - that person you end up sitting next to on a bus or train, the lady in front of you at the checkout who is a few pennies short of being able to pay for her food, the Jehovah's Witness who knocks on your door - it just could be the Holy Spirit putting somebody in your path for you to be the means by which he can invade their lives. What might appear to be an intrusion could be a divine encounter, a miracle waiting to happen.

### September 7, 2012: Don't mess with God

Here at All Nations Church we are reading through the Bible in a year. The last few weeks of the programme have led us through Jeremiah, Lamentations, and we are currently in Ezekiel. To be honest, at times it's been harrowing to read some of the things God said and did to his people; he actually sent them into exile because of their continued, wilful disobedience to his commands and their persistence in worshipping and serving other 'gods'. Many of them were slaughtered or suffered physical degradation by the hands of the Babylonians, and the city of Jerusalem was ransacked and pillaged. The stark and graphic language used by Jeremiah and Ezekiel is often shocking, politically incorrect and intended to offend, so that the people would understand the awful consequences of their decisions.

Despite the ministry of the prophets, the kings, priests and people decided that God would never carry out his threats, or they ignored him altogether, or they thought God would be too kind and merciful to ever follow through on his warnings. But he did.

I am also reading through the book of Acts at the moment. I find the same God at work there as in Jeremiah and Ezekiel. I read about Ananias and Sapphira, who tried to con the apostles by lying and conveying a deception. It was only a lie, nothing too serious, just a white lie, a half truth. Yet God struck them both down and they died. This happened to New Covenant people, it happened in the Church. They didn't kill anybody or teach false doctrine: they lied to God and he killed them.

Also in Acts (chapter 12), we read of Herod, who was struck down by an angel of God and perished because he failed to give glory to God. He died in agony after three days of being eaten by worms.

The wrath of God is mentioned over two hundred times in the Bible - and yes, it's in the New Testament too. The most famous verse in the Bible is John 3:16; just twenty verses later you read:

*Whoever believes in the Son has eternal life, but whoever rejects the Son will not see life, for God's wrath remains on him. (John 3:36)*

We must not only believe in the biblical God, we have to relate to the biblical God biblically. The tendency among modern Christians to deny, downplay or ignore the justice, holiness and wrath aspects of God's nature and how they work towards us leaves us with a god made in our image - a non-god. It leads to a self-centred and self indulgent religion - it is not biblical Christianity. The modern God is a cuddly, fun-loving, non-demanding, cotton wool figure, who demands nothing, understands and overlooks our weirdness, sin, unbelief, fickleness and mood swings. Such a god justifies our actions, no matter how unbiblical and out of line with his character they are. That is the god the Israelites thought they had; then the true God acted against them, and they paid the price for their idolatry.

Don't mess with God. Surely one of the most stupid things a Christian can do is to rob God of his tithe. If you're going to be a thief then the worst person to try and rip off is God! Don't be deceived into thinking that you can continue to get away with things that you know displease God and are contrary to his word and will. Leaders: don't reduce God to a fun evening's entertainment for your church. Don't replace the biblical God with the latest religious psychobabble. Do you think God just sits in heaven and is ambivalent to that? Who do you think he is? If he judged Ananias and Sapphira in that manner for lying to him and deceiving the church, what makes you think he will turn a blind eye to what Christians get up to in his name? Don't throw the grace, mercy and love of God back at me. True grace, mercy and love are the qualities of a holy just God. It's true that he restored Judah, but never forget: he did execute judgement on them.

## September 24, 2012: the secret of Mo

*Obey your leaders and submit to their authority, because they keep watch over you as those who must give an account. (Hebrews 13:17)*

While on holiday recently I had a rare Sunday morning off, and had the television on in the background: the BBC was covering the Great North Run. Double Olympic champion Mo Farah was the guest starter for the race. In the build up he was doing an interview in which he was clearly very relaxed and. He was asked how we was spending his time at the moment, now the pressure and demands of the Olympics had passed. Mo beamed and said that he was enjoying all the things that his coach had forbidden him to eat while in training - fizzy drinks, burgers, and chocolate. He said that there was no way he would ever touch such things while in training because his coach had forbidden him to eat them if he wanted to win Olympic gold. Mo obeyed the wishes and command of his coach - and was successful.

As Dianne and I listened to Mo, she turned to me and said, 'Isn't that interesting? He obeyed the command of his coach. If only Christians would obey their leaders in the same way. Too many Christians regard their leaders as advisers or people with mere opinions, when in fact they should be obeyed as servants of God.'

I mulled this over at length in the following days; Dianne was right. So often the people under our care regard the counsel of their leaders as nothing more than an opinion to be weighed and then disregarded; an attempt to control that must be resisted; a restriction of personal freedom; the outmoded thoughts of a dinosaur. 'Who are you to tell me what to do?'

Our leaders are appointed by God to watch over our lives, to ensure that we live in accordance with all that God requires and desires for us. I am only too aware that leaders are imperfect and fallible: we all make mistakes. I am also aware that some leaders sadly take advantage of the sheep under their care and cases of all kinds of abuse occur. Nevertheless, let's assume that our leaders - the men and women in your church whom you have submitted to, who teach you faithfully the ways of God from the Word of God, who care for you year after year, who fast and pray for you, who cry over you, rejoice over you, are prepared to give account to God for you - are the genuine article, the real deal. When they tell you what you should do, why not receive it as the word of God and obey them? Why not be like Mo Farah, who submitted himself to the word of his coach and succeeded? Submit to the word of your leaders; obey them; stop questioning them or ignoring their counsel. It's not mere advice - it's the will of God for your life.

## October 4, 2012: The delusion of nostalgia
*Don't long for the 'good old days.' This is not wise. (Ecclesiastes 7:10)*

People often talk about the good old days – how things were so much better in the past. The summers were warmer, people were kinder, life was better. It's good to look back at the past, but nostalgia does more than reminisce: it looks back to the past as if it were some kind of golden age. Nostalgia tends to make you live in the past, rather than the present. Charles Kettering said: 'You can't have a better tomorrow if you're thinking about yesterday all the time.' It seems that too many people get nostalgic about a lot of things that in fact weren't so great the first time around. Nostalgia is nothing to do with age; you can be nostalgic at twenty-one, if you find yourself looking back to something you experienced when you were fifteen as the highlight of your life. People talk about 'in my day' or they speak of the past as the best days of their life. However, for Christians, every season of life should be the best days and the years to come will be even better. For a Christian every day is 'my day'.

Nostalgia is a form of unbelief, and unbelief is devoid of hope. Nostalgia makes it hard to believe that God will do something now; it makes God only a God of the past. Nostalgia locks you into an idealised past that never existed. The Israelites who left Egypt with Moses became nostalgic about an imaginary past. They looked back to their life in Egypt through the lens of their current experience and concluded they had left behind a life that was really good and far better than what they were experiencing in the present:

> *The rabble with them began to crave other food, and again the Israelites started wailing and said, "If only we had meat to eat! We remember the fish we ate in Egypt at no cost — also the cucumbers, melons, leeks, onions and garlic. But now we have lost our appetite; we never see anything but this manna!" (Numbers 11:4-6)*

Their nostalgic unbelief caused them to believe a lie: they hadn't had a good life at all. In reality, they had been slaves who had suffered terribly at the hands of the cruel Egyptians. They had cried out to God to deliver them from their torment! Here they were, reminiscing about a non-existent past in complete and utter unreality. Nostalgia is the curse of faith; it distorts reality and misinterprets the facts of history.

How do you know if you're nostalgic? Answer these questions: Do you look to the past with more affection and pleasure than you do to the future? Do you talk more about the past than the present and the future? Do you wish you could live in your past?

### November 19, 2012: JC+1=0

Christianity is Jesus Christ, nothing more and nothing less. That's why it's called Christianity, and we are known as Christians. The moment we add or subtract from that simple fact, we no longer have Christianity.

Christianity is not adhering to a set of beliefs about Jesus or a code of conduct in which we seek to emulate him by following his example. It's not examining his earthly life and teaching as presented in the Gospels and adopting that as a philosophy. It's not observing special days or wearing special clothes. It's not about attending conferences or having a clerical title.

It's very easy to overlay the essence of Christianity with the trappings of what we think should be Christianity; but Jesus plus anything else actually makes Christianity nothing - or less than nothing.

Christianity is Jesus Christ, the Jesus Christ as presented in the Word of God, who lives his own life in and through his Body on earth - the Church. If what we call Christianity or Church lessens that reality, then we cannot truly call ourselves Christians or define ourselves as his Church.

## November 22, 2012: Reflections on an Anglican week

The Church of England has had quite a week. It formally welcomed its new leader, Justin Welby, as the Archbishop of Canterbury. Its ruling body, the synod, stunned most observers by rejecting again the introduction of women bishops. I have had an interesting time observing all this as I have come to write this piece, because I am no fan of the Church of England, or the entire Anglican Communion for that matter. I have major issues with it biblically and theologically, and struggle even to identify it as representative of the Church of the Lord Jesus Christ. That is not to say there are not Christians within it, of course there are, but as an organisation it is so far removed from a biblical model of the Church as to be unrecognisable as Church.

I am aware that these comments will offend many Anglicans and non-Anglicans; there is nothing I can do about that. But the column inches and news reports in which all sorts of people within and without the Church of England have been pontificating and commenting on the events of this week have ranged from the nonsensical to the irrelevant, stopping off at the laughable and heretical. To listen to some of the bishops and priests you'd think they never read a Bible in their lives. What it has demonstrated is the diminished value such people place on the Word of God.

The spiritual leader of the Church of England, and thus the locus of unity for all Anglicans worldwide, is, to all intents and purposes, appointed by the Government. I know there is a process within the Church, but in reality no Archbishop will enter office without the endorsement of the Prime Minister and the approval of Her Majesty the Queen, who is the supreme governor of the Church of England. With great respect to the PM and Her Majesty, that is nonsense and cannot be justified from the Word of God. The office of bishop itself, as practised by the Church of England, is unbiblical. The New Testament knows nothing of such an office; so the question of whether a woman can occupy it is a non-question. The whole matter of clergy and laity, bishops and priests, clerical garb and a claimed apostolic succession cannot be justified from the Word of God. I am not a non-conformist curmudgeon: I have studied Anglican theology in depth and its claims concerning its ministry structures. I am not convinced by them. Furthermore, it would be interesting to examine the doctrinal positions of the bishops concerning the Word of God, the uniqueness and deity of Jesus Christ, salvation and the Trinity. These things are fundamental to the essence of Christianity.

The outgoing Archbishop, Rowan Williams, was not a happy man when he gave his farewell address to the synod yesterday. He said something that, for me, encapsulates the issue of where the true Church of Jesus Christ stands in relation to the world. Commenting on the synod's decision to reject women bishops, he said: 'We are willfully blind to the trends and priorities of wider society...we've lost a measure of credibility in our society'. Is the Church's role to be credible to society? Should the beliefs and practices of the Church mirror the trends and mores of society? Does the Church need to be 'in touch' with the world, or should it exist as the polar opposite? The values of the world and the values of the Church should be diametrically opposed to each other. If the Church is not the prophetic voice of God to the world, to society, then what on earth is it for?

I am conscious that this article may not win me friends. Please don't think I have it in for Anglicanism. We non-Anglican Christians cannot sit smugly if we have practices and traditions that contradict the Word of God. I reject the whole reality of the office of bishop: but what about those of us who call ourselves Reverends, Senior Pastors, Worship Pastors and other man made titles? Why do we use descriptions like Baptist, Presbyterian, Evangelical, Charismatic, Calvinist, Lutheran, when really we are just Christians? Why subdue and subjugate people because of their gender, social standing or race? Why yield to the pressures of society and put people into functions that are not open to them?

The issue of the role of women in the Church is an important one; but let's not get all politically correct about it. I notice a trend among certain churches to abandon biblical practices concerning women, which will rebound on those churches. Neither let us dig our heels in to hold on to unbiblical practices (where women can't even open their mouths in church gatherings). The church should never be reactionary, but prophetic and true. Its first relevance is not to the world and society, but to God.

### December 11, 2012: Good riddance to religion

The results of the UK 2011 census are published today. Apparently, the cities of Brighton and Norwich show the highest percentage of people with 'no religion' at 40%, and the national average has risen to 25%. That is excellent news.

'What?' I hear you cry, as you splutter into your coffee. A rise in people with 'no religion' is excellent news? Yes. How can I say such a thing? Because religion is one of the greatest hindrances to real Christianity. Religion and Christianity are not the same: religion masquerades as Christianity and portrays itself as representing God and Jesus Christ. Its paraphernalia, systems and philosophies are not even pale imitations or accurate replicas of the real thing. Religion is a sham; it deludes people into thinking that they are right with God. Worse: it presents a Jesus Christ who doesn't exist and who is therefore irrelevant. It perpetuates the lie that the Church is a building where one goes to perform rites and services, with a special class of people called clergy who do the business of God for us.

That's why I'm thrilled that there is an increase in people in the UK who have turned their backs on such a ridiculous thing. It clears the decks for true Christianity to shine, for the real Church to stand up and be counted, for real Christians to be listened to by the media, for a clear prophetic voice to be heard again in the nation, for Jesus to be seen and known for who he really is! Church: we have work to do.

### December 21, 2012: The world will end, but not today!

The world will end - but not today! It's been quite an apocalyptic week, with the news reports full of people getting ready for the end of the world, which was due today. It's all down to various interpretations of the Mayan calendar, which predicts a shift in time today. It's amazing how many people have taken this seriously, with many people spending immense amounts of money (which means others have made immense amounts of money) on survival pods and stockpiles of rations. It's like Y2K all over again.

Christians are not immune to this craziness. I was raised with the belief in a secret rapture: that Jesus would return secretly and whisk a declining and weak church away before a Great Tribulation and the rule of the Antichrist. Then I began to read the Bible properly and learned from good Bible teachers that yes the world will end one day, and Jesus will return, not for a battered bride waiting to be delivered, but for a glorious bride, which has made herself ready for her Bridegroom. Jesus will return to wind up human history when all things spoken by the prophets have been restored (Acts 3:19-21).

So today I'm looking forward to tomorrow and the day after. I'm especially looking forward to my Christmas dinner on Tuesday! And I'm looking forward to the end of the world - and the age to come!

## February 7, 2013: Redefining marriage is impossible

This week has seen a sea change in British politics and the continued decline of the moral and spiritual health of the nation. On Tuesday the Conservative-led Coalition successfully negotiated the latest stage in its same sex marriage Bill through the House of Commons. The irony of the proceedings was the fact that more Conservative MPs voted against the Bill than for it. PM David Cameron had to rely on the votes of the Opposition parties to get his majority. He now leads a party in disarray, divided at its core. He stands discredited, presiding over a party riven with schism and division. And we all know what happens to a house divided against itself.

The issues for opponents of the Bill have been varied; in fact, it's been fascinating to hear atheists, homosexuals, liberals and Muslims, as well as Christians, vociferous in their campaign to halt this foolish legislation. Admittedly, their reasons for doing so are also varied, but it does demonstrate that the issue of same sex marriage is not universally agreed on, even among non-Christians. That should tell us something. Polls reveal that the country is more divided on the question than certain parts of the media would have us believe.

For Christians, the fundamental issue is not about marriage per se; it's about God and the authority of his Word, the Bible. In his Word God once and for all, 'in the beginning', defined marriage as a covenant between a man and a woman. He has never changed that definition, and never will. Marriage is symbolic of the relationship between Jesus Christ and the Church: he is the bridegroom/husband, the Church is his bride/wife. This eternal motif is fundamentally important in understanding the purpose of the Church, and of the marriage covenant between a man and a woman. This excludes all other definitions of marriage, including polygamy and same sex. No secular government or power has the authority to redefine what God has eternally defined, for in defining marriage in the way he has God has also defined something of himself to us. And he never changes. In attempting to redefine marriage, the UK government is actually trying to redefine the nature of the unchanging God. That is extreme folly.

Furthermore, marriage cannot be redefined by the Church. The Church is defined by God as the bride of Christ, the wife of the Lamb. It too has no authority to discard that definition by removing one of the foundations of its own identity that marriage between a man and a woman conveys. When the Church makes marriage less than God has made it, then the Church ceases to be the Church. Therefore, any so called church that accepts same sex marriage is no longer the Church of Jesus Christ; it is apostate. When I see so-called Christian leaders pontificate on how each of us should be able to express ourselves in the way we see fit and condone same sex marriage I am grieved - and angry. They not only contradict the clear, consistent message of the Scriptures, they slander the nature of the God they claim to represent and practically deny the authority of the Word of God. Let me make it clear: homosexual marriage is not marriage in the eyes of God. And that is important to stress; even if the UK government eventually passes legislation to legalise and enforce such 'marriages', God will not recognise them, neither will his Church. Call it what you will; pass your laws; but God still says no. And so does his Church. Religious leaders who support and advocate this legislation will pay a terrible price when they stand before God to justify themselves.

The question before the Church, therefore, is: how eternally authoritative is God's Word? It teaches categorically, consistently and permanently, that marriage is a covenant between a man and a woman. It teaches that homosexuality is sin, in both Old and New Testaments. It doesn't recognise same sex marriage as marriage. It celebrates and honours marriage on God's terms, even the marriages of those who don't believe in God. God is for marriage; he thought of it, and he officiated at the very first one! If we really believe the Bible is the God-breathed Word of the living God, then we will conclude that marriage as God defines it is the only true expression of the relationship. No government dare tinker with it or play God. Who do they think they are?

### April 9, 2013: The courage of conviction

Yesterday saw the passing away of Margaret Thatcher, the former British Prime Minister, aged 87. The news of her death sparked a widespread and wide-ranging outpouring: of grief, appreciation, measured assessment, objectivity, spiteful celebration, vituperation, adulation and suppressed anger. This article is not an assessment of her policies; however, something in all that took place yesterday was a provocation and a reminder of what it means to be a disciple of Jesus.

As in life, Baroness Thatcher in death elicited love and loathing, probably in equal measure. For those who could rise above their stark prejudices, both from right and especially from the extreme left, and offer some kind of objective thoughts, three words kept ringing throughout the media storm: belief; truth; conviction.

The reason why Mrs. Thatcher elicited such reactions and responses, not only yesterday, but also throughout her long political career, was that she was no populist politician. While she was prepared to make concessions on policies, she always resolutely refused to compromise her political beliefs for the sake of expediency or popularity. She was a conviction politician; she firmly believed that what she stood for was right and true. As such she was a formidable and respected foe to her opponents and a terror to those of her own party who failed to hold to their convictions, even if they clashed with hers. She could not abide compromise or a lack of conviction in others, no matter their political hue. Nobody in current British politics since she left power, certainly no PM, has been prepared to stand up for their convictions like she did. It's the age of the men in grey suits. Conviction demands courage: Margaret Thatcher had it in spades.

We could say that this situation is mirrored to some degree in western Christianity. What is needed today is a conviction Christianity: one that stands for something, that believes in something, that refuses to waver in the face of opposition, that stands against the tide of compromise from within and attack from without. We need a Christianity that proudly and humbly declares its adherence to eternal, objective truth as found in the Word of God, that doesn't cave in to the spirit of the age and to the religious men in grey suits who all too swiftly abandon their principles and once-held cherished beliefs because they want to be popular or sell their books, or be famous, or are afraid of offending their members and thus emptying their church buildings of people who will take their money elsewhere.

As I travel and meet Christians of many nations I am encouraged because I discover that there is a generation - mostly but not exclusively young men and women - who are conviction Christians. The future belongs to them, their time is now. Even though I am in natural years older than many, I am of the same generation: the generation of Jesus Christ, the ultimate man of conviction.

## April 11, 2013: A matter of honour

The behaviour and attitude of certain Christians this week has been deplorable and quite ungodly. Their responses to the death of former British Prime Minister Margaret Thatcher have demonstrated a clear lack in their understanding of God and the principles of his kingdom. Their hatred of Baroness Thatcher has overflowed in cruel, salacious, crude and vitriolic attacks on her as a person. I have seen social media posts by so-called men and women of God that have made me wince, cringe and drop my jaw in horror that my fellow believers could say such things. They should be ashamed of themselves.

Perhaps they should take a leaf out of King David's book. For most of his early public life, David was hounded by his own father-in-law, King Saul, who, once he realised he could not manipulate David, made David his enemy. Twice he tried to personally murder David; having failed to do so he conducted a long campaign to seek and destroy a man who had done him no harm. He even killed those who sheltered David. Twice David had the opportunity to kill Saul: once when Saul went into a cave to go to the toilet, without realising David and his men were hiding there. Saul did his business and left without David's killing him. In fact David did sneak up behind Saul and cut off a piece of his robe, only to be convicted by the Holy Spirit of doing even that. The second time David's opportunity came he found Saul fast asleep. Again, David refused to kill his enemy, the man who had treated him like a common criminal.

Eventually, Saul died and the news was brought to David. You'd think that David would celebrate and throw a party, just like some of my Christian brothers are advocating now regarding Margaret Thatcher. But David was a spiritual man, and he responded accordingly. He refused to speak ill of his enemy; on the contrary, he killed the man who claimed to have killed Saul. In his song of lament for Saul and Jonathan (note that: he lamented the death of his enemy), David spoke of Saul:

> *Saul and Jonathan, beloved and lovely! In life and in death they were not divided; they were swifter than eagles; they were stronger than lions. You daughters of Israel, weep over Saul, who clothed you luxuriously in scarlet, who put ornaments of gold on your apparel. How the mighty have fallen in the midst of the battle! (2Samuel 1:23-25)*

David refused to speak ill of his enemy, the man who had abused him, tormented him, and who'd tried to kill him. Even though that man was now dead, David retained his dignity and chose the way of the kingdom, the way of the Cross ('Father, forgive them, they don't know what they are doing'). He even ensured that Saul's body was buried with respect.

If you take time to read the Bible you will find that David never spoke ill of Saul the rest of his life. He always honoured Saul for what he was: the Lord's anointed (the Lord's Messiah). David wasn't naïve: he knew what Saul was like, but David understood something about honour, something that certain Christian brothers and sisters need to grasp in these days. Let me say this: to you who behave with such hatred, I'm not asking you to love the lady, but give thought to your conduct. You dishonour not only the person of the late Prime Minister, you demean yourselves and worst of all you dishonour God. Please bear that in mind when you are tempted to make foolish comments.

### April 12, 2013: Speaking truth to power

My previous two articles this week have elicited a considerable number of responses and reactions. Thanks to all who took the time to read them, and to those who felt they wanted to respond. They evidently provoked thought and debate. It's good to have healthy, constructive discussion about issues.

I want to deal with one aspect of the matter that was raised, especially after my piece about David and Saul: as Christians can and should we ever criticise our leaders, political or otherwise? Is there a time and place when we don't behave as David did after the death of Saul? It's an important question. My simple answer is yes, there are times and places to do that very thing.

I believe in the importance of speaking truth to power, but that speaking should be done with the interests of God. A proper reading of the Word of God demonstrates this vividly; many of the Old Testament prophets, such as Jeremiah, Amos and Hosea, railed passionately against the rulers of their day, even prophesying the death and destruction of some of these men. Perhaps the most striking example of this was Elijah in his dealings with Ahab and Jezebel (I deal with this at length in my book *The Elijah People*). When we come into the New Testament we discover John the Baptist castigating King Herod regarding his illegal marriage; and even Jesus himself called Herod 'that old fox.' Even though in all these examples we find withering denunciations of improper, autocratic and despotic rulers, we also always find that the representative of God speaks truth to power, with the interests of God. That is the point. I do not advocate a pacifist acquiescence to those in government, or even those in church leadership, but I still maintain that the point I made regarding David and Saul has merit, even for today.

I am concerned with the inner being of believers, of matters of the heart. I believe that we have the right and responsibility to speak as God's representatives to the powers of government, business, church, entertainment and media. God is not excluded from his world; he has something to say. My concern is that what we say is purely in God's interests, and not our own particular political view or take on the events of history. (It's been interesting to see some of the comments made in the media this week about the 70s and 80s, were made by those who were not even alive during that time). We as Christians are bigger and better than that: we are the sons of God, and the creation is awaiting our maturity.

This week I have even been described as a Thatcherite: I am not. Neither am I a Blairite, a Brownite, or a Churchillian! I was born in 1952 from left wing (even Communist) political stock on my father's side (he came from the Welsh valleys), when Churchill was Prime Minister. Like the Queen I have lived through the Premiership of eleven people; they have been a true mixture. I have experienced the benefits of their successes and suffered through their blunders. They all got things right and they all got things wrong. Both Conservative and Labour Prime Ministers took this country to war in my lifetime; both parties made policy decisions that affected hundreds and thousands of us for the best and the worst. In my working life I have been a Trade Union representative and worked in the private sector. My standard of living has changed many times because of the good and bad decisions made by Labour and Conservatives. I have little or no respect for some who have held the office of PM; I admire others. At various times over the years I have spoken in support of Prime Ministers, at others I have challenged them through my correspondence. If we were to be completely impartial, then there could just as easily have been street parties following the death of certain Labour Prime Ministers, who, in the eyes of many, almost destroyed this nation.

My aim in this week's articles has been to appeal to my fellow believers: to be radical and to live with courage of your convictions, and to conduct yourself in that radical conviction with dignity and not with spiteful, sarcastic, cynical invective. That is all I ask.

## Quotable Quotes & Musings
*Occasionally in Stars and Sand the article consisted of a one or two sentence thought; here is a selection of the most popular.*

The man of the Spirit does not judge nor decide anything by his natural senses; for to him all is spiritual and he judges and decides all things only by the Holy Spirit.

\*

Faith means you can face the future with hope and laughter.

\*

You are only ever one heartbeat from eternity.

\*

Don't put off till tomorrow what you can do today; if you enjoy doing it today, you can do it again tomorrow.

\*

God blesses only that which he approves; don't waste his time or yours by asking him to bless or condone what he never told you to do.

\*

Sometimes you can see a lot just by looking.

\*

Peace can only be with you if the Prince of Peace is within you.

\*

Don't allow your past to control your present and so determine your future.

\*

People of faith have a total disregard for the impossible.

\*

I don't want to read about a God who is miraculous in the Bible but not in the world today.

*

The tragedy of the church in Laodicea was that when Jesus knocked on the door of the church nobody knew he wasn't inside.

*

Always remember that when you're slinging mud, you're losing ground.

*

God always deals with you only on the basis of who you are in Christ.

*

Too many people are shaking their fists in anger at God when they should be lifting holy hands to him in gratitude.

*

If someone is gossiping to you about somebody, rest assured that they will also be gossiping to somebody about you.

*

A miracle is just God's way of acting as God.

*

You need to know not only what Jesus has saved you from, but also what he has saved you into.

*

Your new birth launched you into a life of the supernatural.

*

Truth without love is brutal; love without truth is sentimental.

*

When you dream God's dream, you die to every other dream.

*

Unbelief not only says the impossible is impossible; it says the possible is impossible.

*

If you don't discover the difference between the shakings of God in your life and the attacks of the enemy on your life you will end up fighting against God.

*

The Lord's Table is an invitation and summons from heaven, for us to meet Jesus face to face and receive directly from him all the benefits in full of his broken body and shed blood.

*

Don't give your life for anything that is not worth your life.

*

Faith sees the invisible; faith hears the inaudible; faith touches the intangible.

*

The only status quo worth maintaining is the will of God.

*

We are truly free only to the extent that Jesus is free to be himself as Lord in us.

*

The Christian is truly free only when he becomes a slave of his Master.

*

Christian freedom is not self-expression or self-determination. It is the Lord Jesus living His life freely through us.

*

The Church is God the Father displaying his Son through people filled with his Spirit.

*

No matter what others think of you, let God be the One who defines you.

*

Be the friend to others you want them to be to you.

*

God the Father's purpose is in Christ, is through Christ, is Christ.

*

Speaking in tongues is your supernatural communication line to God!

*

The Bible is not just the Book of God: the Bible is the Voice of God. Have you heard God's Voice today?

*

You can worry. You can trust God. You can't do both.

*

You're only young once but you can remain immature all you're life.

*

You can't be in Christ and live like you're in Adam.

*

You can't love like God and not forgive like God.

*

Jesus is Lord, not a life coach. He is God, not a self-improvement consultant.

*

If you want to know somebody's mind, listen to their words.

*

Your yes to God is also your no to the world. Sin is your yes to God's no and your no to God's yes.

***